C000216494

FREDERICK WILLIAM DWELLY
FIRST DEAN OF LIVERPOOL, 1881–1957

BY THE TENOR *of these presents* **We John William** *by Divine Permission*
BISHOP OF CARLISLE *do make it known unto all men that on* *Sunday — the*
Tenth _____ **day of** *June* _____ *in the Year of our Lord*
One Thousand Nine Hundred and *Six* _____ *WE the Bishop before mentioned*
holding a *public* _____ **Ordination** *under the Protection of the Almighty in*
our Cathedral Church at Carlisle _____
did admit our beloved in Christ *Frederick William Dwelly of Queens'*
College Cambridge _____
_____ *(of whose Virtuous and Pious Life*
and Conversation and Competent Learning and Knowledge in the Holy Scriptures
we were well assured) into the Holy Order of *Deacons* *according to the Manner and*
Form prescribed and used by the Church of England and him the said *Frederick*
William Dwelly _____ *did then and there rightly and Canonically ordain*
Deacon *he having first in our presence made and subscribed such Declaration and*
taken and subscribed such Oaths as are by law in such case required.
In Testimony *whereof we have caused our Episcopal Seal to be hereunto affixed the*
day and Year above written and in the *Second* _____ *Year of our Consecration.*

Jw   Carliol

Temporary
Seal

Frederick William Dwelly
First Dean of Liverpool,
1881–1957

PETER KENNERLEY MBE

WITH A FOREWORD BY CANON DR DONALD GRAY CBE

Carnegie Publishing, 2004

Other books available from Carnegie:
Peter Kennerley, *The Building of Liverpool Cathedral*
Prof. John K. Walton, *Blackpool*
Peter Aughton, *Bristol: A People's History*
Dr John A. Hargreaves, *Halifax*
Dr Andrew White (ed.), *A History of Lancaster*
Peter Aughton, *Liverpool: A People's History*
Prof. Alan Kidd, *Manchester*
Dr Jeffrey Hill, *Nelson*
Prof. David Hey, *A History of Sheffield*

Forthcoming:
Peter Kennerley, *A Short History of Liverpool* (2005)
Janet McLarney, *Liverpool and Slavery* (2005)
Dr Graham Davis and Penny Bonsall, *A History of Bath* (2005)
Prof. Carl Chinn, *Birmingham* (2007)
Dr Derek Beattie, *Blackburn* (2005)
Dr John Doran, *Chester* (2007)
Dr John A. Hargreaves, *Huddersfield* (2007)
Prof. Trevor Rowley, *A History of Oxford* (2008)
Dr Mark Freeman, *A History of St Albans* (2007)
Dr John B. Smith, *Wolverhampton* (2007)
Prof. Bill Sheils, *A History of York* (2007)

Full details on www.carnegiepublishing.com

First published in 2004 by
Carnegie Publishing Ltd
Carnegie House
Chatsworth Road, Lancaster LA1 4SL
www.carnegiepublishing.com

Copyright © Peter Kennerley, 2004

ISBN 1-85936-133-1

All rights reserved

British Library Cataloguing-in-Publication data
A catalogue record for this book is available from the British Library

Designed, typeset and originated by Carnegie Publishing
Printed and bound in the UK by The Bath Press

Contents

For
Ronald Woan
and all who have helped
to create, preserve and develop
the great Liverpool Cathedral tradition

Foreword by Canon Dr Donald Gray CBE

I T IS A HEARTENING FACT that in these days of much statistical gloom for the Church, our cathedrals and collegiate churches are emerging as significant growth points, not merely as places to visit, but also for worship and devotion.

It was not always so; in the nineteenth and into the twentieth century they were often dark, forbidding and unwelcoming. Dean Bennett is rightly celebrated as breaking that particular mould by making Chester Cathedral a place of both interest and welcome. Chester was, of course, the product of one of Henry VIII's better ideas – the subdividing of large medieval dioceses. He could not have known that years later a clutch of even newer dioceses would be necessary, each needing its cathedral church. One of those was the rapidly growing city of Liverpool and its surrounding townships.

The story of how Liverpool chose to build, rather than adapt, is well known, and Peter Kennerley has already put us in his debt with his fascinating account in *The Building of Liverpool Cathedral*. What has not been fully explored, until now, is the way in which that unique edifice built on St James's Mount began to be used. We now have the facts. It was almost single-handedly the work of one man, Frederick William Dwelly. His vision, liturgical expertise and ability perceived a cathedral which, without abandoning the traditions of the past, would speak to the people of his day. Bennett opened the doors of his Cathedral to the visitor, the enquirer; once they were inside the new Cathedral in Liverpool, Dwelly designed services and occasions which would give them a glimpse of the infinite, the eternal.

Dwelly's work was not always appreciated. In a service reminiscent of the Venetian ceremony in which the Doge affirms that city's undeniable marriage to its surrounding sea, Dwelly had the Lord Mayor standing on the Rankin Steps throwing a wedding ring in the general direction of the River Mersey. *The Church Times*, then in its high days of Tractarian conservatism, commented that it only remained for the Lord Mayor of Manchester to make an honest woman of the Ship Canal!

It is easy to poke fun, yet the fact is the 'special service' has for many years now been a staple of our cathedrals, collegiate and civic churches' mission and outreach. Dwelly 'invented' the special service and designed them with a flair which subsequently inspired others.

We should be very grateful that Peter Kennerley has elegantly brought to the fore the life and achievements of a priest whose honoured place in the history of our cathedrals was in danger of being overlooked and forgotten.

Donald Gray

Preface

FIFTEEN YEARS AGO, when I began the research which led to the publication of *The Building of Liverpool Cathedral*, I realised how little primary source material there was in the Cathedral relating to the life of Frederick William Dwelly, the first Dean. The cathedral – the largest in Britain – had been the inspiration of Francis James Chavasse and was designed by the architect Sir Giles Gilbert Scott. Its physical presence is overwhelming and it is destined to stand unignorably on the city skyline for a thousand years. A cathedral, however, should be a living entity and it was Frederick Dwelly who first breathed life into this most magnificent of buildings. Dwelly created and directed the worshipping life of the Cathedral for almost thirty years: he more than any other man or woman influenced indelibly the life and liturgy of the Cathedral. At the time of his retirement in frail physical and mental health, a biography was planned, to be written by the Rev. Ralph Dawson, a friend and devotee of Dwelly's over many years. Dawson died; no biography appeared and there was a reticence which dissuaded more than one person from undertaking further Dwelly research.

Dwelly was not a liturgical scholar in the traditional sense: he published one slender book of devotions and was thought to be the anonymous compiler of a book of services for broadcasting. In the estimation of many eminent figures in the Church of England, however, Dwelly was a liturgical genius whose life history could so very easily be lost. When I began the first chapter of *The Building of Liverpool Cathedral*, most of the detailed research was already completed; the bones of the story were well ordered and preserved in the computer. As I begin chapter one of the Dwelly book, I am uncomfortably conscious of the serious gaps in my research findings. The cautious part of my personality warns me that I am not ready to undertake the work; my realistic self challenges me to move without delay, while the few people remaining who knew Dwelly are still able to inform and support me. I was uncomfortably conscious that my academic and professional background was not ideal for this subject, but I was 'on the spot'. I worked in the building which was quite literally his home (my office was his wartime bedroom), bound volumes of his service papers lined the shelves, and I have sorted and filed all the primary and secondary source materials. I have even almost mastered the difficult hand writing.

Two activities in 1998 proved to be the final spur to undertake this project. Firstly, I supervised an undergraduate dissertation on the life of Dwelly by my friend and colleague Nicholas Basson. His painstaking textual research for an excellent piece of academic work began to sift and analyse the existing materials. It was also the centenary year of Emmanuel Church in Southport, a Dwelly church, and Nicholas Basson and I were invited to contribute to those celebrations. We wrote and performed 'Drama for Dwelly', a dramatic reconstruction of his life using primary source materials. That two-hour-long presentation made a powerful impression on both performers and audience. The dissertation and the dramatic performance together seemed to demand that I undertake this book.

Any biographer of Dwelly also has to accept the challenge of writing about the worship and liturgy of a great twentieth century Cathedral, because man and Cathedral are inextricably linked. The Cathedral was his life and a contributory factor in his death. He was almost destroyed by what he had created. The foundation stone of the new Cathedral was laid in 1904 and the first services in the newly completed Lady Chapel were held in 1910. It was only with the completion of the chancel and eastern transepts in 1924 that the enormous challenge of this vast worship space became apparent. That was the year in which Dwelly, then a local parish priest, was invited by the Bishop to devise a suitable service of consecration: no Cathedral had been built on a previously unconsecrated site since Salisbury in 1225. Dwelly's imaginative genius and organisational abilities made him an obvious choice as first Dean following the formal establishment of Dean and Chapter in 1931. During the thirties and forties, under Dwelly's deanship, Liverpool Cathedral was at the centre of liturgical development in Cathedrals the length and breadth of Britain.

Dwelly has been dead for nearly fifty years; most of his personal papers were removed from the Cathedral at the time of his retirement and would-be biographers have not been encouraged to research all aspects of his life. However, through the support of a wide range of people, I have been able to gather together twenty-four files full of Dwelly papers, as well as a range of oral history. I am attempting to gather and set down for posterity the facts relating to his life and his work and I am struggling towards an understanding of the whole man. At this moment, there are still serious gaps in the material and I run the risk of making some false judgements. Though he died almost two generations ago, people are still aware of him and his influence is everywhere. In his life there is tragedy, and yet there is exuberance, delight, sparkling humour, joyful creativity, dynamic leadership. He was tender, caring, devoted, faithful, magnetic, whilst at the same time being obtuse, autocratic, unbending, stubborn and harsh. He lead and inspired and supported the Cathedral for over thirty years and his close Cathedral company guarded and supported him through his decline into physical and mental frailty. If the Cathedral was his life it was also his death.

In all my writing to date, I have had a clear understanding of my readers. The Cathedral book was to satisfy the curiosity of those visitors to know how, why and when? My impulse was that of the story teller and I made no claims to historical or architectural expertise. If I try to be scrupulously honest, I have to admit that I am writing the Dwelly book not just to record his achievements for posterity, but also to satisfy my own curiosity, to understand more clearly an extraordinarily talented and enigmatic man. I intend to make maximum use of a wide range of primary sources so that Dwelly, his critics and his devotees, can speak for themselves and that Dean Dwelly of Liverpool may start to come alive through the chapters of his life and the pages of this book.

Acknowledgements

I have been at work on this biography for so long, and I have received the support of so many people, that I know my list of acknowledgements will contain omissions, particularly of some of the people with whom I had conversations over ten years ago. In a variety of ways I have been helped by all of the following: Nicholas Basson; Rt Rev. Gordon Bates; Dr Judith Blezzard; Very Rev. Mark Boyling; Patrick David; Rev. Canon Myles Davies; the late Dr Frederick Dillistone; Professor Alan Dronsfield; John Dwelly; Vernon Dwelly; Very Rev. Nicholas Frayling; Canon Dr Donald Gray; Edward Kelly; Miss Elizabeth Kennerley; Mrs Jean Lee; librarians at Lambeth Palace Library; John Lloyd; Mrs Diana Luck; Rt Rev. Hugh Montefiore; Mrs Patricia Mollinson; Rev. Prebendary David Nash; Very Rev. Edward Patey; John S. Peart-Binns; the late Gordon Pemberton; Rev. Colin Pope; Mrs Ann Prest; Peter Rae; Miss Mary Raven; Noel Rawsthorne; Miss Carol Reekie and other staff at Cambridge University Library; Miss Ann Rigby-Jones; Very Rev. Ken Riley; the late Geoffrey Rimmer; Mervyn Roberts; Miss Mollie Rogers and the staff of the Radcliffe Library; Alan Topping; Dr Leonard Wilkinson; Ronald Woan.

The house where Fred Dwelly grew up. The sign, Dwelly & Co., Carriage Builders, is still visible behind the garage sign.

Chard School, founded in 1671, provided Dwelly's early education.

CHAPTER ONE

Chard

C OVERED WITH DUST, on one of the most inaccessible shelves in the Cathedral archives, was a filing box labelled Family Papers and Affairs of Dwelly Family in Chard. The bulk of the contents were made up of yellowed newspapers, some of which had already begun to disintegrate. *The Chard and Illminster News* of 26 May 1900 gave an account of the town's spontaneous rejoicing at the news of the relief of Mafeking. The same paper devoted one of its four pages on 26 January 1901 to a report on the death of Queen Victoria. On February 9 1901 there was a lengthy report of the meeting of the Chard Town Council, at which Councillor Robert Dwelly, to the Mayor's annoyance, spoke four times. A Sunday School Class Register for 1893 gives evidence of large classes and high attendances. The texts of some of Councillor Dwelly's speeches in Council are laboriously recorded in black ink in a powerful hand. There are a few rather insignificant legal papers and a clutch of newspaper cuttings referring to the work of the youngest son of Councillor Dwelly, whose family papers and affairs have escaped the fire or the rubbish tip for a hundred years because that son went on to become the Reverend Frederick William Dwelly, M.A., DD., first Dean of Liverpool.

There is nothing in the family background to suggest such future eminence. An unnamed newspaper cutting from 1865 reports:

On the 26th Inst, a marriage was solemnised at the parish church by the Rev. Canon Burn between Mr. Robert Dwelly, of Puckington, and Miss Caroline Cooper, youngest daughter of Mr. T. Cooper, of this town. The bridesmaids, four in number, were Miss Cooper, sister of the bride, Miss L. Cooper, Miss Wyatt, and Miss Perry. There were also present Mr. Cooper, sen., father of the bride, Mr. W. T. Cooper, who officiated as bridegroom's best man, Mr. T. Dwelly, brother of the bridegroom, and Mr. W. Cooper of Bath. The happy pair left in the afternoon for Clifton. In connection with the interesting ceremony we must not omit to notice that a beautiful and costly workbox was presented to the bride by the teachers and children of the Illminster Church Sunday Schools, together with an appropriate address.

That marriage was celebrated in the magnificent Parish Church in Illminster on 26 December 1865. Further evidence of this event is recorded in an imposing, ornate little book produced in 1915 to mark the celebration of their Golden Wedding Anniversary. Further genealogical information about the Dwelly family can be gleaned from the *Compendium of Notes of the Dwelly Family* compiled by E. Dwelly, F.S.G., printed and published by the compiler at his office in King's Road, Fleet, Hants, in 1912. Though an unusual name, E. Dwelly produced evidence of branches of the family in a number of parts of the West Country, as well as a John Dwelly at Lancaster in the seventeenth century whose descendants sailed to America. The details of the relevant branch of the family are recorded in more detail by E. Dwelly in *The Dwelly Family Pedigree*, an undated copy of which is held in county records in Taunton. 'Dwelly of Stocklinch, Barrington, Chard, North Curry, Puckington, Etc., Somerset' reports the birth of Thomas Dwelly in 1810, and of his future wife Betsy in 1802. Robert was buried in Puckington on 7 June 1854 while his wife lived until October 1883. The family kept the Rock Inn at Curry Mallett where Robert was born in 1842, followed by his brother Thomas in 1844.

Even today, the area of Somerset a few miles to the south of Taunton is predominantly beautiful, undulating English countryside of mature trees, hedgerows and fields. It is essentially an agricultural district with small villages and isolated farms. Even Chard, the largest centre of population, never had more than 6,000 inhabitants at any time during the nineteenth century. There is no scrap of evidence to suggest that a member of the Dwelly family might go on to become one of the most influential clergymen of his day.

The Rock Inn is now a private house, in a fairly isolated position near a T junction, overlooking open country. Many years later, and certainly after 1914 as an old man, Robert made some pencil notes about his life at the prompting of one of his sons (punctuation considerably edited):

My Dear Boy, you have asked me more than once to write the history of my life. To do so I think it first my duty to give my parentage of our excellent Father & Mother. My Father was the fourth Son of Robert and Ann Dwelly of Barrington. My mother was the only daughter of John and Betty Chislett ... My Father & Mother['s] first home was Rock House which was built in two parishes Curry Mallett and North Curry. I was born in Curry Mallett Parish 31st Dec 1842 as a few years since could be seen cut on bedroom door my only brother Tom was born 3 April 1844 ... Some of my first recollections of childhood's days I have often wished I could banish forever from memory. These incidents have convinced me how children take notice and form impressions here. In later years I has been always very careful what I say or do before the youngest of children ... I can only remember one incident that was of a drunken man who became quarrelsome. They turned him out of the room; as he would not leave the house my mother broke his head with a stick. My father carried on stone quarrie Lime Burning and Farming. Well do I remember the men bringing in large ash faggots and building up the chimney corner ... Another incident I was sent by Father to a field to bring home the sheep. The ram which was with them attacked me, got me down no doubt would have served me bad if a friend had not come to my rescue and helped me to get them out of the field. On arriving home, Father asked me what was the matter. On telling him he got an oak stick with a very large knob to it. He said, 'Take this and come with me. When the ram comes at you smack him in the face with this.' I had to do 3 times before the ram shook his head turned tail and gave up the fight. I shall have to give other instance how my Father taught his boys to face our fears.

One more incident perhaps interesting any how I was taught such a lesson I have never forgotten. I with a lad several years my senior was set to watch the sheep in a large field which was occupied by several occupiers but there was no hedge or other means of dividing ... The sheep was feeding very quietly so we ramble away to some hedgerows for flowers. Among the many was a very lovely Oxlip. The other lad out ran me and picked it just as it was the sheep began to break we knew they had left the lawn So ran back to get them in their proper place. After so doing the chap says you must not tell your father the sheep broke. I said I must. After some time he said I will give you the Oxlip if you will promise not to tell ... That night Father said Well Robert did the sheep get out at all. I said no. He quickly answered which by his manner I knew I had to acknowledge they did get out. I expected to have a whipping and sent to bed without any supper ... Next morning before I had been out in the field where the chap was ploughing my father stopped the horses ask the chap why he taught his boy to tell lies ... and told him to leave the field ... I never knew my Father a healthy man and Mother was so very full of business in door and out ... I was sent to 2 Dame schools but I fear made little progress so was afterwards sent to Barrington under a master ... he was a very old man The only two things I can remember that is his very long stick by which he used to knock our heads, the other I jumped of[f] the front steps and fell and cut open one eye ... Lady Day 1851 Father left Rock House and took ... [?] Barrington with about 30 acres of ground.

At some point after their marriage in 1865, Robert and Caroline Dwelly moved to Chard. *Kelly's Directory of Somerset* for 1886 makes reference to one Thomas Cooper, coach builder in Fore Street. By 1883 the firm and family house had moved to East Street, where it still operates as a garage. By 1897 the firm is listed simply as Dwelly & Co.

I suspect that not even the inhabitants of Chard would attempt to describe their little town as being especially picturesque or beautiful, though the borough is a very ancient foundation. By the last quarter of the nineteenth century the London and South Western Railway had run a branch line to Chard and the Great Western ran a line from Taunton. 'The town is paved, lighted with gas, and supplied with excellent water.' 'By the Municipal Corporation Act the government of the town is vested in a mayor, four aldermen and twelve councillors.' (*Kelly's Directory of Somerset*, 1883). Robert Dwelly served several terms as a councillor and one term as an alderman, and a visitor to the town today might be interested to discover Dwelly Close, a collection of 1960s residences of little character or charm, but whose name gives some indication of Robert's standing within the town.

Robert and Caroline were staunch members of the Church of England and all ten of their children were baptised in the font within the ancient Parish Church of St Mary, though three died as infants and one as a young married man. The last child was born on 9 April 1881 at the house in East Street and was baptised Frederick William (the same name as another of the Dwelly children who had died in 1871 at four months) on 29 May by the Vicar, Rev. W. E. Buller. Always known as Fred to his family and friends, we know that he attended the Endowed Grammar School in Fore Street, not far from his home and the family business. The building is still there and still functioning as a school. Towards the end of Frederick William's time there, the establishment was described as follows:

Chard Endowed School, in Fore Street, was founded in 1671 by W. Symes of Poundsford. The school-house, a building of squared flint with Ham stone dressings, bears the date 1583; the old school-room, probably built in 1670, has annexed a modern dining-hall & classrooms, & attached is a gravelled playground, playing field & lawn tennis court, etc. There are three boarding houses, under the charge of the Headmaster, Mr. A. H. Town, B.A. & Mr H. E. Armstrong, B.A., & a detached building is available as a sanatorium for infectious cases. There is also a spacious gymnasium, with a carpenter's shop attached. Thomas Wakley M.D., M.P. For Finsbury, founder of 'The Lancet' was educated here ... Rev. C. F. A. Wimberley, M.A. Of Durham University, head master; A. H. Town, B. A. J. F. Harrison B. A. H. S. Dale drawing master; F. C. Mastrale, french & german; W. Giles shorthand; Wm Pilton, sergeant-instructor for drill and gymnastics.

During his years in office, Councillor Dwelly appears to have taken his duties very seriously and the archive box preserves some of the speeches he made in council. He took a particular interest in the future of the town's water supply. The strength of his religious beliefs is indicated in a remarkable letter to the Right Honourable Earl Poulett on 8 January 1894:

To the Glory of the Lord God of Heaven and for the Poor of Chard some of the weakest members of the Chard Town Council take this liberty of addressing your Lordship. Having heard at our last meeting it was your Lordship's intention to make further search on Chard Farm for water I felt it to be my duty to lay before your Lordship a dream which I had of a most bountiful clear sparkling stream of water the goodness of which I seemed never to have tasted such before. On telling my dream to Mr Phelps who can use the divining rod he resolved to come down and try. On the 16th of last August by permission of Mr Lawrence (but wishing to improve the force) I took him to a higher level than where I saw the water and he said most probably water could be found at such a spot but before it was tried he advised the calling in of another to confirm that his suggestion was right. Your Lordship caused his men to cease digging by the Kiln and commenced at the spot suggested by Mr Phelps which as yet has been a failure. Allow me to say My Lord I feel if water was revealed to me it was also revealed to me in that dream. It was to the Glory of the Lord God of heaven and earth and for the special benefit of the Poor of Chard.

> I am your Lordships
> Humble Servant
> Robert Dwelly.

Though the letter might have the tone of an Old Testament prophet, many of his speeches were well researched and were concerned with the economics of various water schemes. The speeches are undoubtedly those of a powerful figure, persistent and determined, ready to stand firm for his beliefs – beliefs which reveal a zealous Christian well versed in scripture.

> Mr Mayor,
> In my opinion Messrs Bailey Dinton Lawford and Co have shamefully fooled the council, and their works have more than justified my criticism of their schemes. A copy of my letter on it was sent to each member of the Town Council 30th May 1906.
> For 15 years I have held and expressed by belief in the God of Nature's excellent and bountiful provision of water for Chard and where it can be got by the council making a fair trial. The scheme is the Lord Jehovah's – Whether intentionally or unintentionally I know not. Anyhow when the Council in 1905 uncovered Nature's bosom in Summer Field and there saw every sign of an abundance of water, they would not use any effort to draw from it, but rather adopt abortive schemes, which has cost the town not much less than £1000, the whole has proved absolute failures – aye – and any other I believe will so long as the council will ignore or wilfully try to deprive God of his Honour and his people of his life giving water. It will be sad – very sad – if this council do persist in kicking against the pricks. If you will I am convinced neither you nor your engineers will prevail more than Pharaoh of old did in keeping God's people in bondage. To the Honour and Glory of God and for the benefit of this town (which we all love) I ask you now to make a fair trial in summer field so all may see, drink and sing Praise God from whom all blessings flow.

If Robert Dwelly had been an Archbishop or some other high dignitary in the church, far more might have been recorded about him and his family and how they lived. As it is, over a century later, we have to use whatever scraps of evidence still exist to help to establish and clarify the early background of a future Dean. From snippets in Frederick William's writings at a much later date, we are made aware of the strength of his ties with his family.

July 14, 1917

On the hill where Father played as a boy – overlooking Barrington Church and village.

Here 60 years ago my Father played and worked below, only a few yards he lived, his father died – the baby's coffin was discovered – and now, we wander together over these parts and he is boy again as he walks and talks of his walnut tree and that old flail shed – whilst I, his baby boy, baby of 10, feel old, mightily old because tomorrow by the will of God I am to preach in my old Parish Church, the church of my christening and confirmation – church of my choir boy's devotion – dear old church – and today I feel very old as I sit here looking at my father's old home parish church – by the grace of God he has surpassed his wildest dreams – by the same grace, cause of my feeling of age, I am to fulfil the last point of my parents ideals – to be ordained – to have a parish of my own – to preach in the old church at Chard – it seems too easily to have one's wishes granted and yet so like the Heavenly Father – all my life he has enriched me – to Him here and now I would – I do – dedicate my life.

Frederick W. Dwelly

Even many years after the death of his parents, he continued to return to Chard. *The Chard and Illminster News* for 12 July 1941 reported on the celebrations to mark the twentieth anniversary of the induction of Rev. Prebendary G. H. W. Mallett as Vicar of Chard. A number of people spoke at the reception after the service, including Dean Dwelly:

The next speaker was Dr. Dwelly, who had come the whole way from Liverpool to be present. He said how delighted he was when he received an invitation to come to Chard and how honoured he felt to think that the congregation had felt that he would like to come. He was speaking on behalf of two groups of people who were represented in his own person: the old ones, those who had gone before, such as his wonderful mother and noble father; in him they came to give thanks to Vicar Mallett for all that he had done; and also he spoke for the naughty ones, who had gone away from Chard. He had been naughty in all sorts of ways. He asked the congregation if they remembered 'old Sims, the organist'. He remembered on one Fifth of November, when he was a choir boy, putting a large cracker under the organ stool during choir practice. Even now, when one of his choir boys at Liverpool Cathedral was brought to him to be punished he often remembered that scene and the boys got off with a warning. There was another burst of laughter and cries of 'Yes' when he asked if anyone remembered Johnny Doddle. Did they remember how Johnny Doddle always chipped in with an 'Aymen' or 'Alleluia' when he approved of what was said? He had found Johnny Doddle very useful when he was speaking as a 'distinguished visitor' in the U.S.A. He had explained how he had interrupted and had asked his audience not to copy his example or it would spoil his style.

The ancient parish church of St Mary, Chard, the exterior unchanged since Dwelly's days as a choir boy.

The obituary notices of Robert, and then Caroline, Dwelly have been preserved in parish magazines and are a further insight into the character of the family home and of two people who had exerted powerful influences on his development:

Chard Parish Magazine
August, 1927
Robert Dwelly, 1843–1927
After months of suffering endured most patiently, Robert Dwelly passed to his rest on Friday, 22nd July. He was probably the best known, and certainly one of the most respected men in Chard, and will be long remembered. There is a phrase in the Apocryphal second book of Esdras, which has often come into my mind when I have been thinking of him. It is this – 'Them that stood stiffly for the Name of the Lord.' The whole passage is worth quoting, for it seems so well to fit the occasion (II *Esdras* ii: 42–48)
'I Esdras, saw upon the Mount Sion a great multitude I could not number, and they all praised the Lord with songs. And in the midst of them there was a young man of high stature, taller than all the rest, and upon every one of their heads he set crowns and was more exalted: whereat I marvelled greatly. So I asked the angel, and said, What are these, my Lord? He answered and said unto me, These are they that have put off the mortal clothing and have put on the immortal, and

The interior of the church of St Mary, Chard, was reordered towards the end of the twentieth century. It is a remarkably spacious building.

The font in which the Dwelly children were baptised. It was moved to the east end of the church as part of the reordering.

have confessed the name of God; now are they crowned; and receive palms. Then said I unto the angel, What man he is that setteth the crowns upon them, and giveth them palms in their hands? So he answered and said unto me, It is the Son of God whom they have confessed in the world. Then began I greatly to commend them that stood so stiffly for the name of the Lord.'

That last sentence well describes the attitude of our friend, Mr. Councillor Dwelly. In season and out of season, he stood stiffly for what he thought to be right. He was no reed shaken by the wind. His life was governed by rule. Who has not seen him day after day taking his regular exercise in spite of his lameness? We could always count on his place in church being filled on Sundays and Wednesdays. Others might be kept away by the weather or caprice, but he was there, a witness and an example to us all. In so many ways he stood stiffly for the name of the Lord. Let us thank God for his consistent example, and let us not fail to pray for those who must miss him so much, and especially for her who for more than sixty years was his loyal and loving helpmeet.

Less than a year later his widow died. The Church of the Good Shepherd, Furnham, Chard, was just across the road from the Dwelly home, and we might assume that Caroline Dwelly worshipped in the church most convenient to her home.

The Church of the Good Shepherd, just across the road from the Dwelly house. Mrs Dwelly worshipped here regularly in her later days.

A very wooden studio portrait of the Dwelly brothers with their mother. Fred is on the right, the earliest existing photograph of him.

Mrs Caroline Dwelly, to whom Fred was devoted the whole of her life.

The Good Shepherd Parish Magazine
  March, 1928
  In Memoriam
  Caroline Dwelly
  Passed at time of Evensong
  Quinquagesima Sunday 1928
  Her ways are ways of gentleness
  And all her paths are peace.

While we were singing Evensong on Quinquagesima Sunday there passed to the Better Land one of the most beautiful, saintly, heroic souls it has ever been my privilege to know.

Mrs Dwelly was one of the oldest and most faithful members of this Church; she had an intense love for the Master, always trying to follow His steps, and do

His Holy Will in all things. She was a most regular and devout Communicant, and never missed the daily Evensong. She was my Mother's greatest friend, and to me she has been as a Mother, to whom I could go and tell all my troubles and difficulties, and be sure of perfect sympathy and understanding and the wisest counsel and advice. She took the keenest interest in everything that was happening, and especially all that concerned the welfare of the Church.

Full of the love of God, she was always happy and bright and cheerful, and with a great sense of humour which enabled her to see the funny side of things, and so she was constantly making the most delightful little jokes. Her later years were made specially happy by the intense love and affection shown to her by all her many friends and especially by the wonderful devotion of her Children of whom she was so rightly proud. Her dear body rested in her beloved church Tuesday evening. There was a celebration of the Holy Communion on Wednesday, and the most beautiful and touching service at 12.30, when we were glad to have the Vicar of the Mother Church joining with us. The committal of the body was by her son, Canon F. W. Dwelly.

We praise God for the example of a real Christian life, so humble and gentle and strong. We shall miss her visible presence very much, but we rejoice that she has found her rest, and higher, nobler work; and are sure that in Paradise she will always remember and help those she loved on earth.

LAUS DEO

Everything about the funeral service paper speaks of Dwelly of Liverpool: the paper, print, design, the prayers, and the character of the whole, from 'O Jesus, thou hast promised' at the start, to 'The strife is o'er, the battle done. Alleluia!' at the end.

After a visit to Chard in 1993, I was able to make an appeal in the *Furnham Magazine* for any information relating to the Dwelly family and received this most informative letter from Mrs Evelyn Hounsell:

I am now 84 years of age and when I was a child I lived in Bath Street, Chard, where our only supply of water was from a pipe or shute as we called it, bringing lovely spring water from the hills at the west of the town and which was always icy cold and never dried up whatever the weather.

Now I remember clearly Alderman Dwelly coming frequently to drink that water. It was usually early morning. He carried a small Gladstone bag with a glass tumbler inside and he used to take out the glass, fill it with the spring water and stand there and drink it, put the glass back in the bag and go home again. We lived directly opposite only 3 or 4 yards away and I have seen him do this many times. He used to say it was the purest water for miles around. He was a very nice gentleman and always wore black clothes and a round fairly flat crowned black hat with a brim. Unfortunately owing to new rules and regulations the water was cut off by the 1940s, blocked and diverted.

The Dwelly family were greatly respected in the town. I can remember well,

Miss Dwelly who always seemed to wear a long flowing coat. She was a very staunch church woman who used to help a great deal with the Sunday schools and the Girls Friendly Society. My husband who is 90 said the coaches Mr Dwelly turned out were really perfect specimens, he was very thorough and proud of his work. The man who worked for him on the painting of the coaches was called Mr Pike ...

All my old friends and relatives who knew a lot more than I do have passed on so there is no one I can ask for more information.

After the spring of 1898, Fred Dwelly left Chard, although thereafter visited his home town frequently. His departure was marked by his friends at the Parish Church:

FAREWELL TO A SUNDAY SCHOOL WORKER

On Sunday, after the evening service at St Mary's Church, a special Sunday School teachers' meeting was held for the purpose of bidding adieu to Mr F. W. Dwelly, who is leaving the town. On behalf of the teachers, the Vicar handed him a travelling clock. The recipient suitably acknowledged the gift, observing that in the past 34 years scarcely a Sunday had passed without one of the Dwellys having attended the Sunday School. The clock bore the inscription 'Presented to F. W. Dwelly from the teachers of the Parish Sunday School, Chard, April 9th, 1898.'

As far as written evidence relating to Dwelly's departure from Chard is concerned, we have to wait for details in one of the many obituary notices after his death in 1957:

Frederick William Dwelly was born on April 10, 1881, son of Robert Dwelly, a Somerset carriage builder, a religious and forceful character. The lad, at a late stage in his education at Chard Grammar School was a frequent truant, with the excuse of listening to music. Though the headmaster was indulgent, the facts eventually came to his father's knowledge, whereupon the admonitions were so severe that (it appears with his mother's connivance) the young Dwelly left home for London.

Family oral history corroborates this account but adds nothing by way of detail. One of his oldest, closest and most distinguished friends was to write of the early years that they were, 'without any special advantages of birth or prestige or privilege. Schooled for business ...' (Charles Raven)

What facts remain from this crucial boyhood stage of his life have been recorded here. From many later pieces of written evidence, Dwelly's dedication to his family and his old friends becomes one of the most powerful features of his long, distinguished, and enigmatic, life. This writer has no false notion that he can judge his subject and write a definitive statement. All he can do is to make available the results of his research to a wider audience.

The famous mathematical bridge over the river Cam at Queens' College, Cambridge.

Freshmen at Queens' College in 1903. Dwelly stands, determined not to look at the camera, at the end of the back row.

CHAPTER TWO

London and Cambridge

F RED DWELLY LEFT THE FAMILY HOME in Chard in 1898 at the age of seventeen. To date, research has yielded little information about the developments of a future Dean over the next eight years. An obituary notice gives an unadorned and unconfirmed outline:

> ... the young Dwelly left home for London. For some years he earned a livelihood by working in a large draper's shop, devoting his spare time to religious and social work in slums and adding to his knowledge of the arts, though not in a systematic study of them. Through the advice and intervention of a business man he went to Queens' College, Cambridge, and became reconciled to his father, of whom he always spoke with admiration.

We may never know for certain why his first destination was London but in at least two letters which refer to the London period his brother Bert is mentioned. Herbert Dwelly was nine years his senior and we know that he married Florence May Peryman at St Michael's Church, Stonebridge Park, Harlesden, in 1908. Fred might have moved to London because his elder brother was there already working as a teacher. John Frederick Dwelly, Herbert's son, is still alive and has reported that Fred obtained a post with Marshall and Snelgrove. 'He spent many weekends amongst the underpriviliged and criminal classes doing "good works" in the East End of London.'

As well as having difficult handwriting, Dwelly had the bad habit of not dating his letters, but undoubtedly the following letter to his mother dates from the London period. He wrote from an illegible address in Hampstead and gave his new address as c/o Rev Whaller, St Catherines, Broxburne.

> My dearest Mother,
>
> Once again the date reminds me of the richest earthly blessing bestowed on one that of the never ending Mother's love and one cannot not only make the somewhat conventional remark 'Many Happy returns of the day', but turn it into a sincere prayer, for I do so hope that for a long time to come you may be spared

to cheer and encourage the lives of your children – dear little Mother mine I fear you had a troublesome life with us all, but this much should comfort you that you have the fullest of children's devotion of boys and girls who would do anything for you.

Bert and I were talking on Sunday and comparing many Mothers to our own Mother and we both came to the conclusion that there isn't another Mother going like ours is for you are the real best and as for Dad's – well may we say Thank God for good Father and Mother.

And now Mother dear be very happy on your birthday as we shall all be praying for you more than ever, may the sweet consciousness of his nearness fill up the gap of our absence.

Will you accept that little table as a token of my love and good wishes, I know you reverence it – and please tell me of something else I can send as a token.

My very fondest love to you and Daddy.

Your very devoted

Baby boy, Fred.

One letter to his parents written after he had preached for the first time in Westminster Abbey makes one brief reference to his London days: 'I thought of those days gone by when I went to the abbey out of work and prayed for a job.' There is also a reference to Bert being present at the service together with Fred Cooper.

The London and Cambridge years may well remain one of the dark rooms in Dwelly's life. At the present time the only primary sources extant from the period are a freshman's photograph taken at Queens' College in 1903, and the records of his examination performance:

The only College archives for Dwelly's time at Queens' relate to his examination results and these do not suggest that he was in any way outstanding academically. He was awarded his B.A. in 1906 on the results of a second class pass in Part I of the Special Examination for the ordinary degree in Theology and third class pass in Pt II of the same examination.

M. M. Scarr, Liaison Officer, Queens' College Cambridge, 24 June 1993

It is certainly not clear how or when Dwelly's vocation to the priesthood came about and we have to be content with F. W. Dillistone's brief comment in his biography of Charles Raven:

A native of Chard in Somerset he had moved to London after leaving school to work as a salesman in one of the great stores near Oxford Circus. He became associated with All Soul's Langham Place whose incumbent at the time was a noted Evangelical leader, Prebendary F. S. Webster. Evidently realising the potentialities of the young man who has passed though a crisis of religious experience, Webster encouraged him to go up to Cambridge and prepare for ordination.

The Cambridge of the turn of the last century was very different from the

Two views of Queens'
College. Unfortunately very
little is known about his
Cambridge years.

The chapel at Queens', where Dwelly became dissatisfied with the character of the services.

Cambridge of today. A very self-conscious looking Dwelly can be seen on the freshmen's photograph, rather ostentatiously on the end of the back row in profile while everyone else looked at the camera – there were only twenty-six men in all. The college itself runs along the side of Silver Street and down to the river, which is crossed by the famous mathematical bridge. The 'English domestic' brick of the architecture has none of the grandeur of King's or Trinity but the scale is as comfortable as the colour and texture of the brick and the half-timbering. Erasmus had lodged in the college during a time in England. Of all unlikely sources, the *Yale News* for 4 March 1925 comments on some of Dwelly's experiences from this time. Dwelly had gone to America in 1925 to give a series of lectures at the invitation of the Berkeley Divinity School. The headlines to the article are very interesting:

CANON DWELLY IS SPEAKER IN DWIGHT HALL TONIGHT
  Studdert-Kennedy's Successor is U.S. Considered Fully as Striking a Personality

FIGHTS UNREALITY IN RELIGION
  While in College Opposed Artificiality in Chapel Services

While in college Canon Dwelly carried on a vigorous protest against unreality in college services ...
  An English correspondent writes of Canon Dwelly: 'He set out in life with the

intention of being a shipper. Interest in the dockhands led him into the slum areas of Spitalfields, East London. Here he received great surprise ... he discovered there was reality in prayer, and creative reality in religious fellowship. The church life had never revealed this to him, and yet he could not resist the appeal of the potentialities of the church. He wanted to recapture for the church the reality of prayer and the creative reality of spiritual fellowship. He threw up his brilliant business prospects, entered college, and there carried on a vigorous protest against the unreality of college services.

This is a secondary not a primary source (references to shipper, dockhands and brilliant business prospects may all be suspect) and yet the main thrust sounds typical of much that we shall observe later in Dwelly's ministry. At Queens' he would have encountered rigid adherence to the *Book of Common Prayer*, a book which Dwelly never rejected but early in his ministry he saw the need for the enrichment of the traditional services. Later in his career we shall examine his friendship with Percy Dearmer, his involvement with the National Mission, the Life and Liberty Movement, the *Grey Book*, the lead up to the *1928 Prayer Book*, his own *Acts of Devotion*, his editorial work on *Songs of Praise*, and all his liturgical experimentation in the famous services in Liverpool Cathedral and further afield. Some of these concerns may well have been rooted in worship during his undergraduate days of compulsory attendance of chapel services.

For this writer the most important insight into the development of the undergraduate Dwelly came about almost by accident in conversation with Canon Huw Thomas, then Canon Treasurer at Liverpool and subsequently Provost of Cairo. He had come across a brief reference to Dwelly in Adam Fox's *Dean Inge*, 1960. Only several years later when I read some of Inge's work did I begin to realise the significance of this find: so much of the very essence of Dwelly's later work can be traced back to the lecturing and writing of the man who was to become such a famous Dean of St Paul's.

William Ralph Inge was born in 1860, the son of a parson, later to become Provost of Worcester College Oxford. Throughout his education at Eton and King's College Cambridge, he showed academic brilliance in everything he undertook. In 1889 he became a Fellow of Hertford College, Oxford. After his marriage and two years as vicar of All Saints, Ennismore Gardens, he became Lady Margaret Professor of Divinity at Cambridge, and finally Dean of Saint Paul's. His early academic success was as a brilliant classicist but by the time he was elected to Hertford he was moving in the direction of neo-Platonism and the Mystics. His biographer declared him to be 'by temperament mystical and intuitive', 'decidedly a liberal', and in 1899, during the period when he was beginning to clarify his strongest convictions, he delivered the Bampton Lectures, published immediately as *Christian Mysticism*. Later, in *Confessio Fidei*, he was to write that 'Faith needs the help of imagination to make its affirmations real ... The true religion for each of us is the most spiritual view of reality we are able to realise and live by.'

In the first decade of the century, Inge was clearly a thinker and speaker of considerable significance. A committee of resident graduates of Cambridge invited him to deliver six lectures in the University during the Lent Term of 1906. The Victoria Assembly Rooms were filled with between 250 and 300 students (mainly undergraduates) on Wednesday afternoons to listen to *Truth and Falsehood in Religion*. In the Inge biography, Fox was later to report:

> One of those who heard them wrote some months later and said he could not express what he owed to the lectures; he had given up thoughts of ordination, but after hearing them he had determined to be ordained, and was ordained at Trinity. This was F. W. Dwelly who afterwards did such a remarkable work as Dean of Liverpool.

As a third-year undergraduate Dwelly would have been steeped in Biblical Studies, Church History, theological dogma. From what we know of so much of his ministry, he would not have found satisfaction here and from the opening moments of the first lecture he might well have found Inge's words and approach just what he needed: 'It is a perplexing age for those who need guidance. The simple expedient of obeying orders, of believing in authority, is difficult when they are so much in conflict ... I think I shall have a better chance of interesting some of you if I follow my own bent, and tell you how some of our most pressing problems appear to me.' I have no background in academic theology but even in the early years of the twenty-first century I find a vigour and freshness in his words, and from all my researches into Dwelly I feel certain that Inge's ideas would have set him alight.

> It is almost frivolous to make the whole truth or falsehood of Christianity turn upon the historical truth of a particular miracle, or the authenticity of a particular document, when among the real questions at issue are the character of the relations between the spiritual and the natural world, and the difference, if any, between revealed and natural religion. Until we have satisfied ourselves on these great general questions, it is useless to argue about the virgin-birth or the manner of the resurrection.
>
> If, then, I avoid these points of current controversy, it is not from cowardice, but because I wish to go behind them. I wish you to dig deeper among the foundations of religious belief, to consider what faith means, and what is its essential content ... I shall ask you to accompany me in an impartial and dispassionate survey of religious belief as a historical and psychological fact.
>
> ... I wish to remind you that, as a historical fact, the artistic sense has played, and still plays, an important part in the development of religion. Ideas, as we know, must be given through something. Language, if we analyse it, consists almost entirely of metaphors, that is, of calling things something which they are not, but which they resemble. Poetry affects us more than prose, because it is more lavish in the use of symbols or metaphors; a parable often 'hits him whom a sermon flies'; a concrete image impresses us more than an abstract truth; an overt

act, whether done or witnessed, though it may be a very poor and imperfect example of an ethical principle, lays hold on us and becomes part of us to a far greater extent than a general maxim, however wise and noble. And it is natural to some persons, and to some races, to express their feelings about the Divine by sensuous images – pictures, statues, architecture, music, orderly and solemn ritual, as it is to others to rely only on the spoken or written word, and on efforts to impress the Divine image on the order of events. Nor is it necessary that the symbolism should have any close connection with morality. The appreciation of beauty is itself an act of worship, and has been felt so during the greater part of the history of religion ... The beauty of God is a symbol of His righteousness, and His righteousness a symbol of His beauty. All religious art, whether painting or statuary or architecture or music or ceremonial, should be transparent. It should not be complete and satisfying in itself. It should suggest something behind, which it cannot fully express. This mystical quality (I use the word mystical of that which, in being what it is, suggests something beyond itself) – belongs to all religious art, and is its distinguishing feature. It is educative, not in intention so much as in fact, because it awakens in the beholder a sense of the hidden harmonies of things, and of depths of reality lying far beyond the ken of the common surface consciousness. The proper course for the worshipper of heavenly beauty, is, as all Platonists tell us, from the many to the One, from the variegated and scattered pictures of beauty with which the phenomenal world is full, to the Eternal Source of beauty and goodness, in whom beauty and goodness are one.

Quotation at such length from Inge at this point in the biography of Dwelly may seem a digression, but for me, after struggling towards some understanding of Dwelly for nearly ten years, Inge's words and ideas are like a floodlight: so much of Dwelly becomes clearer.

Religion must come down to earth, and mix with men. It must speak in their own language to the men that sit on the wall ... If human minds are weak, it must appear to share their weakness; if they are offended, its cheek must burn in sympathy.

Religion is pledged to the service of truth as yet but dimly seen; it pursues an ideal which is not yet an object of knowledge. It makes no pretence to be a complete and rounded theory of existence, which leaves nothing unexplained ...

Religion does not profess to explain everything. It is precisely because there are ragged edges in our experience, places where our consciousness is at discord with itself, that religious faith is needed.

The image of 'ragged edges' of experience seems most fitting when considering some of Dwelly's sermons in which he seemed to be engaging his congregation in his innermost thoughts. As Frederick Dillistone was to write many years later, 'Dwelly captured his audience by his sheer informality of approach, talking to them as friends for whom he really cared, about important matters which they had not perhaps sufficiently taken into account.' His sermons did speak to people 'in their own language' and he filled churches with people anxious to hear him. His deep concern for the importance of the arts permeated all aspects of worship for which he had responsibility: sermons on Shakespeare or Browning, poetry within the service, the language of intercessions, response to great architecture, sensitive and imaginative use of music in worship, and, maybe more important than anything else, brilliant use of human movement in meaningful ritual and ceremonial.

An early photograph of the Rev. F.W. Dwelly, probably taken shortly after his ordination.

CHAPTER THREE

St Mary, Windermere

'**B**Y THE TENOR OF THESE PRESENTS We John William by Divine Permission Bishop of Carlisle do make it known that on Sunday the Tenth day of June in the Year of our Lord One Thousand Nine Hundred and Six We the Bishop before mentioned holding a public Ordination under the Protection of the Almighty in our Cathedral Church at Carlisle did admit our beloved in Christ Frederick William Dwelly of Queens' College Cambridge (of whose Virtuous and Pious Life and conversation and Competent Learning and Knowledge in the Holy Scriptures we were well assured) into the Holy Order of Deacons according to the Manner and Form prescribed and used by the Church of England and him the said Frederick William Dwelly did then and there rightly and Canonically ordain Deacon he having first in our presence made and subscribed such Declaration and taken and subscribed such Oaths as are by law in such case required. In Testimony whereof we have caused our Episcopal Seal to be hereunto affixed the day and Year above written in the second Year of our Consecration.'

Dwelly was licensed to perform 'the office of Curate in the Parish of Saint Mary Windermere in the County of Westmoreland on the nomination of George Crewdson, Clerk M.A. The Incumbent thereof.'

Dwelly was one of three Cambridge graduates to be ordained at Carlisle on that day. We have no evidence as to why his ministry started in this way but we do know that the news of his ordination was known back in Chard because it is recorded in the magazine of the Church of the Good Shepherd across the road from the family home:

> It was a very great pleasure to all of us to hear a sermon at the Church of the Good Shepherd from Rev. Frederick Dwelly, the son of our fellow townsman, Mr Dwelly, on Sunday evening. He had been ordained at Carlisle on Trinity Sunday, so we had the privilege of hearing his first sermon, and a right good one it was. The parish that he goes to work in is Windermere in the beautiful lake country in the north. We heartily wish him God's speed.

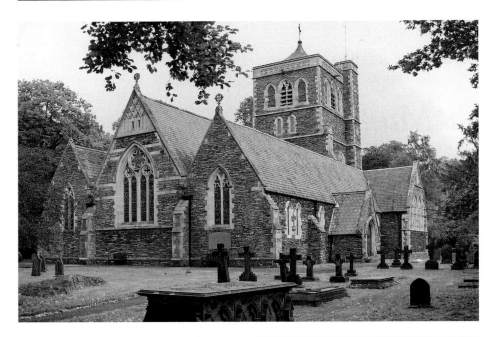

St Mary's Church at Windermere, quite an imposing church begun by the Rev. J.A. Addison with his own money.

Dwelly went straight from a degree course in Theology into the practical work of a parish with no professional training of any kind. He had to acquire his practical skills in the parish. There are only a few written sources by which to trace the progress he made and these are all from the latter part of his five years in the parish.

We do know that on 3 January 1907 Dwelly married Mary Bradshaw Darwin at Christ Church, West Didsbury. She was daughter of Major and Mrs Darwin of 1 Lethbridge Road, Southport. From the extant photographs, Mary Dwelly, known as Molly in the family, was a handsome young woman, accomplished as a water-colour artist, embroiderer and musician. Much of my knowledge of Mrs Dwelly comes from conversations with a niece, one of her two surviving relatives.

Giving news of Dwelly's departure from Windermere in 1911, *Pulman's Weekly News* reported that: 'For some time past Mr Dwelly has had the sole spiritual care of the parish as curate-in-charge' after the retirement of Canon Crewdson. This interesting note was to be paralleled in his next parish where, as a result of the vicar's ill-health, Dwelly ran two significant churches. As will be seen in detail later in his ministry, Dwelly was always the man who made the decisions. It is interesting to note that even as a curate, he was given considerable responsibility.

A significant signed carbon copy exists from James Carter, Parishioners' Warden, St Mary's Church, Windermere, 9 July 1910. The opening sentence might well indicate that the report was written in support of Dwelly's application for a new post. The paragraphs form such a thorough review of the man's ministry that they have to be reported in full.

Pleasure and regret struggle for the mastery as we pen this tribute to the Rev. F. W. Dwelly; It is a pleasure to remember all that he is and has been to this place, and it is a regret to feel that a change is anticipated, which will carry him to another sphere.

1. He is a Parish Priest of great power and ability, he stands before the world with a standard of lofty ideals, and he demands and receives, both within and without the Church, the homage and respect which belong to his character and sacred office. He is courageous, and yet tender, he has won the hearts of the children, of the young men, and indeed of the whole place, with the possible exception of two or three old women. He is a great comforter, and full of compassion for the sick and dying.

2. He is a born Organizer and is eminently practical, and the following are a few of the schemes he has initiated here.

(a) Boy Scouts and Young Men's Institute. These are two separate agencies, and the latter is the first really successful effort in this parish to cope with lads at a difficult age.

(b) Men's Society. This activity was formed to develop a more social and corporate feeling among the older men, and during the winter months some sixty or seventy men have weekly been drawn together, and have eagerly listened, it is no exaggeration to say for hours, to his able, profound and

Dwelly married Mary Bradshaw Dawsin in 1907. She is seen here with her grandmother.

fascinating lectures on 'The Religious Beliefs of the East' and other subjects. To see men, today, listen with sustained attention, and for so considerable a time to an avowedly religious address, and further, during the same session to see the clamour for a repetition of the same addresses, is to be conscious of a supremacy over men, and of a triumph indeed which few can claim.

(c) Girl Guides. A Guild to enrich and give purpose to the lives of young girls, it has met a greatly felt want here.

(d) Sunday Schools. These have been entirely reorganised, and for the last three years the children have been taken away to the seaside for the annual treat. This effort has been quite novel here, and very successful.

(e) Choir Trip. For the last three years, the trip has been extended. To plan and successfully organize a trip to London for say thirty choristers, covering as the distance does, roughly five hundred miles, and done withal with limited means is an achievement of great moment.

(f) Parochial Finances. These have been reorganised throughout, and placed on a sound working basis, every account is now clear of debt, and when one remembers that before the vestry meeting of 1908, there was an accumulated balance on the debit side of over two hundred pounds, and that it was Mr Dwelly's zeal, enthusiasm, and compelling faith which cleared the debt, one feels quite naturally proud of him.

(g) Parish Magazine. This has been placed on an entirely new basis, and for the first time ever in its history, it is self-supporting.

(h) Whitehaven Colliery Disaster 1910. During the enforced absence, through illness of the Vicar, who is also Rural Dean, Mr. Dwelly, as the Rural Dean's Secretary, and entirely on his own initiative, organized a fund for this disaster ...

(j) Ordination Fund. This scheme it outside the ordinary parochial machinery. Two lads are now at the moment at Cambridge University, one has recently obtained honours in the Theological Tripos there, and these lads after taking their degrees are ultimately to take Orders. This effort, this wide outlook, this regard for the church at large, and her needs, is specially noteworthy. Without Mr. Dwelly's loving heart, and vigilant eye and gift for arousing the sympathy and co-operation of wealthy members of the Parish, these lads would have found it impossible to realize their vocation, through lack of means. Turning to the Schools, one Pupil teacher has already been provided with the means to qualify at a Training College, and is now able to take a much better position.

Charity Organization. This valuable attempt to solve the difficulty of overlapping and indiscriminate charity, has already proved of great benefit, and the care and trouble taken by Mr. Dwelly to investigate individual cases is known to all the parish.

(k) London Slums. He has an extraordinary love for this work, and he has succeeded in evoking a large amount of genuine and practical sympathy, which has been productive of much and lasting good, both to the slums, and to this parish.

To summarize, Does one overstate the case? Is he not a born organizer?

3. He is a preacher, at once able and eloquent in the pulpit, having a mind enriched with the wisdom of the ancients, an extraordinary grasp of the tread & movement of contemporary scholarship and modern thought, having a great width of vision, and a profound spiritual intuition, he can and does interpret the deep things of God in a language, and by a mode of thought which palpitates and throbs with life, and which make the Eternal Verities and the Church of God a living reality, and force in this twentieth century of ours. Should this diocese lose him, it will lose indeed a 'Priest of the Most High God', a Priest whose prayers and availing presence can wrestle in the heavenly places, and prevail, it will lose a man, nay, a Prince, nay, a King with a great and a wide spiritual dominion.

This would be a remarkable testimonial even for an experienced priest: for someone in his first post it would seem to hint at a future career of some distinction.

The Liverpool Echo for Friday October 14, 1955 carried a letter from an Ex-Scoutmaster, 1st Windermere Scouts, the contents of which underline Dwelly's staying power and loyalty to friends and causes:

I wonder if you would be interested to know that the Rev. F. W. Dwelly became Curate at St Mary's Church Windermere in 1906 his first curacy. Two years later his great friend Mr. J. Mortimer Sladen started the first Windermere Sea Scouts and Dr Dwelly became its Chaplain. From then on, until 1938, I cannot remember him missing a single August Camp with the troop at Fellfoot on Lake Windermere, where he took part in all the activities of the camp. There on sports day he met the parents of the scouts, and very many friends he had made during his curacy. It was always a great day in the scout year.

The day he was made Dean car loads of the 1st Windermere Rovers, all of them scouts of 1908 or later went to Liverpool ... From then on until 1938 the Windermere Rover Scouts went to Liverpool and slept on the floor of the old wooden refectory, so that they could be present at the anniversary service on the following Sunday morning.

Through the years since then the Dean has kept in touch with the troop and he is still an honorary member of the Rover Scout Guild. Dr Dwelly was a great inspiration and influence on his old fellow scouts and this inspiration still pervades the training of the 1st Windermere Sea Scouts. At the Annual Rover Scout supper he is always remembered and stories about him are recalled and talked over.

It is usual for the departure of a clergyman from a parish to be marked by some form of presentation. The presentations to Dwelly, however, were remarkable and included a silver ink-stand, a leather bound *Britannica*, a gold stop watch, a grandfather clock, a cheque for £420 and a diamond and sapphire pendant for Mrs Dwelly.

For many years Dwelly
attended the annual scout
camp at Windermere.

The monetary value of all of these gifts was many times the average annual stipend for a young curate at that time.

The *Westmoreland Gazette* for December 17, 1910 gives extensive accounts of those final social events which Dwelly attended before his departure from the town. Thirty members of the St Mary's Men's Society gathered for a hot-pot supper and smoking concert at which their presentation was made. The newspaper devoted considerable space to the event and we can only assume that a reporter took notes in shorthand because speeches are reported lengthily and Dwelly spoke several times during the evening, as well as singing *John Peel* as part of the concert.

Mr Dwelly at this point he had from time to time said some rather nasty things about the North Country. But now I am leaving it I will say it is perhaps not so bad, you know. I don't like climbing down; it is not my nature; but all the time, while I have been trying to get at them, my object has been honestly trying to make the North Country better than it is. To tell you the honest truth, I think the hearts of Westmoreland and the heart of the North country is a heart that is real, and a heart that is true, and a heart that is generous and good. (Cheers) Nobody taking my job, that of a clergyman, could say anything else after asking for £250 and getting £400. No one could do what one has tried to do – and doing it rather frequently, without coming to that conclusion about Westmoreland people. I have come to the conclusion after all these nice things you have said about me that as a matter of fact it proves that there lies within the men of the place a responsiveness, a readiness, a reciprocativeness, a heartiness, a willingness that has done a great amount of good and will do greater good in the future.

The presentation was made by F. H. Walker, the Secretary of the Society, and parts of his speech also throw light upon parts of Dwelly's ministry as a young curate.

If we go back a year or two, when the society had its birth, we remember that it was entirely Mr Dwelly's idea. The two main ideas in beginning it were (1) that many of us men wished to have a better knowledge not only of religious matters but to have it put into a form which, perhaps, we could more easily understand at first hand. (2) Mr Dwelly also had the idea, and I think it was fairly prevalent at that time, that we men in Windermere should get to know each other better, that there should be more brotherliness, and that we should be able to meet together and discuss things and in that way to promote a better feeling among the men of Windermere. [Applause] There is no question that it has proved most successful; but I may say that out of that there has grown something greater, and that is the ideal which has grown up in this society – an ideal which we must carry forward to the best of our ability, one which we must take outside this society and apply to other people in our own personal everyday life ... It is unnecessary for me to tell you what Mr Dwelly has done; everyone knows the enormous amount of work he has got through, the enormous amount of sympathy he has given out. We all regret his departure; we shall miss seeing him in the street, shall miss the familiar figure at St Mary's – [Applause] – standing erect against that stone pillar and lashing out at something which he hates. I feel that I may not say all that I should like to; my admiration of him is unbounded and I know that so it is with every member of this club.

Much of Dwelly's ministry was before the days of easy and effective sound recording and for this reason any fully reported speech or sermon is valuable in revealing an important aspect of the man.

There is a peculiar atmosphere about this room that makes it not quite so difficult for me to acknowledge this kind of gift of yours as it has been in the case of the other presentations I have had to pass through. I say 'had to', for while one values tremendously all the kindness that has prompted them, you must realise that it does mean something to one to think that with the boys whose faces one has looked upon for the last time one has been able to mould their characters in some small way. There I have been the clergyman; here, gentlemen, I have been just a man. [Applause] My greatest pleasure has been the feeling that I could set aside, as it were, my collar and come here as a man and feel that you did not expect me to be a parson but that you are here with me, that together we can help one another with friendship, with comradeship, and talks over different matters. You have been kind enough to ask me at times 'What is a Christian?' And I have occupied a lot of your time in telling of the growth of Christianity, and how we got our Bible, and in a comparison of Christianity with other religions of the world and the hypothesis with it provides for building up the greatest of character. But while you have given me that privilege, one I value so highly, you have given me far more. As I have said in the *Magazine*, whenever the grumblers have come and made one sad, it is to some one or other of you that I have turned off to, perhaps jumped off my bicycle in the street and talked about it, – perhaps in a kitchen or a library, a school, a shop or office or bank, on the station platform, in the street – in one place or another one has always turned in, and come out feeling happier. Strange to say, much as one values one's work, somehow or other it costs a great deal; it is hard to do your best and be understood. But you men – I thank you for it – you have ever given me your trust, you have ever allowed me to say things you didn't perhaps quite understand or approve of; but at any rate we have felt as we left these rooms on a Friday night, that every one of us means the best and means right. [Applause]

As I leave Windermere, it is with the consciousness that I have had much help from you, that I owe you men more than I can say, for the friendship, the manly strength, the magnificent help, the real grit you have thrown into my work when I have asked you to do it. The clock will remind me of the saying, sometimes, at half past ten, 'Now we must be off home,' or of the saying at 11.30, 'What will your wife say, Mr Dwelly?' I am grateful to you for this kind gift to my wife. Some people have been unkind enough to say that she cares not for the great Master's work because I have now allowed her to act as most clergymen's wives act. But, gentlemen, let me say this, – forgive me for being personal – my wife has had many many meals alone; often she has allowed me to be out, night after night, haunting homes or doing something until perhaps four o'clock in the morning; and as needed strength – for you cannot give out your best without needing it – she has given it me back. I thank you for this kind thought of yours for my wife.

These are not the words of a remote cleric: he had clearly established a vigorous, open, direct, very down-to-earth way of speaking. Throughout his life there is evidence of a genius for forming strong relationships and unshakeable friendship. In this speech we have the first extant reference to his wife. Certainly in both of his next parishes Mrs Dwelly's work was to feature, but by the Cathedral years there were discernible signs of breakdown in their relationship. There were no children of the marriage and, in the light of Dwelly's natural talent for communicating with children, this would seem a tragic gap.

On the Tuesday evening, the day after the Men's Society meeting, the final parish presentation was made in 'the institute'. The newspaper account of the setting is of interest.

The hall was sumptuously furnished and decorated for the occasion and its appearance was transformed to a wonderful degree. Large palms, sprays of bay leaves, begonias, chrysanthemums, etc. brought from the nurseries of Mr Mawson were skilfully disposed along the platform, and about the hall. In the middle of the floor space, overhung by the curving fronds of giant palms, the gifts of the different parochial bodies were disposed on or around a large writing table. The amplitude of floral decorations was supplemented by special electric lighting arrangements, producing a charming and fairy-like effect. Lamps of delicate tints, chiefly red and green, were artistically disposed among the palms and other plants. These illuminations were excellently carried out by Messrs J. K. Thornborough and Co., electrical engineers, a portion of whose premises is on the ground floor of the building. A band from Messrs. Forsyth's of Manchester, was seated in the gallery, and played several selections of choice music as the guests assembled and again as they partook of refreshments in the earlier part of the evening.

It is interesting to note Alderman Robert Dwelly was present together with Mr T. Dwelly, presumably the eldest son who had been born in 1866.

A number of speeches marked the occasion, in the main extolling qualities in the man and his ministry which have already been emphasised. However, part of Church Warden James Carter's speech stresses an aspect whose relevance may well be seen twenty years later.

One thing, I think, has been emphasised more than any other during his tenure of office; we have almost ceased to remember that we have belonged to this or that denomination, or to remember that there are such names. We have been taught by precept and glorious example the nobility and grandeur of the Christian calling, which shall break down every animosity and all this strife and shall one day knit the family of men into one great Divine Brotherhood. He has accomplished this not in the obvious way, not by whittling down his own convictions by a profound and tenacious grasp of the principles which he believes to be true; and the very force and power of that tenacity has shown to others who think differently from him the necessity of a great and wide toleration which will allow to every man, no matter who he may be, the same liberty of thought which he claims for himself. He has broken down the sectional feeling which paralyses our work, but he has done it, I say, by a way not obvious, but by tenaciously clinging to his own opinions, and that has enabled him to give to others the same liberty he has claimed for himself.

It is interesting to think back to this statement at the time of the Unitarian Controversy at Liverpool Cathedral and the Dean's close friendship with Rev. John Wilkinson, a free-church minister.

The Rector of Windermere, Rev. E. J. Nurse, spoke briefly and commented on what someone present had said: 'A lady said to him that night, "This meeting is quite worthy of a Bishop is it not?" He replied, "And he is going to be a bishop." [Applause]' He also made reference to the absent Mrs Dwelly. 'Before sitting down, he would like to mention Mrs Dwelly, who was unable to be present – they would all have liked to see her that night, if she had been in Windermere, although it would have been a trying ordeal for her to go through.'

A. R. Sladen who formally made the presentations had been present on the previous evening to hear Dwelly's comments on the attitudes towards his wife, and in his presentation speech he makes much of her support for her husband. He also makes pertinent comment on Dwelly's skills with people.

We must all feel from the bottom of our hearts that in losing Mr Dwelly we are losing a friend. The greatest thing in the world is a real friend; and we can honestly say that in his departure we are losing one. Not only has he given us his help and sympathy and advice in every way, but he has had that rare gift, one which few persons possess, of extracting the best out of other people if other people will only let him.

Some of Dwelly's words of thanks are quite revealing; there is no intention of staying with comfortable words or non-contentious issues.

Whenever I have come and pestered you in the last four years I have sometimes come in fear and trembling; yet you have always given me what I have asked for, and when I have asked you to work you have nearly always responded. Although once or twice in a kindly way you would wish I would stop begging, you have continued up to the last month to give.

His thanks for the overwhelmingly generous gifts are heartfelt:

I value them tremendously. That desk there – the boys' book the little Scouties –
I have it before my eyes; it tells me some of those rows we had, of the many ways
in which we have tried to rub off each other's corners. We lads – for after all I am
only a lad – have tried to travel together the upward path . . .

I came to you quite as a novice. You know a curate is supposed to be an appren-
tice, and I have been one. You have taught me sometimes by failure, sometimes by
a little success, how best to find out the secret of the Master in your hearts. Often
I have blundered; I can see now before my mind's eye many men and women
whom I have spoken to as I ought not to have done. Remember, please, it was only
an apprenticeship, and forgive me, let me carry away your forgiveness . . .

For the second evening in succession he refers to his wife and to people's implied
criticism of her.

Let me pass for one moment to one who would have liked to be here but her
health did not allow. I must say, though it may seem unkind, that frequently some
ladies have suggested that my wife did not care for my Master's work. It has given
me the greatest pain to hear this. One could not help not doing one's best, yet one
would not have been able to give all the time, strength and energy as one has tried
to give had it not been that behind there was someone doing all the mechanical,
hard, dreary drudgery – the unseen work of the Master – She whom the world did
not see was working for Christ but who in my weakness became my strength, who
in the hours when I could not have written or spoken, wrote for me, spoke for
me. I thank you very much that you have not forgotten the one who works behind
the scenes. I am very grateful.

From another fragment of news we learn that even Dwelly's physical departure
from the town was marked by crowds of people who assembled at the railway
station. The departure must have been surprising and noisy through the use of fog
signals detonated to herald his train journey to his new parish.

CHAPTER FOUR

St Mary, Cheltenham

T HE PARISH MAGAZINE of the Parish Church with St Matthew's, Cheltenham, announced the appointment of a new senior curate:

> The Rev. F. W. Dwelly, M.A., has accepted the position of Senior Assistant Clergyman on our Staff. He has since Ordination held the Curacy of St Mary's Church, Windermere, and from accounts I have received, he has done excellent work for our Heavenly Master. We cordially welcome his wife and himself to our Parish, and we earnestly pray that the blessing and inspiration of God the Holy Spirit may rest on his ministry in our midst.

Dwelly's licence from Edgar Charles Sumner by Divine permission, Bishop of Gloucester, is dated 20 May 1911, almost five months after his departure from Windermere. His new post carried a stipend of £180. The archives give no evidence of what he was doing between his departure from Windermere and licensing in Cheltenham.

St Mary's Church is the oldest building in Cheltenham, the only surviving medieval building in the town. There is late-Norman work to be seen at the west end and at the tower crossing, though most of the present walls are fourteenth century. Galleries had been added early in the nineteenth century without due attention to foundations. In 1859 the church had to be closed, condemned as unsafe and unsanitary. Because of the weight of the galleries, the floor of the south aisle collapsed into the crypt. Some people wanted to demolish the church and build a new and larger church on the site, but instead the church was restored and a much larger church was consecrated in 1879. St Matthew's, only a couple of hundred yards away, is a vast Victorian building with seating for 1,800. The Rector, Canon Francis L'Estrange Fawcett, focused his attentions on the congregation at St Matthew's and wished to appoint a senior assistant curate to devote his attention to St Mary's. Dwelly was appointed to that position and lived at Hazeldale, Hewlett Road, and worked with three other assistant curates.

In Dwelly's own words, 'Canon Fawcett ... charged me with the spiritual revival

St Mary's Church, the only
surviving medieval building in
Cheltenham.

The interior of St Mary's was
regularly packed to the doors
when Dwelly preached.

of the old Parish church – to work among boys – and to work among girls.' A short article has been preserved from a Cheltenham journal of January 1916 which is a useful starting point from which to consider Dwelly's ministry.

The peculiar difficulties of the incumbency of Cheltenham are well known. With two churches to be kept going, within the proverbial stone's throw of each other, there is always a danger lest the interests of the one should be advanced at the expense of the other. When Canon L'Estrange Fawcett filled the Rectory, however, he determined that the old Parish church should not be depressed for the aggrandisement of St Matthew's, and while devoting his own energies princi-pally to the service of the latter church, he sought and obtained a very able coadjutor in the person of Mr Dwelly to undertake the corresponding position at St Mary's. And it has further to be said in praise of the attitude of the late Rector that he gave his colleague a free hand in the arrangement and carrying on of his work. This was the way to secure the very best results, and success which has attended Mr. Dwelly's labours is in no small measure due to the liberty of action which was given to him. A man of unbounded energy, Mr. Dwelly would have made his mark in any vocation, and his love for the calling to which he has devoted his life has found expression not only in the earnest pulpit ministrations but in the organisation and conduct of not a few agencies which have helped mate-rially to attract and attach to the Parish Church large numbers of the young people of the town. Among those associations may be mentioned the Parish Church Boy Scouts, a numerically strong force which has given between thirty and forty of its members to the Army, and the Parish Church Girl Guides, an organisation which boasts of some three hundred members. It is, however, Mr. Dwelly's pulpit gifts which have restored the congregations at St Mary's to something like the propor-tions they bore before the erection of St Matthew's drew away the larger part of the people to that church, which the late Canon Bell at once made in effect, if not in name, the chief of the two churches of which he had the oversight.

As had happened at Windermere, here again Dwelly was to be given more freedom and opportunities for personal initiative and leadership than were then presented to most inexperienced assistant curates. With the same 'boundless energy' which had marked his labours in Windermere, he began to make himself an un-ignorable presence in Cheltenham, and within a year one of the local papers was remarking upon his wonderful achievements:

The collections in the Parish Church on Sunday, both morning and evening, were on behalf of the work among lads, the troop of Boy Scouts, with bugle band, attending the morning service. Very crowded congregations were present on both occasions, especially at the evening service, when hundreds failed to gain admit-tance. The Rev. F. W. Dwelly preached the sermons, and they gave fresh evidence of his deep-seated sympathy with boys; for he understands and loves the 'human boy' as it is given to few grown-ups to do. There is no doubt that the Rev.

F. W. Dwelly is the most eloquent of the many eloquent preachers who occupy our local pulpits at the present time. Numbers of people come from all parts of the town to hear his sermons. It is not only the fluency of his words which attracts, but the obvious sincerity and earnestness of the man. Though his words may be many, he has no difficulty in retaining the attention of all until he brings his discourse to a close. At the end so interested and absorbed are his congregations that they can hardly tell whether the sermon was long or short. When he preaches there are no constant and furtive glances at the watch, nor are there scarce smothered yawns. Mr Dwelly is evidently marked for early preferment; but when the day comes for him to be called away, the parish will sadly miss his untiring work and his instructive eloquence.

There is evidence of the very long-term influence of Dwelly on the members of his congregations at most times in his ministry and at this point it is interesting to note that someone who remembered him from his few Cheltenham years took the trouble to write to the *Cheltenham Echo* late in 1955:

Sir, – About a month ago I remember seeing in your 'Gossip' column a short notice of the retirement of Dr Dwelly from Liverpool Cathedral. This revived memories of a personality who drew a really large number of people to St Mary's and St Matthew's Churches round about the first world war and a few years preceding it.

So appealing were the sincerity and earnestness of the man that at whichever church he preached there was never a vacant place. During a series of sermons given on some Victorian poets at the Parish Church many had to be turned away. Although he was appreciated highly by women, he was a man's man, and his sympathies were of the broadest, and no one ever went to him for counsel in vain. The war killed a great number of young fellows who came under his influence. His sermons to troops when stationed here, and an afternoon service to volunteers to the Colours, when both the high galleries at St Matthew's were packed to the last seat, are still vividly remembered.

One of his very young Cheltenham parishioners wrote him a letter nearly forty years later which gives a wonderful personal glimpse of a very memorable character: 'Your name always brings back such happy childhood memories of Cheltenham. How adept you were at writing your name in treacle on bread and butter! I still have my school girl autograph book in which you wrote a quotation from Robert Browning. The date is February 1916.' (Edna Banks, 24 June 1955)

The pulpit of the ancient Parish Church gave Dwelly a prominent platform from which to speak out on issues that he regarded as important, and he seems to have been quite fearless of public opinion:

Many people tell us today that England is degenerating, but no, no, never will I believe that to be so; never will Englishmen allow the glory of our country to fail.

REV. F. W. DWELLY,

Senior Curate of Cheltenham Parish Church, who is leaving to-day to take th
Vicariate of Emmanuel Church, Southport. He has made himself greatly beloved b
his congregation, and a series of valuable presentations were made to him on Wednesda
last. The photo, specially taken by our photographer this week, shows him at the doc
of our beautiful old Parish Church.

Dwelly outside the west door.

Yet in the same breath I would tell you that it is true, that England is degenerating, and you need go no further than this town of Cheltenham to prove it. So many men follow their political party whether they agree with it or not. They do not work things out for themselves; they are content to follow others. I cannot but believe that any man who has the interests of his town and country at heart has not an ideal for it. Then sit down in silence, and think out your ideal, think and plan until you find a way in which it can be realised. All through history it is not the men who have been accessories to any particular party who have made our empire what it is; it is men who have thought and worked in silence and then struck out a new line for themselves. What matter if your party gives you up? Strive to realise your ideal. Work alone if necessary until you find someone who thinks with you, then throw in your lot together and you will conquer. (Dwelly, 5 December 1912)

Preaching at the annual parade service of the Ancient Order of Foresters, a local friendly society, Dwelly was scathing about organisations with secret practices: 'Your men resolved that there should be nothing but free, open dignity. Some of you may be still hankering after the secret signs and forms. Let me tell you as a minister that there has been nothing which has come between husband and wife, father and family, more than those wicked systems which suppose to make men have secrets apart from their wives. You have done honorably and nobly in turning from such babyish things which belong to the early days when faith was a mere superstition.' (Dwelly, 29 September 1913) The same sermon contained strong words critical of what he saw as irrelevant bickering between members of the local political parties. Here was a preacher not afraid of public opinion and of the opinion of some of the powerful groups in society.

He might have been in danger of offending some of the most xenophobic members of society by his words in a very balanced service delivered after the outbreak of the war in 1914:

And then towards the foe. Let us see to it that calm restraint be ours. Let us not forget ourselves and use some hateful expressions towards the Germans. Remember that they, too, are 'children of God and inheritors of the kingdom of heaven,' though for the present day they have fallen from their goodly heritage. The idle gossip which indulges in invectives against them does neither them nor us good ... To look down often means the giving up of a struggle, to look round often means discouragement, but to look up means quiet strength and ultimate success.

The *Record* for 24 June 1915 announced the immediate resignation of Canon L'Estrange Fawcett on the grounds of overwork and breakdown in health. Once again, Dwelly was to find himself curate-in-charge of a demanding parish, this time with two churches to be supported. As seems to be customary in the Church of England, an assistant curate moves on near the time when a new incumbent arrives,

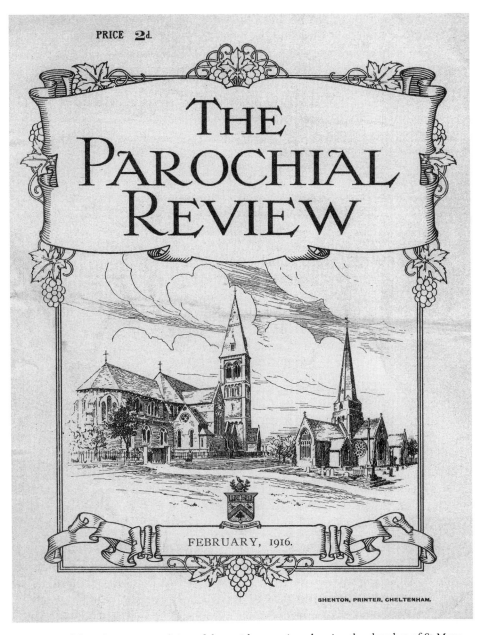

The cover of the February 1916 edition of the parish magazine, showing the churches of St Mary and St Matthew.

but Dwelly supported the parish and all its work until the eve of the arrival of the new man. Boy Scout and Girl Guide troops were founded during his time. As with the Windermere boys, Dwelly was the life and soul of the summer camp of his new troop. Mrs Dwelly was involved with the Guides, who numbered three hundred by the time the Dwellys departed.

Only two copies of the *Parochial Review* are extant within the Dwelly archive but their contents give further evidence of the extraordinary energy and drive which marked his ministry. Even the list of the standard weekly services at St Mary's gives some idea of the demands made upon the clergy team.

SUNDAYS

Holy Communion every Sunday at 8.00 a.m.

Second and fourth Sunday at noon.

SERMONS AT

Morning Prayer 11.00: Men's Service 3.00

Evening Prayer 6.30

INTERCESSION FOR RELATIVES AT WAR

Daily at 12.00: 5.30. Sundays at 8.00 p.m.

Tuesdays: 7.00 a.m. With Holy Communion

HOLY COMMUNION

Tuesdays 7.00 a.m.: Thursdays at 12.00 noon

Saints' Days 12.00 noon

The *Southport Guardian* reported that Dwelly had been invited by the Principal of the prestigious Cheltenham Ladies College to conduct a regular week-day service, and on top of all this and the parochial organisations he had the reputation for being a very regular visitor. When he returned to Cheltenham as a visiting preacher in the autumn of 1916, he managed to visit the homes of over fifty parishioners during one weekend.

The *Gloucester Echo* for 30 December 1915 announced that it was the 'End of a notable curacy' and the article is reminiscent of words written or spoken in Westmoreland a few years earlier:

It does not often fall to the lot of a young clergyman in his curacy to leave so large a mark of his connection with an important parish as has been the case with Mr Dwelly. The circumstances were unusual, and the man was ideally constituted to turn them to advantage rather than be overwhelmed by them. And by advantage we must not be taken to imply personal advantage, for one of the most charac- teristic features of Mr Dwelly's labours has been a high degree of loyalty to his work and the ideals which he has kept before him, although the following of them may not always have led him along the 'primrose way' to popularity. The fact of the Parish of St Mary having two large churches, and that fine trait in the char- acter of the last rector, Canon L'Estrange Fawcett, which allowed him to give his capable curate full scope for his very marked individuality and great energy in the entire charge of the old Parish Church and many of its agencies, was one of the unusual circumstances to which we refer. Another was the fact of the long period during which the duties of the rectorship practically devolved upon Mr Dwelly in consequence of the illness of Canon Fawcett, and then during the several months' interregnum which will not really be at an end until the induction of the new Rector next month.

Dwelly was quite clearly an extraordinarily successful curate-in-charge and the reports of his final Sunday in office, 31 January 1916, are remarkable. The most touching is a hand-written letter from W. Ayres of Leeswood, Montpellier Drive, Cheltenham, dated February 1 1916:

My dear Mrs Dwelly,
I must this morning write to tell you a little about yesterday – it is quite impossible for me to describe it – but oh! How proud you would have been of your Fred. At the morning service we were crowded out but my word in the evening was really the time – at half past four I am told people commenced to congregate outside St Matthew's – by 6 o'clock it was packed like sardines in a tin – hundreds were turned away, not being able to get near the doors, much less inside. We had to have an overflow service at the Parish Church after the ordinary Evensong when Fred again preached. I shall never forget it. In Canon Bell's most palmy days there was nothing to touch the scene. Please forgive haste etc but I do so want you to know about it – a paper follows so with kindest regards to Mr Dwelly Caroline and yourself. Believe me Yours always sincerely.

The *Cheltenham Chronicle and Gloucester Graphic* for 12 February 1916 delivers a fuller account for its readers, including what it describes as a summary of the sermon:

In the evening a crowded congregation was expected at St Matthew's, but few perhaps were prepared for the sight which met their gaze. As early as half past four, or two hours before the time of the service, people began to form up in a queue on the footpath outside the church, and long time before the doors were open there were more outside than could be accommodated within. Mr Wethered (church warden) and his efficient staff of sidesmen managed to seat over 2,000. This could only be done by placing 500 chairs in the aisles and on every other bit of available space; and even then large numbers had to stand throughout the service, while many more could not get inside the church.

Not even in Canon Bell's time, it is said, was there ever such a crowd at St Matthew's. The church wardens sent the overflow to the Parish Church with the promise that Mr Dwelly would preach there immediately after his sermon in St Matthew's. But even after the Parish Church was also filled awaiting the overflow service, crowds stood in the aisles of St Matthew's.

THE EVENING SERMON
From the pulpit of St Matthew's Church on Sunday evening, the Rev.

F. W. Dwelly preached his valedictory sermon to his Cheltenham congregation. Before delivering his text, the reverend gentleman said he would be grateful if they would do for the new Rector of Cheltenham what scores of people in his new parish had done for him. During the coming week the new Rector was bound to feel a little sad at leaving a place where he was loved. It would be very nice if everyone sent him a postcard 'Welcome to Cheltenham', and put their names on it, for a postcard from all of them would brighten him, and help him enormously to do the work God had called him to do.

Preaching from the text 'Finally, whatsoever things are loveable, think on these ... The peace of God, which passeth all understanding, shall keep your hearts and minds in Christ Jesus' (Phil. iv., 7–8), he said St Paul was not leaving so much a parish as a church. He thought he would never get out of the dungeon into which he had been thrown, and so he wrote continually to his people 'Rejoice, rejoice'. No Christian minister was ever happy to see his people sad, for the Church of Christ was a Church which was continuous in its creative power, and it was various in its expressive power. There could be no end of a ministry, and there could, therefore, be no farewell sermon. The Church was one foundation, and in ministry it was not one body of people, it was not one set of ordained clergy; but it was Jesus Christ.

It was their privilege on Saturday next to welcome God's new minister in their midst, and they would say to him 'Lead us onward; we are one, no longer divided, no longer a strange set of heterogeneous people, but our faith is one.' He remembered that it was a year ago that day that he who taught Cheltenham the great truth that it was not their opinions that counted, but the Church of Christ, preached his last sermon in that church. They had learnt it. Those who would not lay aside their opinions could be done without, for the great cause of Christ must and would prevail.

What, then, should be their message? Surely to try and gather up for themselves what St Paul found necessary to give to his people the thought furniture of the soul. Was it not that every one of them desired to be the finest stamp of a Christian that could be found. The one thing for which they prayed was that they should live as God would have them live. Why was it, then, they failed? What was wrong? Was it not that somehow or other, at a weak moment, they were caught napping, and some temptation trapped them? Why did people speak uncharitably to their fellow Christians? Their thoughts were badly furnished; they had no stock of the commodity called charity. They did not mean to be cruel. The more one had of the commodity that was loveable the easier it was to live near Jesus Christ. The Lord emphasised more than the words could tell the necessity of their thoughts being pure. One's speech was held in check by the outside world. One dared not say what one thought of some, for there was a law of libel; but there was no check for the thoughts. His thoughts were his own, and no one could judge him for them. Did they not see how essential it was, if there was no guardian of the thoughts, that they themselves should provide one? They must train the thoughts, so 'finally, whatsoever things are loveable, think on these.' There were none so sour-hearted that they did not love the loveable, and the more they thought of them the more they became like them. There was never a fault in their lives that did not commence with thought, and no one sarcastic expression but was first in thought, and came out just when they did not expect it. The little act which they regretted so much was nursed in the mind, thought out, perhaps, when they were alone, and what had been nursed in one's mind must come out. Those must be revealed in the Great Day of Judgement.

The peace of God passeth all understanding and shall guard your hearts, but we must guard our thoughts. The promise is sure, it is the peace of God; but do not let us even think we can understand it, nor lose our peace by vain attempts to understand. We cannot hope to understand God. Do men understand their fellow men? Do they understand their wives? Do the women understand their husbands and lovers; and do they understand themselves? He (the preacher) did not understand himself. How then, if they understood not their fellow men whom they had seen, how could they ever hope to understand God, whom they had not seen? What were they, then, to do? We do not understand our nearest on earth; we just fold them in our hearts and love them, and peace between us is ours, though we do not understand. We do not understand the dormant nobility of our soldier or sailor lads, we think of their loveableness, and are peaceful again. So let us fling ourselves into the arms of the Blessed Lord, then think of the loveable in life, and we shall experience the peace which passes all understanding.

The sermon was closed with five minutes' thanksgiving for the 'loveable' of life, after which, all kneeling, was sung "Jesu, Lover of my soul" – a most impressive close to a memorable evening.'

Even the appearance of the parish magazine became more professional under his direction and before he left the *Parochial Review* had an eye-catching front cover with excellent line drawings of the two churches.

Windermere had seen a very successful start to Dwelly's ministry. The ancient Parish Church of Cheltenham had given him a wider audience, but neither church had given him much physical space to begin to develop the visual liturgy which was to be his greatest gift to the church. His next parish church was to have space, space which some of the parishioners believe to have been the training ground in which he was being prepared to take responsibility for the worship in the largest Cathedral in Britain, and one of the great churches of the world.

Diocese of Liverpool.

FORM OF SERVICE

FOR THE

INSTITUTION

BY THE

Right Reverend the Lord Bishop of Liverpool,

AND

INDUCTION

BY THE

Venerable the Archdeacon of Liverpool.

OF THE

REV. FREDERICK W. DWELLY, M.A.,

TO THE BENEFICE OF

EMMANUEL, SOUTHPORT,

On FRIDAY, FEBRUARY 18th, 1916,

AT 5 P.M.

Liverpool:
THE CHURCH PRESS, Church House, South John Street.
1916.

Rights of alteration reserved.

CHAPTER FIVE

Emmanuel Church, Southport

T HERE IS A DANGER of Frederick Dwelly's life and ministry to date being seen
in a rather parochial and provincial way, seemingly divorced from the whole
Church of England in which he was functioning. This biographer is not an appropriate person to attempt to write with any authority about the Church and liturgical
developments during the first quarter of the twentieth century, but it is not possible
to understand the man or his later liturgical achievements without attempting, very
simply and briefly, to place him on a wider ecclesiastical canvass.

This was a period of considerable liturgical ferment, with the hooligan Riots of
Kensit and the Protestant Truth Society on one side, and a Royal Commission on
the other. Dwelly the theology student at Cambridge and young curate in
Windermere and Cheltenham was obviously aware of the activities and publications
of the Bradshaw Society and the Alcuin Club. The names of Charles Gore, Walter
Frere and Percy Dearmer were influential in the land and, years later, Dwelly and
Dearmer were both heavily involved in the production of *Songs of Praise*. The 1908
Lambeth Conference was unequivocal on the matter of revision of the *Book of
Common Prayer*:

> The growing experience of the Anglican Communion in different parts of the
> world and among different races has pointed to the necessity for the adaptation
> and enrichment of forms of service which have come down to us from other times.
> Such adaptation and enrichment are advisable, and indeed essential if our church
> is to meet the real needs of living men and women today.

The outbreak of war and the need for appropriate forms of worship for the men
fighting in the trenches put another strain on existing texts. In 1915 Archbishop
Randall Davidson set up a committee to report entitled 'The Spiritual Call to the
Nation and the Church – what is being done by the war and what should be done?'
The Committee recommended a National Mission of Repentance and Hope to be
held in the autumn of 1916: a mission in which Dwelly's popularity as a preacher was
going to be heavily in demand. Three army chaplains formed part of the committee:

'In the light of their experience in France, the *Prayer Book* failed to meet the spiritual needs of the nation. Apart from its liturgical defects, it was too intellectual, it lacked homeliness, and it failed to express the needs of ordinary people.' (Jasper 1989)

No exact date of publication has yet been uncovered, but it was about this time that *Acts of Devotion* appeared – a collection of responsorial prayers, clearly intended to enrich public worship. Over seventy years later they may well sound stylistically remote and rather long but they are rooted in common humanity, and the book remains one of the few that Dwelly published.

ON THE GRACE OF CHILDHOOD

For His tender compassion towards them; for His burning indignation against those who do them wrong; for His deep and overflowing love, drawing them with irresistible attraction to Himself; for His message of their nearness to the Father of all

Alleluia. Blessed be God, Eternal Friend of Children.

For the beauty of children and their joy in all beautiful things, for their mirth and laughter, and for the joy and light they bring into the world.

Alleluia. Blessed be God, Eternal Friend of Children.

For their enthusiasm, their abounding energy, and their love of the heroic and adventurous; for their candid trust in those around them, and for their quick response to calls of love and service.

Alleluia. Blessed be God, Eternal Friend of Children.

And as we give thanks for the infinite value of children, so let us pray for Fathers and Mothers and for all of us through whom children receive their first thoughts of God.

That by the Inspiration of Thy Loving Spirit we may direct the thoughts of our children through curiosity to wonder, through fairies to angels, through the imagination to the delights of playtime to the worship of the joys of the Eternal.

Amen; Amen in Jesus the Everlasting Child.

Let us, in silence, remember before God all children born with some defect of body, or hindered by their environment, all orphaned, homeless or unwanted children, all children of loveless homes.

O Heavenly Father, make our hearts to burn within us for the unlovely lives of the children of our dark places; let Thy Loving Spirit breath into us a living renewal, that with unflagging confidence, with wise statesmanship and readiness to combine with others, we may turn to good account every law for the welfare of children. Amen.

From

A LITANY OF REMEMBRANCE

From weariness in continuing struggles; from despondency in failure and disappointment; from self-conceit; from delight in supposed superiority; and from all the harms and hindrances of offensive manners;

Save us and help us, we humbly beseech Thee, O Lord.

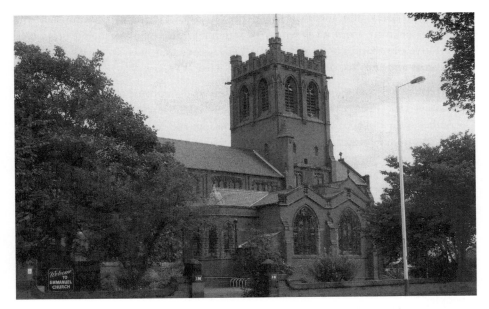

Emmanual Church, Cambridge Road, Southport, a large and imposing building, which must have encouraged Dwelly's liturgical experiments. There is seating for over a thousand people.

From all hasty utterances of impatience; from the retort of irritation and the taunt of sarcasm; from all infirmity of temper in provoking or being provoked; from love of unkind gossip and from all idle words that may do hurt:

Save us and help us, we humbly beseech Thee, O Lord.

The *Southport Guardian* for 1 January 1916 had reported that the living of Emmanuel had been offered to Dwelly who had preached there 'on Sunday, December 19th, and at St Cuthbert's in the evening; and on these occasions he made a most favourable impression, his reading of the lessons being described as "exceedingly fine", while his sermons were, it is said, "delivered extempore, and in such a way as to rivet the attention of his hearers". His style is attractive; the treatment of his subject original and imaginative; while throughout the spiritual seems to dominate the whole discourse.'

The earliest surviving letter to Dwelly from Francis James Chavasse, Bishop of Liverpool, was written on 10 January 1916:

I was much interested in reading the newspaper which you sent. It is pleasant and encouraging that you are leaving Cheltenham with the goodwill of so many of its people.

I hope you will look upon me as your father and friend. The temptations to vanity and self-assurance will not be few at Southport, but I know that you will be able to put God in place of Self and to give him the glory. You will also have much to humble you, and you must not allow yourself to be discouraged by rebuffs any more than you allow yourself to be elated by flattery and praise. May God richly bless you and Mrs. Dwelly.

As Dwelly was to spend the rest of his life in the Liverpool diocese, it is important to place him against the background of the diocese as a whole and its partly built Cathedral in particular. The Diocese had been carved out of the diocese of Chester in 1880 with John Charles Ryle, famous evangelical scholar and preacher, as its first Bishop. Liverpool was a city of wealth: second city of the land, handling a greater tonnage of cargo than the Port of London. The wealthy traders and ship owners had built their elegant town houses in the wide, tree-lined roads and beautifully proportioned squares. However, although the rich might have been living in comfort and prosperity overlooking Joseph Paxton's Princes Park or the riverside residences of Grassendale and Cressington, thousands of young, old, sick and destitute lived rough, sleeping out in the streets. The slum conditions in the courts and cellars were as bad as could be found anywhere in Europe. But the Diocese extended way beyond the city boundaries and contained much rich South Lancashire farmland, small mining communities to the east near Wigan and to the north the well-to-do seaside township of Southport developed rapidly in the late-Victorian and Edwardian period.

During its early years, Liverpool did not have a Cathedral and had to rely upon a rather cramped and architecturally undistinguished building on one of the main shopping thoroughfares. The foundation stone for what was planned as the largest

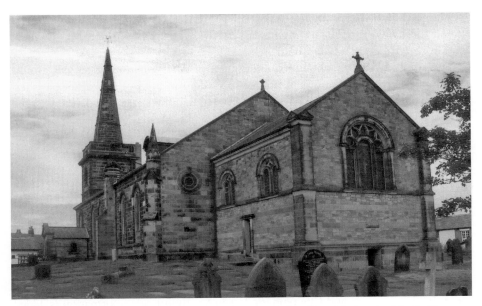

Despite the new chancel added in the nineteenth century, the old parish church of St Cuthbert was too small for the rapidly expanding population of the north end of Southport.

Cathedral in Britain was laid in 1904 at about the time Dwelly was completing the first year of his undergraduate studies. In the summer of 1910, when Dwelly was planning his move from Windermere, the Lady Chapel was consecrated, and during the war years building work on the chancel was slowed down through lack of funds and skilled labour.

Emmanuel was also a new church. The Rector of North Meols served a very large and disparate parish, now divided into St Cuthbert's, St Simon and St Jude, and Emmanuel. The foundation stone was laid in 1895 for a very splendid and spacious church on the wide and prosperous Cambridge Road. The essential parts of the building were to cost £12,000 and seat almost 1,200 people. St Cuthbert's was inadequate as a church for a parish so large and socially varied:

> Then there was the great diversity of occupations and residents, with merchants and gentlemen in the new villas of Cambridge Road, artisans and railways workers at High Park, Meols Hall estate workers at Churchtown. Farmers and fishermen at Marshside.

The scheme to close St Cuthbert's was vehemently opposed with the result that the original parish was divided into three parts in 1905. Emmanuel lost about a third of the originally intended catchment area; no vicarage was provided; the Rector of North Meols provided £100 a year towards the vicar's stipend; and all else had to be raised by the church itself. In 1916, Dwelly was to become the third incumbent of a very large church with immense potential. There is no evidence as to why he was offered the living, though his parents-in-law, the wealthy Major and Mrs Darwin, lived in Lethbridge Road, Southport.

The Dwelly traits of unbounded energy and a determination to see all groups actively involved in parish organizations, so evident in both of his earlier parishes, are discernible in even greater measure here. He became deeply involved with the Guides and Scouts again, becoming District Scout Master and recipient of the Queen's medal; the Mothers' Union flourished, as did the Galahads – a weekly Sunday School group for the smart 'church end' of the parish; and at the same time he was much in demand in the wider field of the National Mission. He was appointed a Bishop's Messenger for the Dioceses of Bath and Wells, Gloucester, Manchester and Liverpool. In the parish magazine for December 1916 he was able to announce: 'With one exception, the privileges and responsibilities of the Vicar in connection with the delivery of the National Mission addresses throughout the country is now over.' For those who love statistics, it will be a matter of interest to know that he had delivered 147 addresses on the National Mission.

Reports of Dwelly services became as common in the local paper as they had been earlier in Windermere and Cheltenham, but in Southport this information is added to in an important manner through the pages of the monthly *Emmanuel Church Parish Magazine*, fortunately now all bound and preserved at the church. Amazingly, over seventy five years after Dwelly left Emmanuel he is still remembered and talked about; partly because such a dynamic character remained in the memories of those who knew him, and partly because the legend has been passed on to later generations by word of mouth and through the traditions which he established, together with some of the features of the church for which he was responsible. Music was important in the services and as well as strengthening and supporting the robed choir for all the regular services, he founded the 'great choir' with up to 150 voices, initially for National Mission services, but then ready for those special services which would benefit from large choral resources.

In Windermere and Cheltenham Dwelly regularly ministered to packed churches, but neither of the St Mary Churches gave him much scope for the movement and pageantry which was to become such an important part of his later ministry. Emmanuel is a vast church and Dwelly, through liturgical experiment, learned to use the space. There are still some Emmanuel families who boast of the fact that Liverpool Cathedral was later to learn and benefit from the Dwelly experiments at Southport. It may well be that the idea for the famous Liverpool Cathedral Holly Bough service originated in the Emmanuel Wreathing service:

'The old-fashioned Wreathing Service will be held in the afternoon at 2.30; all worshippers are invited to bring a length (about one yard) of wreathed evergreen.' 'Very reverently, and in a quaint old-world way, the members of the schools, the Galahads, and Bible classes moved to their several little bits of wreathing to the singing of the carol, "Noel, Noel". Only four of the verses of "Once in Royal David's

City" were required to accomplish the entire wreathing of the church, not a single portion of the church being left unwreathed, the pillars included, which accomplished, the whole congregational choir grouped around the Star of Bethlehem, and burst forth into singing "Halleluia Chorus". The effect was wonderfully inspiring. The choir seemed to number about 180.' Dwelly liked the use of banners, and choir and clergy regularly processed around the imposing building.

An example of a typical piece of 'Southport Dwelly' is the celebrations for Peace Day, 19 July 1919.

My dear Friends,

Saturday next is Peace Day. Some of us may be tempted to be so critical of the terms of, and parties to, the peace that we lose our sense of proportion and forget that it is a return to a state where equilibrium may be attained, and therefore Peace Day is of the greatest importance. Further, to Britons it must be a day of rejoicing for we are a Peace loving people; let us avow it by our celebration.

The Mayor is caring for the old folk and part of the children; but what about all the others – and especially do I think of the gentlemen who have won Peace for us, the returned soldier and sailor? I feel we must do ourselves the honour as a parish of entertaining them. It will be expensive. No one wants to do catering that day, but I have secured the Prince of Wales Hotel for this, and though the cost is great, I do not fear but you will be proud that I have done it in your name. We must entertain those who have returned in a royal manner. You will be so good as to send me a cheque for the purpose; also I would like the men of the congregation to buy a ticket and come along to swell the welcome, for without a number of hosts we cannot raise a cheer for the returned.

Then I want your help for a jolly procession. Will you decorate bicycles or cars or carriages and meet at Bradstock Lockett Home at 4.25 (prompt) to make a triumphant Peace procession, and if you cannot have any decoration, will you and your friends hire a trap or landau or motor and join in the procession, for there will be many there that are only decorated with a flag. There are already a large number of entries – it is now a secured success (if fine) – but I feel you and your friends can make it an unprecedented success worthy of the mighty occasion.

One other matter of detail, as you are the hosts, you ought to know, and so be able to acquaint everyone that conveniences and accommodation will be adequately arranged near the Joy field kindly lent to us by Mr. Henderson. Also a canteen will be arranged in the field.

Praying that we may all have a spirit of rejoicing on Peace Day.

Yours sincerely,

Frederick W. Dwelly

The great day was reported on in the magazine and is relevant to our attempts to understand this man:

The Judas spirit in our hearts almost held us back as it held back many another community – 'why all this waste, when it might have been given to the poor?' – but – Blessed be God, His spirit prevailed and our people poured out their treasures.

I cannot tell you how proud I felt, as standing at the Luncheon to returned heroes, I said, 'Gentlemen, in the name of the people of Emmanuel, I have the honour to welcome you back from those heroic sufferings that you have borne to save us, our country, and liberty. We thank you and thank God for you.' Then we all stood for grace, and our grace was this, 'For Victory and Peace, for the men who have died to win it, for these our friends and for the means whereby we can enjoy this day. Thank God. Amen'. During the luncheon one after another came and said, 'We have done the right thing. It would have been a shame if no Welcome home had been given today.' 'There is no doubt about it.' 'I was glad you gave the lead.' 'I have enjoyed being a waiter.' 'This is what I call a gradely Peace Day.' Then. 'How about expenses?' To which question I now with rare pleasure, make reply, 'It's all paid for by your donations.' 'Good.'

Dwelly while in Southport, one of many photographs of him with dogs and puppies.

There is so much in these words and sentiments which we now see to be typical Dwelly. He thought and planned on a large scale: other churches might have tea-parties and hot-pot suppers, while he arranged a lavish lunch in the foremost hotel in the town, and then mobilised a high proportion of parishioners for a huge decorated procession through the district. Everything was undertaken 'with style'. His prose style, whether in report, letter or sermon, is readily identifiable. Through use of first-person pronouns he identifies with his readers and cajoles them into identifying with him. He must have sensed opposition to his Peace celebration but people are won over to his side: 'Some of us may be tempted,' he said, not 'Some of you.' 'I do not fear that you will be proud that I have done it in your name. We must entertain those who have returned in a royal manner.' The same rhetorical question features throughout his career: '... but what about all the others ...?' His Vicar's letters in the magazine are full of enthusiastic exhortations and peppered with exclamation marks and frequent use of capital letters and bold type. In all things his enthusiasm seems to be boundless. In his words, whether written or spoken, you hear a warm, generous, vigorous, determined, exuberant personality, who seems to be making a direct appeal, not to the whole congregation, but to the individual. I have spoken with more than one person who has declared Dwelly to be the most influential figure in his life.

By the end of the war, over fifty Emmanuel parishioners had been killed, and under Dwelly's driving force the church decided to embark upon a very elaborate war memorial chapel to be sited in the south transept and called the Chapel of Victory and Peace – now referred to more simply as the Oratory. It was to be richly and elaborately furnished and everything paid for by voluntary contributions from the congregation. Throughout the war, Dwelly had been zealous in his ministrations to the bereaved and there were regular ceremonies to remember the fallen. I do not think there is any doubt about his motives in the whole venture but the tone of some of what he wrote in the magazine reveals an almost ruthless determination to shame people into contributing. There is a determined and even ruthless element within his character which reveals itself clearly in all the litigation in which he was engaged during the nineteen thirties.

Here at least I present you with a joy for ever. Less than the best I have never given you, and, knowing that if you care to choose the best you can afford it, I should insult you if I offered you a less worthy memorial. In its wealth of symbolism you will not find it excelled anywhere. I am proud of the scheme. I wait with curious interest to see who there is among us who will rise to it and who there is that will deny to their better spirit an expression of the wonderful things it has experienced.

We must express our finest feelings or those fine feelings will be quenched. Selfish interests will suggest all sorts of excuses. This memorial ideal will mark the rise of many, and the fall of many.

Since it cannot be that selfishness has died entirely, I beg one favour of those who intend to fall by selfish considerations, please do not weary us with excuses. This memorial is only intended to provide an opportunity for the grateful hearted to express their spirit in such a beautiful manner that after generations might say, 'What mighty days those must have been. See how thankful and relieved they were with Victory and Peace'.

I am told by friends in the south that this is too full of beauty and loveliness to appeal to a Lancashire parish, and that Lancashire folk would begrudge money for ideals and beauty. I laughed at them; they do not know you as I think I do.

Many of you complain to me that I do not say what I want. Good people, I want you to rise to your highest and best. It is not for me to say how much, it would be an impertinence, but I do know that all of us whose income is over four hundred a year can, if we choose to pinch ourselves, make a really handsome gift

Dwelly while in Southport

to the Memorial Chapel or hand over a goodly number of war bonds to endow the annual memorial prizes, instead of spending it on our persons or houses, or increasing our death duties.

The estimated cost of the whole scheme was to be over £4,000: it has never been completely finished. Jean Lee, historian of Emmanuel, was to remark wryly that in November 1919 the Church Council resolved to approve the establishment of the Memorial Chapel: 'Just as well, as work had already begun, and gifts for use in the chapel had already been given and dedicated for use.' I have immense admiration for Dwelly; many of his great schemes were visionary and right but some of his means might be seen as dubious and he tolerated no opposition. He was autocratic to the end.

The Dwelly of later years is remembered for his determination that Liverpool's new Cathedral should be seen as welcoming to nonconformists of the Diocese and the pulpit was made available to two eminent Unitarian ministers. His views during the Southport years are not in any way sympathetic to the Anglo-Catholic end of the Church of England and the Roman Church. Readers of the magazine cannot have been oblivious to his uncharitable scorn.

I was taught that 'Anglo' means 'English', but all this stuff is anti-English in character ... it is not even Italian. The Roman Catholics would be bilious with it. 'Catholic' in my dictionary means 'universal', including the past and future – but what was said in the Congress concerning the state of the dead is utterly alien to what our Lord taught, and, surely, He is the best of the past and the end of the future. I pin my faith in the Blessed Lord and the interpretation of His Gospel as is given in the New Testament in preference to the stunt which arrogates to itself the name, 'Anglo-Catholic'. What impudence! ...

Now for Roman Catholics, 'Mass' and 'Pater Nosters' are as they should be, for Rome has never been reformed, Rome trades upon ignorance, but for people who profess to be of the English Church to go and cadge the uniform and the college songs ... well ... for goodness sake let them be honest and go over to Rome.

Then again in a later article:

It is sheer nonsense to talk about being charitable when Principles are at stake ... Let us make no mistake: opinions, arguments, excuses are curses when they have no foundation of Principle. Yes: Principles, not sentimental emotionalism or unintelligent propitiation.

There is some confusion in the remaining papers over Dwelly's thoughts on the interchange of pulpits with nonconformist ministers. The magazine for October 1920 announces that three ministers were to preach at Emmanuel and that Dwelly was to preach in return at Chapel Street Congregational Church – all this because the Lambeth Conference had proposed such a form of invitation. The article makes it clear that the arrangement was not to Dwelly's liking. While writing positively of the work of Marshside Primitive Methodist Church he comments: 'Such souls would find our form of worship rather a hindrance than a blessing, and therefore I have argued that the clergyman should minister exclusively to those whose form of worship he finds most direct to the Heavenly Father.' Bishop Chavasse wrote to Dwelly on 25 October and his letter gives a slightly different impression: 'I must certainly have written awkwardly and ambiguously to have left one impression in my mind and quite a different one in yours. Let your third engagement stand, as it has been made under a misconception.'

One item on the Parochial Church Council meeting of 3 June 1921 gives some indication of Dwelly's attitude towards women in the church. The council was being asked to respond to a letter from the League of the Church Militant asking for support on 'Ministrations of Women in the Church'. There is no report of anything that Dwelly might have said, but one cannot imagine the council making a formal response which did not have his active support:

(1) That this Church Council affirms and asserts the principles of the Catholic church as to the fundamental equality of all baptised persons, and we entirely repudiate the assertion that any Christian soul is considered on grounds of sex incapable of receiving any Christian gift or grace.

(2) That this Church Council strongly urges the Lambeth Conference Resolutions on the Ministrations of Women in the church shall be put into practice forthwith without limitation or hindrance.

The report gives a detailed account of Mr Farrer-Morgan's statement to the Council, which includes the clearest recommendation for the revival of the order of Deaconess in the church. Some words from his final paragraph might seem to suggest that, in good time, matters will be taken further.

When this is accomplished, the future will take care of further developments. It is pure folly to hustle the matter. The Holy Catholic Church has been exclusively man administered for nearly 2,000 years. When one looks out today upon the deplorable state of Christianity in this and every other country, one is driven to the conclusion that what the church needs today is the active ministrations of God-fearing earnest women. They may reach and hold people men have failed to reach and hold.

There is not the slightest doubt that at Emmanuel Dwelly had become a very successful vicar in a thriving parish, but Southport, though it had high opinions of itself, could never be regarded as a town of any significance as far as the Church of England was concerned and it must have been clear to his parishioners that his time with them would be limited. A short letter has remained with the family papers from Chard. In the top corner is a hand-written note by Dwelly: 'send this on to Bert when you have read it, cos I know he would love it. Fred.'

The letter is from Fulham Palace and dated 16 July 1923.

Dear Sir,

The Bishop of London desires me to invite you to preach in St Paul's Cathedral on Sunday evening September the 16th at 7 o'clock. The Bishop very much hopes that your engagements may make it possible for you to accept this invitation.

He obviously did accept, though no account remains in the archives of Dwelly's reactions to the occasion. What we do know is that he must have communicated without delay with his parents who both reply in separate letters.

17 September 1923

My Dear Boy,

It gives me great joy to hear you was blessed with grace courage strength & wisdom to deliver the message in St Paul's it gives me great pleasure to read your manuscript your letter brings tears of grateful thankfulness for our Heavenly Fathers loving kindness to in giving us this un surpassable pleasure and joy to HIM be all the Honour & Glory & Praise. The congratulations to me have been very numerous ... That I should be spared to know one of my children was doing the Masters Service which I so feebly tried to do truly when I have been weak He has been strong. David was not permitted to build the Temple but the promise was his Son should. May you my Dear Boy be held from falling as that Son did after his great work. I think I have to watch and pray(er) more earnest than ever that my footsteps do no slide. We all join most heartily in your joy.

With fond Love from

Your Affectionate Father

R. Dwelly

In a little envelope marked 'To be kept. My mothers letter on S Pauls' is the only letter in the archives from his mother:

My own dearest one

I am to overcome to write much thank you thank you thank you for his guidance and goodness to you I am so thankful and shall write again to you We shall never forget Mollies goodness she has been good to wire and now a lovely letter.

May God bless My Freddie.

The same year brought an invitation from Bishop Herbert Ryle to preach at Westminster Abbey on 9th March 1924: 'Our congregation is a very ordinary one and not at all formidable. It is large and neither learned nor aristocratic.' The service in the Abbey was reported to the family on six tiny sheets of Langham Hotel note paper in dreadful writing.

Dear all of you –

It's over – I loved it – loved it. Not a bit nervous after the beginning.

The Dean was most kind, I told him before that I was nervous & he said I should not think very much of you if you were not for it is a red letter day in any mans

life the first time he preaches in the abbey. I have a copy of the service the first
time I preached in the Abbey.

This put me at my ease.

Then after other talk his butler robed me and we proceeded down the winding
staircase to the Abbey – his private door comes out immediately opposite the
Warrior's Grave …

When we arrived at the deans stall under the organ the Dean bowed to me and
his verger then took me to my seat by the Altar so that to walk all that way alone
oh – golly – I was nervous.

The Dean came to read the lesson which he had asked me to choose – then I
was conducted to the pulpit – & alone I shivered feeling that packed congregation
– I thought of you & how you would be praying for your baby – I thought of the
days gone by when I went to the Abbey out of work and prayed for a job. & then
of how this was the place where the sermon in preached at Kings at their coro-
nations to Queen Victoria and right back to Edward the Confessor – I thought of
how the Royal tombs are around me and then I looked deliberately & saw dear
old Bert and underneath me dear old Fred Cooper – then the Anthem stopped &
I prayed – then began my sermon – the Dean moved to where he could see me –
& after that I forgot all in the love of my Saviour – my church – & my country.

I never felt so proud of my church and my country as I did preaching for her –
speaking for her in the old abbey.

Then a hymn & then a great surprise -

The Dean walked to the chancel steps & said 'My friends we have heard tonight
a call to dedicate ourselves afresh – let us in silence pray to be worth to that call',
& you can imagine how I well nigh choked as he mentioned the chief points of
my sermon in a appeal for prayer.

So the service ended & I walked back behind the verger the whole length of the
Abbey – then into the Deanery – The Dean put his hand on my shoulder & said
'Dear Lad you have given us a message – come again we want such words.'

Wasn't it lovely of him – at supper we talked lots and it was all lovely.

I am so happy – I do hope it has given you some happiness.

I am your most loving who owes all to you.

Fred.

It is interesting to be able to put a letter of this nature alongside a hectoring or
sarcastic statement in the *Parish Magazine*. The Abbey letter reads as if it were a letter
from an excited teenager rather than the forty-three-year-old Vicar of Emmanuel,
but a boyish excitement seems to have been maintained by Dwelly for almost the
whole of his life. Both playfulness and severity seemed to have inhabited the same
personality. The big special occasion always appealed to Dwelly and it was to be his
genius at rising to the major challenge which was to bring him such prominence in
the Church of England, particularly in the nineteen thirties. His powerful memory
of his lone walk from stall to pulpit for the sermon may well have been echoed only

a few months later when the Bishop walked 'alone and unattended' right through the chancel to the sanctuary in a splendid new Cathedral in Liverpool. The importance of the Southport years in the growth of a flamboyant, enigmatic, imaginative, strong-willed, enthusiastic, ebullient, warm-hearted, tireless, engaging, magnetic, talented and totally dedicated Dean of Liverpool must never be overlooked. The Emmanuel parish magazines record more of his thoughts and words as a priest of the church than any other source which has yet been uncovered.

Emmanuel Fellowship Gazette for April 1920 affords us another important insight into Dwelly's vision of God:

We have forgotten what the God we preach is really like. We are obsessed at present with a system, and leave so very little room for God. Our Lord never once in all his teachings spoke of God in ecclesiastical terms. He spoke of the sheep and cottages and market places, and showed how interested God is in them. He went about the earth doing good: not from any theological motive, but because he loved men and women. He gave the lonely his companionship, moving about in other people's homes. He gave the 'outsiders' back their self-respect; He brought hope to the despairing, purpose and meaning into aimless lives; A Gospel of joy to those who were down and out; power and restoration to the sick. He brought laughter back to earth again (there was no laughter in the ancient world). He told men that there is a God who loves them, and showed Him to them by His life of kindness and His royal love for other people. It was in Our Lord that men found God. In the life he lived was revealed the glory of the Father. He showed men God in the language of human life. What He is, God is; God is what Our Lord is. In living as He lived, He showed men God. He defines the meaning of 'Divinity.' The answer to 'What is God like?' is, 'Like Him.' That is the meaning of the Incarnation, in which the church each day professes faith.

We have managed to obscure our Lord, and so we have made God remote and dull, and not essentially adorable. The Church is never going to save the world, or redeem men from their loneliness, or bring God into hungry, longing lives by any preaching of Theology. It must be doing what its Master did. It must show men God in the healing hand, in kindness, service, personal affection. That, I take it, is what St Paul was saying in the most famous chapter that he wrote (1 *Cor.* xiii) He was discussing the value of different 'gifts' for the extension and consolidation of the Christian Church – that is, in the end, for the Redemption of society. Preaching is, he says, an 'excellent' thing, but there is a 'way' which is 'superlative.' Obviously what follows is intended as a description of the Master's character. The beauty of the A.V. is intoxicating, to those of a literary turn of mind. An attempt is worth while making to translate these incomparable phrases, with every care to preserve the balance and exact shade of the meaning of the Greek, into the English of the Tube and Smoke-room. In that language, this is what he wrote:

'If I have all the gifts of a revivalist and have not love, I am merely a braying trumpet, or the clapper of a bell. Though I am a preacher and know all God's secrets, all the theology there is, and though I believe in God so much that I can remove mountains, but have not love, I do not count. Though I spend all my income on philanthropy, though I am even ready for the stake, but have not love, there is nothing in it. Love does not take offence, is always trying to do good turns to others. Love is not jealous, does not swagger, does not stand on its dignity, always behaves like a gentleman, never plays for its own hand, does not get peevish, is glad when other people find the truth, never loses courage, never loses faith, never loses hope, always sees it through to the end. Love never lets you down. If it is sermons, they will be out of date; if it is emotionalism, it will stop; if it is Theology, it will be superseded. For our knowledge is fragmentary, and our preaching is fragmentary. When the perfect whole has come, the fragmentary will be out of date. When I was a child I used to talk like a child, I used to think like a child, I used to reason like a child. When I became a man I found children's things out of date; for now we see but a blurred reflection, but then face to face. Now my knowledge is partial, but then I shall know fully for myself, just as God already knows me. These are the three things which stand the test: faith, hope, and love, but the biggest of these is love.' ('Love' – the Character of Our Lord.)

All of us can recognise these people. Reckless Bill, who never manages to have more than a shilling in his pocket, but will always give you sixpence of it. Then there is old Mrs. Motherly, who just pops in to mind the baby, or to help to cook the Sunday dinner in times of sickness. Mr. Unassuming we all know. He'll never 'thrust' or advertise himself, never stands upon his dignity, or thinks it necessary to be pompous. Yet he has such a simple, natural dignity that no one ever 'takes a liberty,' or, because he's always affable, thinks he can be turned into a mascot. There's a sense of power about him. (Naturally, because it's God!) Mr. Righteous Indignation is often heard at Parish Councils, or orating in Trafalgar Square, standing up for the unprivileged. We dismiss the man as an 'agitator.' (Just as though our Lord were not!) Mr. Self-forgetful, Mr. Whiteman, Mr. Great-heart, Mr. Hopeful, Mr. Valiant-in-difficulty, – we come across them all each day we live. We do not always recognise God in them; yet that is what the Church is meant to be – the fellowship of people who love like that, just because they are full of the Master's Spirit. How to do that is for the church to say.

'These are the three things that stand the test – faith, hope, and Christlikeness: the biggest of these is to be like our Lord.'

Because Dwelly was an extempore preacher, we have only a few direct texts of any of his sermons, and even some of those are filtered through the pen of a journalist. It is for this reason that some of these Southport magazine articles are so important in helping towards an understanding of his theology and his approach. The magazines are also a lead-in to Dwelly's involvement in some significant movements within the Church of England. The magazine for August 1917 carried a short note:

'Life and Liberty for the Church'

Is a demand made by some of the finest clergy in the church to-day. The meeting in Queen's Hall, London, was packed out.

Life and Liberty for the Church was resolved upon, at all costs.

This also is the spirit of Emmanuel in Southport; our services are real because of it. 'Where the spirit of the Lord is, there is Liberty' – 'He is our Life.' If we have had any troubles in the administration they have been of the nature which will always be found by every community that refuses to be tied and bound with the chains of tradition.

The 'life and liberty' movement is led by the Vicar of St Martin's-in-the-Fields, whose church we have more than once recommended Emmanuel people to attend when they are in London.

The movement is essentially big and out for business: the Editor has a feeling that here are disciples who will think God size enough – believe Jesus like enough to create that universalisation of soul, that solidarity of worshipping humanity which will overcome the weary spectre that threatens a war-satiated world . . .

Dwelly had been heavily involved in the National Mission and it seems clear that the impulses behind Life and Liberty were an inevitable outcome of the Mission which had: 'left the Church in a state of chastened discontent with itself, combined with a sense of frustration that baulked and halted all efforts towards a full recovery.' (Iremonger, 1948) Rev. H. R. L. (Dick) Sheppard was a moving force at the start, together with Rev William Temple, the future Archbishop. The first meeting of the movement was held on 29 March 1917 in St Martin's Vicarage and the need for speedy reforms in many aspects of church life were called for. No reform of any kind was possible without the agreement of Parliament and as Iremonger wryly recorded it had taken 'nine sessions of Parliament to settle the salary of the Archdeacon of Cornwall'. No movement could make its presence felt without a suitable name, and Life and Liberty was the suggestion of the Headmaster of Rugby, Dr A. A. David, a few years later to move to the Liverpool Diocese as its Bishop.

The first official public statement from the organisation appeared in the *Times* on 20 June 1917 under the heading 'Movement for Reform':

But as soon as we consider the changes that are needed to make the church a living force in the nation, we find ourselves hampered at every turn by an antiquated machinery which we are powerless to change except by a series of Acts of Parliament. Every one sees that the House of Commons is a highly unsuitable place for the settlement of questions affecting the church's life and work; and even if it were suitable in its composition it has no time . . .

If the Church is to have new life, even if it is to maintain the life which it has, it must have liberty. Those who are promoting this Movement are convinced that we must win for the church full power to control its own life, even at the cost, if necessary, of disestablishment and of whatever consequences that may possibly involve.

The inaugural meeting of the new Movement reported by Dwelly in his parish magazine was held in the packed Queen's Hall in London on 16 July. At this moment, the author has no way of knowing whether Dwelly was present at that meeting or not but we do know that Dwelly and Dick Sheppard were close friends. Leadership of the Movement was taken up by William Temple who resigned from his living, St James's, Piccadilly. Later events will reveal the ways in which Dwelly was to be involved in the movement and came into working contact with a future Archbishop.

The year 1923 was significant for Dwelly and Life and Liberty, and a small clutch of letters in the Cathedral archive indicates the high esteem in which Dwelly was held by the senior members of the organisation.

29th September 1923
My dear Dwelly,
This is good news indeed. I am simply delighted, and I will write at once to David, and as soon as I hear from him I will let you know again. I am cram full of hope about the Movement, and we will look forward to many happy days work together.
Yours ever,
F. A. Iremonger

4 Oct 1923
My dear Mr Dwelly,
I know that the Life and Liberty Executive were going to ask you to do half time work for them, and I have already told them that if arrangements could be made to secure that your parish will not seriously suffer I should encourage you to accept the work. I am quite sure that the effort in which you are invited to join is of the utmost importance to the Church at large, and I also believe that the effect of this activity of yours will be wholesomely felt at Emmanuel after and even while you are engaged in it. It does us all good, and it is good also for those with whom we work, that we should maintain contact with the bigger movements outside our actual sphere ...
I am glad that you are consulting your Parochial Church Council before making your final decision. Perhaps you would like to read them this letter.
I am sure they will appreciate, as I do, the compliment that Life and Liberty have paid you.
Yours sincerely,
Albert E and I (the future Bishop of Liverpool)

Rev. C. F. Twitchett, Clerical Secretary of Life and Liberty, and a future Archdeacon of Liverpool, wrote to Dwelly on 3 November 1923:

I saw Freddy Iremonger yesterday and had lunch with him, and I made him see the urgency of your free leadership if your contribution to the Movement is to be of value. Duncan-Jones went back on fire with enthusiasm after the Office committee and I think that you will find every sympathy in that quarter now.

As was mentioned earlier, Dwelly had, since his undergraduate days at Cambridge been critical of the total inflexibility of the *Book of Common Prayer*. Prayer Book dissatisfaction was one of the areas of concern among members of Life and Liberty. One of the significant names who had made considerable contributions to Anglican Worship was the former Vicar of St Mary's, Primrose Hill, the Rev. Percy Dearmer, author of *The Parson's Handbook*. Dearmer was twenty years older than Dwelly and a considerable liturgical scholar but he was not one of the original supporters of Life and Liberty. None of the correspondence between the two men remains in the Cathedral archive, though they were to collaborate on a number of significant matters – ranging from hymn tunes to vestments. An interesting fact has been recorded by Nan Dearmer:

> Percy had not at first been in sympathy with the Life and Liberty Movement ... and he owed it to Canon Dwelly that he was finally dragged into it. Once in the movement he grew enthusiastic and became fertile of ideas for its expansion. (Dearmer, 1940)

Detailed examination of Prayer Book revision in the nineteen twenties is too extensive a subject for consideration in this book – as well as being beyond the capacity of this writer to produce it. However, an important part of Dwelly's interests lay in this field and there must be at least brief reference to this complex area if the man is to be understood. It is important to recognise the national significance of some of the work undertaken by Dwelly when still a parish priest in an insignificant seaside town in the North of England. It is also important to note the fame and calibre of many of the figures in the church with whom he cooperated, even before Liverpool Cathedral cast a spotlight on his work.

The 1922 meeting of the new Church Assembly accepted an important proposal concerning Prayer Book reform that 'any revised forms of service should not be incorporated into the Prayer book, but should be in a separate volume and sanctioned for use for a specific period.' (Jasper, 1989) Activity was considerable and varied but the three most significant publications became known as the Green, the Orange and the Grey books – the only significance of the titles rested in the colour of the covers.

The Green Book emerged from the Catholic end of the Church and was published by the English Church Union in 1922. The Orange Book, largely the work of Frere, contained the Alcuin Club's proposals. The Grey Book, with the overall title *A New Prayer Book* with a foreword by the Bishop of Manchester (William Temple), was published in three parts between April and June 1923, along with introductory pamphlets. The Grey Book had its official roots in the Life and Liberty Movement and the proposed services were the work of Percy Dearmer, R. G. Evans, later a Bishop of Southwark, F. R. Barry, later a Bishop of Southwell, Leslie Hunter, later

Bishop of Sheffield, Mervyn Haigh Bishop of Winchester, and Frederick Dwelly. The pamphlets were the work of Mervyn Haigh, Oliver Carrick, R. G. Parsons, H. J. Matthews, Percy Dearmer, F. R. Barry, H. R. L. Sheppard, Tom Pyon, Edward S. Woods, Harold Anson, Leslie Hunter, and Fred Dwelly. The actual wording of the services remains anonymous but, with only slight modification, some of Dwelly's prayers, previously published in *Acts of Devotion*, appear in the third volume, *Short Services for Occasional Use.*

The preface to this third volume states the intentions of the writers and compilers succinctly:

> The services which follow are intended for use at Morning and Evening Prayer, and at other times as occasion requires. The compilers of this book believe that there is a need for more experiment and freedom in worship in the church. This means not only more elasticity in the regular services, but also a greater variety in the services provided: special services for those who do not come to the usual offices, services of preparation for communicants, services for guilds and fellowships and for special occasions.

It is interesting to compare these sentiments with Dwelly's ideas about the formulation of special services set down by Stanley Morison in *English Prayer Books*, 1943, and with some of the actual services devised for use in Liverpool Cathedral in the thirties and forties.

The writers of the preface acknowledge that many of their published devotions 'approximate to the type of devotion generally known as extempore (a type which should have a larger place in public worship) and they do not even claim that limited permanence which belongs to more formal acts of worship ... we are ... convinced that the church will be wise to reserve within her ordered garden of prayer a corner where the more simple natural thoughts and emotions in the hearts of our people, which are at present rather repressed in the worship of the church, may find some kind of expression.'

The preface to the second volume comments first on Mattins and Evensong and makes practical suggestions: 'Ways of shortening both services have been suggested ... We have also felt that it was desirable to break away from the present uniform introduction, which is apt to be unreal ... We have ventured ... by way of experiment to provide a different set of versicles and responses for Mattins, and a different arrangement of collects. In the revision of the Occasional Offices, the aim has been to shorten and simplify and to introduce a more human note where we felt it was needed. It has to be remembered that many hear the Baptismal, Marriage, and Burial Offices, who are not in the habit of attending other services and are not familiar with the teaching of the Church. It is very necessary, therefore, that these services should be made as intelligible to such people as is possible.'

Even as a devotee of BCP Mattins and Evensong, particularly when they are well sung, I find merit in the suggestions for Mattins. Three alternatives are suggested by way of introduction in place of Exhortation, General Confession, Absolution and Lord's Prayer. The General Confession is maintained for festivals but the shorter, less linguistically complex confessions, have much to recommend them.

Almighty God, Lord of heaven and earth, we confess that we have sinned against thee in thought word and deed, and that we have not loved our neighbour as ourselves. Have mercy upon us, O God, after thy great goodness: help us to overcome our faults and cleanse us from our sins; through Jesus Christ our Lord. Amen.

Almighty God, the Father of our Lord Jesus Christ, of whom the whole family in heaven and earth is named, deliver us now from the vain things that have power over us, and enable us to rest our souls in thee and yield them to the guidance of thy loving Spirit. Make us ready to offer thee the joy that is thy gift, and worship thee with glad and thankful hearts. In the light of thy perfection help us to see our shortcomings and be sorry for our faults; and grant, we beseech thee, that, strengthened by our worship together, we may serve thee and our fellow men more faithfully in our daily life, and come at last to thy eternal kingdom; through the same Jesus Christ our Lord. Amen.

The compilers, while showing their respect for the traditional form and content of the service, have acknowledged the importance of occasional variety to help combat the tendency towards the mechanical saying of words which can so easily destroy the power of the daily Offices. The compilers even offer an alternative Confession of Faith, for saying or singing, alongside the Apostles' Creed, though the latter remains mandatory 'at least for Great Festivals'. It must have been interesting to hear the first responses of the Anglo-Catholics or the Evangelicals to this proposal:

We believe that God is Spirit: and they that worship him must worship him in spirit and in truth.
   We believe that God is Light: and if we walk in the light as he is in the light we have fellowship one with another.
   We believe that God is Love: and that everyone that loveth is born of God and knoweth God.
   We believe that Jesus is the Son of God: and that God has given to us eternal life, and this life is in his Son.
   We believe that we are children of God: and that he hath given us of his Spirit.
   We believe that if we confess our sins: he is faithful and just to forgive us our sins.
   We believe that he who doeth the will of God: shall abide for ever. Amen.

Anyone aware of Dwelly's fondness for conflation of biblical texts as part of great Cathedral services will be interested in this piece.
   Dwelly's significant involvement in liturgical reform on a national front did not

seem to detract in any way from his faithful ministry at Emmanuel, where the magazine was used on a number of occasions to keep the congregation in touch with
national developments, particularly those concerning the Grey Book group. The
magazine for July 1923 carries a very prominent Vicar's letter, taking up a full page,
and printed in large and heavy type.

My dear Friends,
    I must write you a line of thanks for your generous response to my appeal that
you would make yourselves felt in urgent issues that have arisen in the matter of
Prayer Book Revision.
    I have attended four Round Table Conferences since that Sunday, and am more
than ever persuaded that we must be up and doing if the faith so dear to us is not
to be overbalanced.
    Two important movements have been set in motion this month, both of which
are calculated to provide a corrective ... of these and other results I have to report
to you the first Sunday in July.
    The large-hearted Evangelicals without necessarily making any claim to
monopoly of truth must make their influence felt in these critical days. I am
grateful to you for your backing. Yours prayers, please, for all who attend the
several Conferences of the next two weeks.
    Ever your affectionate Vicar,
    Frederick W. Dwelly.

For the congregation at Emmanuel, liturgical experiment and reform were not
simply matters which engaged the vicar's time in London; experimental forms were
actually tried out at Emmanuel, as the magazine for December 1923 intimates:

A fateful time for the Revision of the Communion Service. Very hard and intricate
lobby work; many private conferences; and at last a marvellous persuading of the
Assembly by what seemed to be not less than an outpouring of the Holy Spirit.
The Green Book has had its bitter tendency taken away. The Revision which has
been used as a reverent experiment at Emmanuel has passed.

From the earliest movements towards liturgical reform, all parties realised that
finding agreement over the service of Holy Communion was going to cause the
greatest problems. It is interesting to note how some of the deliberations over a new
Eucharistic Rite at the end of the nineteen nineties occupied the minds of reformers
way back in the twenties. In his more famous Cathedral years, Dwelly is not
remembered for any particular contribution to the Service of Holy Communion,
but he was incumbent before the days when a Choral Eucharist was the principal
Sunday morning service in a Cathedral, just as the Parish Communion was to
displace Choral Mattins in the parishes. Dwelly kept Bishop Chavasse informed of
what he was doing over reform, and a letter of 23 April 1923 thanks Dwelly for
his correspondence. Along with all the other bishops he had received copies of

the Grey Book, but the Communion Service was not acceptable to a fervent Evangelical:

> I am afraid I cannot vote for it as it stands. It recommends Reservation for the Sick, and connects with the Consecration Prayer the Sacrifice of the Elements. You have done your best, my dear brother, to exclude these innovations, and I heartily thank you.

A magazine article for February 1924 devotes a complete page to the revision of the service and it would seem to be Dwelly's fullest extant statement on the Church's most important service. Though the statement is long, its inclusion is, I believe, justifiable because it is such a full summary of Dwelly's liturgical stance at that time:

> The desire to revise the Communion Service is not confined to one section of the Church alone, and it is most important that any changes authorised should not reflect the ideas of one school of thought only. Hitherto it has not proved possible to devise one single alternative Canon which all who desire revision could agree to accept. This being so the only honest and charitable course would appear to be the authorisation of alternative Canons in one and the same liturgy, provided always that these Canons contain nothing that is considered contrary to Holy Scripture, or incapable of defence and explanation by those who definitely prefer some other form. With this object in view the Round Table Conference held during the last Assembly, modified both the 'Green' and the 'Grey' Canons; and those of its members who desire a revised Liturgy are agreed in believing that these modifications make either of the Canons such that they can consent to others using it, even though they would prefer not to use it themselves.
>
> If the defenders of the second or 'Grey' alternative are asked why they are not ready to give it up for the sake of securing a single alternative use, their answer would be that they believe it to be preferable in certain important respects to both the present Order, and the other proposed alternatives. They think -
>
> (1) That it represents more fully and exactly the teaching of the New Testament;
>
> (2) That it conforms more closely in its structure to earlier forms of the Consecration Prayer; as used, not only in the East, but also in the West, before the influence of the Roman Rite displaced other uses;
>
> (3) That it precludes more effectually certain theories as to the mode and moment of consecration and the nature of Eucharistic sacrifice, which were rejected by the Church of England at the Reformation and are not acceptable to great numbers of Anglicans today;
>
> (4) That it emphasis the Priesthood of the Laity;
>
> (5) That it makes clear the inseparable connection between Communion and Sacrifice in the Eucharist;
>
> (6) That it preserves a valuable characteristic of our English Liturgy by keeping

the offering of 'ourselves, our souls and bodies', in its present place, after the Communion.

The 'Grey' Canon alone of the various proposals before the Assembly has received support from Evangelicals and Liberals as well as High Churchmen. It seeks to remove certain blemishes on our present Order which Anglican liturgiologists from the XVIIth century onward have recognised, and in other churches of our communion have sought to correct. But at the same time it deliberately sets out to confirm certain aspects of sacramental doctrine which the Evangelical tradition exists to maintain; and its supporters claim that it is the expression of a spirit which looks for its standard of catholicity not only to the tradition which prevails in the Latin West, but also to the thought and experience of the whole church, Eastern as well as Western, modern as well as ancient, Reformed as well as Orthodox or Roman.

For these reasons the supporters of the 'Grey' alternative desire most earnestly that it should have an opportunity of being put to the test of use and experience in the coming years. They recognise that the other alternative has been made capable of an interpretation no more repugnant to Evangelical Churchmen, and are ready to agree to its being given the same opportunity as the one which they themselves prefer. Nor need the authorisation of different modes of celebrating the Eucharist be regarded as at best a regrettable necessity. If it be granted that they are not doctrinally inconsistent with one another or with Holy Scriptures, though they differ in emphasis and arrangement, the fact of their concurrent authorisation may help Church people to see our differences in their proper proportion and to realise that they are not fundamental. This will open the way not merely to mutual toleration but to mutual trust.

The old idea of rigid uniformity has led in the past to disruption. Its failure is made manifest in the present disorders which we all alike deplore. Is not diversity itself an essential element in the Christian ideal of Fellowship? And if it is, may we not well hope that an ordered variety in worship will lead us to a truer and stronger unity than uniformity is ever likely to achieve.

William Temple in his introduction indicated that the services were founded on the principles of truth, intelligibility, simplicity, uniformity and comprehensiveness. When attempting to assess the significance of the work of the Grey Book team almost sixty years later, Ronald Jasper, a highly knowledgeable and respected liturgical expert commented: 'Liberal in outlook, and often rather precious in language, the pamphlets were in places remarkably forward-looking (e.g. they pioneered the recitation of the Nicene Creed in the plural) and at times very imaginative. Some of the Occasional Services were precisely on the lines advocated by Conron and Milner-White in "The church in the furnace". One noted Evangelical scholar, R. T. Howard, claimed, "The majority of the Grey book proposals satisfy the aspirations of the Evangelicals towards a better form of Common Worship ... There are things ... which Evangelicals find unnecessary, but taking the compilation as a whole it is a new liturgical world to breathe and grow in. There is good fresh air here." This is praise indeed; for on the whole Evangelicals were not enthusiasts for Prayer Book revision.' (Jasper, 1989)

The move towards liturgical revision in which Dwelly was so much involved was of course to continue towards the production of *The Prayer Book as Proposed in 1928*. Dwelly's own liturgical concentration, though he had no idea about it even early in 1924, was needed within his own Diocese, particularly within its partly built and unconsecrated new Cathedral.

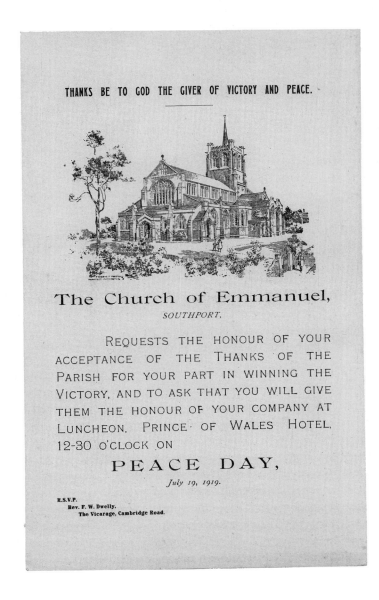

THANKS BE TO GOD THE GIVER OF VICTORY AND PEACE.

The Church of Emmanuel,
SOUTHPORT.

REQUESTS THE HONOUR OF YOUR ACCEPTANCE OF THE THANKS OF THE PARISH FOR YOUR PART IN WINNING THE VICTORY, AND TO ASK THAT YOU WILL GIVE THEM THE HONOUR OF YOUR COMPANY AT LUNCHEON, PRINCE OF WALES HOTEL, 12-30 O'CLOCK ON

PEACE DAY,
July 19, 1919.

R.S.V.P.
Rev. F. W. Dwelly.
The Vicarage, Cambridge Road.

CHAPTER SIX

Consecration

W HEN I FIRST BEGAN TO EXPLORE the contents of the Cathedral archives,
I was introduced by the Precentor to what was affectionately known as the
tin cupboard. It was in reality a drab green cupboard such as might have been seen
in innumerable offices round about the nineteen fifties. In amongst a clutter of
official vellum scrolls and special service papers, I unearthed a handsome and heavy
book, well bound in black leather with lettering embossed in gold on the front. In
the book is recorded for posterity the events of the most significant week
in the whole life of the Cathedral – and at the same time the most significant week in
the life of Frederick William Dwelly. His part in the events of one week in the
summer of 1924 was to change the course of his life for ever. The book is entitled
Liverpool Cathedral Consecration Services, July 19th to 27th 1924. At the bottom of the
cover are the words 'Rev. F. W. Dwelly, Ceremoniarius' and inside on the fly leaf
there is the inscription 'To F.W.D. In ever grateful and affectionate remembrance of
July 19–27, 1924. "A friend is never knowne till a man hath neede". From Albert
Liverpool.'

Francis James Chavasse, second Bishop of Liverpool, the man responsible for
inspiring his diocese to build a Cathedral, retired in 1923 because he wanted a new
Bishop to lead forward the next phase in the life of the Cathedral, the commencement of which would be a great service of Consecration. The new Bishop was Albert
Augustus David, Bishop of St Edmundsbury and Ipswich, a former Headmaster of
Rugby, and a significant force within the Life and Liberty Movement. One of David's
early actions was to appoint Charles Raven as a Provisional Canon of the new
Cathedral. Raven was later to become Regius Professor of Divinity at Cambridge, a
dramatic preacher, and one of the foremost theological scholars of his day. David
and Raven clearly talked together about the challenge to be faced in the production
of a service worthy of the consecration of a great new Cathedral on a previously
unconsecrated site: such an event had not taken place since the Consecration of
Salisbury Cathedral in 1225. Raven understood the nature of the problem:

A view looking up towards the Children's Porch into the Lady Chapel.

It was evident that to mark such an occasion no repetition of a traditional form would suffice; that it would not be enough to collect together a variety of ancient ceremonies and formulae and to combine them into an Office. What was needed was a service which, while fulfilling all that past experience could suggest, should possess a coherence, a rhythm, an appropriateness of its own for the circumstances of today. Such a service must be the work not of a liturgies expert (if this means

View over the rooftops of the city showing the partially built Cathedral. The Lady Chapel is the lower part of the building to the right in this view.

a student of past precedents) but of a creative artist who perceived what the ceremony signified, knew how to interpret its significance in apposite technique, and could enable the congregation to experience and share in the dramatic movement of the whole.

The inside story as to how Dwelly of Emmanuel started the journey towards Dwelly of Liverpool was set down in the *Liverpool Diocesan Leaflet* for October 1955 by his great friend Charles Raven:

His first achievement, the great service of Consecration, was typical of his whole career. He came to it almost unknown; and the circumstances of his coming deserve to be put on record. Bishop David had confided in me, his newly-appointed Canon, that having himself no expert knowledge of liturgics or ceremonial he did not know how to get a service worthy of the occasion. I had spent the first four days of Holy Week at Emmanuel, Southport; and on my last evening there had sat up till after midnight with the Vicar, planning his Easter service. When I went to bed, the script was almost illegible – a mass of corrections and turkey-tracks. With my morning tea, appeared the same script in print and ready for distribution. When I asked Dwelly whether he had a printing press or a tame magician on the premises, he replied, 'You took a lot of interest in the service and I thought you'd like to see it before you left: the local paper is printed on Wednesday night: the foreman printer is a pal of mine: I took down the service on my bike and asked him to send up the printed form with the milk.' Naturally I told this history to the Bishop, and said: 'You've got this man in your own diocese: he knows all about liturgies and church music: he has imagination and a sense of dignity: he will construct your service, produce it, and plan all the details from processions to ceremonial.'

So I was not surprised that the Service itself was superbly designed and executed, and that the arrival of the King and Queen twenty minutes too early, in a programme synchronised to an exact precision, threatened to destroy the sequence of the very many processions, Dwelly rose at once to the occasion, set chairs for the royal visitors in the King's Porch and carried through the whole programme without a sign of anxiety.

From that day onwards it has been the same. He has lived in and for the Cathedral, exercising all his thought and ingenuity in discovering fresh opportunities for it; collecting a vast wealth of precedents, forms of service, music and local knowledge; and gathering round him a great company of artists and craftsmen and women of all kinds devoted to the welfare of the Cathedral and ready to sacrifice time and care without stint in its service.

King, Queen, Archibishop and Bishop depicted in a Liverpool Cathedral window.

When the foundation stone was laid for the great new Cathedral of Liverpool in the summer of 1904, it was acknowledged by Bishop Chavasse and those who supported him in the venture that they were building for future generations, and many knew they would not live to see the completion of their great enterprise. The Lady Chapel was dedicated on St Peter's Day in 1910, and as far as Lady Chapels go, that at Liverpool is one of the largest and most beautiful, and is perhaps also the most prayerful part of the whole building. However, as the walls of the chancel rose higher and higher, the people of Liverpool began to have some notion of the colossal scale of their new Cathedral, and the architect and the builders indicated that about one third of the building would be completed by the summer of 1924. Having constructed the largest Gothic arch anywhere in the world, they bricked this up with a temporary wall so that the High Altar chancel and eastern transepts might be consecrated and taken over for worship while building continued on the other side. A series of temporary walls, of a slightly less solid nature, appeared gradually nearer and nearer to the west end of the building until the west wall itself was completed and the whole Cathedral was dedicated in the presence of Queen Elizabeth II in 1978. To our eyes, the Cathedral of 1924 looks a strangely truncated building, but at the time it stood out on the horizon as a unique and splendid structure, and a structure worthy of a unique and splendid service of Consecration.

Before examining that service, it is interesting to read what Sir Giles Scott had to say about his masterpiece in the *Morning Post* for 19 July 1924.

Liverpool Cathedral. The Expression of Atmosphere.

A Cathedral is a great opportunity for an architect to express an abstract idea in architectural form. The practical requirements are simple and few. The chief requirement is to produce a solemn and devotional effect ...

The aim being to produce a religious atmosphere, it is natural that he should examine existing buildings where this characteristic is to be found, and endeavour to learn how it has been achieved, and to attempt, if possible, to do even better. I feel bound to confess (though with diffidence, be it said) that English Cathedrals, as they stand, do not sufficiently produce this religious atmosphere. The restorer's hand is laid heavily upon them, and incongruous fittings and alterations break up the harmony and tend to destroy breadth and serenity ...

Personally, I think a great deal too much importance is attached to mere style; the really fundamental qualities of architecture are common to all styles. But it does seem to me that certain effects upon the mind are more readily produced by one style than another. One may take it broadly that in Gothic the verticals dominate the horizontals, while in Classic the reverse is the case. Now for some reason, which I have not been able to discover, verticality of expression seems more suggestive of the high aspirations that one associates with religion, and it seems to me easier to get the religious feeling in Gothic than in a style embodying strong horizontals. At the same time, I think that in most gothic Cathedrals the emphasis on the verticals is unduly stressed, and thereby a great deal of calm and serenity is sacrificed, and a feeling of restlessness is imparted to the building, which tends to destroy the repose and peace that in those strenuous days seem doubly necessary in a building devoted to prayer.

It comes to a question of balance, like everything in Nature, and at Liverpool I have endeavoured to combine the uplifting character imparted by vertical expression with the restful calm undoubtedly given by judicious use of horizontals.

Here the architect is concentrating not upon the size, splendour and magnificence of the building but upon the prayerful atmosphere which he has laboured to create. For the liturgist in 1924 there must have been grave danger of over-emphasising the drama and pageantry of Consecration at the expense of the spiritual, and the prayerful. From everything which was reported after the service it seems clear that Dwelly did not fall into this trap.

The Bishop was generous in making public to a wide readership his personal indebtedness to Dwelly for his immense labours on behalf of the new Cathedral. His words are cited in the *Church of England Newspaper* for 25 July 1924.

We have received more help in our task than we can easily acknowledge. But there is no difficulty in singling out one who deserves the chief share of our gratitude, namely, the Rev. F. W. Dwelly, of Southport. He was assisted by Canon Morley Stevenson and Rev. J. W. Tyrer. What they did not know about liturgical details and precedents (which is not a great deal) Mr. Dwelly knew where to find, and he spared neither time nor labour in seeking it. His well-known gift of devotional expression was invaluable in the composition of all the Consecration Services, and we have indeed been happy to find in the diocese itself a contribution of so much sympathy and skill.

The handsomely bound book in the Cathedral archives was a scrap book displaying dozens of newspaper reports and comments on the services, and was made specially as a gift to Dwelly from his grateful Bishop. Alongside this book is preserved *The Consecration of Liverpool Cathedral – The Services of the Octave 1924*. These two volumes, together with a clutch of personal letters give the fullest account of Dwelly's memorable achievements during one week – achievements which were later to give him a Deanery. People have spoken for years about Dwelly's skills in devising the Consecration Service but this is a huge understatement because the book contains twenty-eight services which took place during the Octave and a further two later in the year. All the services are devised quite specifically to be fitting and appropriate for those attending: Service for the Mersey Mission, Shipping and Sailors, for Friendly Societies, for Free Churchmen, for Social Workers, for Missionary Workers, for Sunday School Scholars, for Business Men – the list is long and years later will be seen to be quite typical of Dwelly's genius for devising special services in which Liverpool Cathedral was in the vanguard of experiment in Cathedral Worship across the whole country.

From the existing written evidence, the Bishop seems to have been anxious for the whole diocese to understand and to feel part of the consecration of their new Cathedral. A short pamphlet was issued by Albert Augustus on 11 July 1924. As well as listing the names of everyone carrying out significant formal duties at the ceremony, it lists acknowledgements of those people and organisations whose assistance had provided the foundation upon which the service was built:

Through the Bureau of the Life and Liberty Movement the following have given generous assistance in the compilation of the Service Books, and the precedents involved in the same:

The Dean of Canterbury

The Secretary and Consulting Members of the Alcuin Club

The Librarian of Corpus Christi, Cambridge

The Librarian of Lambeth

The Librarian of the London Registry

The Chairman of the 'Grey Book' Group

The Chancellor of Salisbury Cathedral

The Chancellor of Worcester Cathedral

The Chancellor of Lincoln Cathedral

The Controller of the Oxford University Press

Dr. Percy Dearmer

Martin Shaw has written music for the occasion, and presented the same.

Alan Gray and the Cambridge University Press; also the editors of the *English Hymnal* have given permission for free use of their copyright hymns.

His Majesty the King has graciously approved the following arrangements for the due performance of the ceremonies of the Consecration of Liverpool Cathedral according to the precedents set at:

(1) Canterbury May 4th, 1130 in the presence of Henry, King of England and David, King of Scotland.

(2) No account to be taken of the consecration of enlargements of Parish Churches as at Truro.

The Compiler of the Form of Service, the Reverend F. W. Dwelly, will exercise the offices of Ceremoniarius and Ecclesiarches.

From the *Church Times* of 25 July 1924, a wider public was to learn of the Bishop's determination that there should be broad understanding of the significance of the various elements of the service:

From the first the Bishop has been eager to impress upon the diocese the supreme importance of a right atmosphere for the Consecration ceremony. He felt, and he has warned us, of the danger of being carried away by the spectacular side of the ceremony, and to that end he had arranged for a systematised course of services and addresses to take place previous to the consecration. In the first place, a fortnight before the consecration day, the clergy were supplied with a short but complete synopsis of the form and order of consecration together with an expla-

Before the consecration service began in the Cathedral, the Bishop processed around the outside. Here he moves away from a newly made consecration mark.

nation of the spiritual meaning of the different details of the ceremonial to be adopted. All this the clergy were asked to explain from their pulpits throughout the diocese on Sunday, July 13th, and the majority, I believe, did so.

For anyone knowing anything about the planning and writing of a great Cathedral service, it must be amazing that Dwelly was able to work at such speed on a topic which was new to him. Charles Raven's conversation with the Bishop could not have taken place before Easter – April 20 that year – and yet the service of Consecration was scheduled for July 19. Dwelly wisely consulted those few people whom he believed were capable of assisting him. The Cathedral archive contains one fascinating insight into his consultations, fascinating and enigmatic in the form of fourteen manuscript pages of a letter dated April 29. It is written to 'My Dear Mr Dwelly' from Edenfield, Half Acre Lane, Eccles, but the final page is missing so I do not know the writer of the letter. Parts of this anonymous letter give some indication of how Dwelly approached his task, in that he never made any claims to be a scholarly, academic liturgist; rather he asked for research assistance from those he knew to be knowledgeable. The Dwelly genius lay in using the ancient precedents to produce a meaningful twentieth-century service.

I am sorry to have left you waiting so long – but I was at Buxton when your letter was forwarded to me – Then – I had to write to Worcester to Canon Wilson – as Berties was away – for help. He sent me his copy – of which he has no duplicate

– on the express condition that I do not 'let it out of [my] possession'!! – So I have had to copy it out today (I only got it last night and I was at Macclesfield!) – I think I have copied all that refers to the Dedication Service and I must register the copy back to Canon Wilson tomorrow.

There is not so far as I am aware, extant any copy of the Consecration Service at Worcester in 1218. It would be identical, probably, with those to be found in the earlier printed pontificals ...

There is only one person living who can be relied on to give an accurate answer to questions about what took place at Worcester in the thirteenth century – that is Dame Laurentia of Stanbrook Abbey, Worcester, who has just completed the introduction to the Worcester Antiphoner, which is being printed by the brethren of Solesme – 'I am sure she would help Mr Dwelly'.

There follows several pages of descriptions concerning the preparation for and early part of the service at Worcester in the thirteenth century, the Bishop's entry into the Cathedral to see that all was ready, and then the lengthy processional element which included circling the Cathedral three times on the outside, the triple knocking on the West Doors to gain admittance, the entrance and the symbolic writing in the ashes scattered on the floor. The letter also contains an extract from *Annales of Wigoria* and lists many of the most significant people present in Worcester on 7 June 1218. There is also a reference to a Pontifical which belonged to Worcester in the eleventh century and is preserved in the Library of Corpus Christi College, Cambridge.

Ceremoniarius, Bishop and other diocesan dignatories outside the building.

The anonymous writer of the letter gives an account of Canon Wilson's interpretation of the symbolism of the occasion. Several phrases were used later in explanation of parts of the Liverpool service:

Worcester: 'They lay siege to the natural human soul'
   Liverpool: '– the Grace of God laying siege to the natural man'
   Worcester: '– written with the Pastoral staff to claim for the Church the whole field of learning and of science and art and consecrate it to God'
   Liverpool: '– the Bishop claims for Christ the whole field of learning of science and of art.'

The chanting of Litany, penitential psalms and Benedictus were all part of the Worcester service.

The Cathedral archive contains an undated, typed and duplicated four-page paper by Rev. J. Tyrer, one of the two diocesan clergy who were assisting Dwelly in the whole operation. It is entitled *Liverpool Diocesan Service Book Commission – The Sources of the Liverpool Cathedral Consecration service*. This would be an inappropriate context in which to quote all twenty of the notes but the direct quotation of some of them gives an indication of the depth of researches undertaken into past precedent, and also those points which did not rely on any past precedents. It must be remembered that all of these ancient orders of service were from pre-Reformation days and contained attitudes and ceremonies which would have been unacceptable in Protestant Liverpool in the 1920s.

Knocking at Church door with Ps. 24 seq.
   Found in Pontifical of Egbert (10th-century, not 8th) and in Sarum. Ps. 24 (without knocking) is found here at consecration of Chapel of Wyle-Champflour (A D 1624 – Bath and Wells) and St Catherine Cree (London – A D 1631); but these stand pretty much alone. But whole of Ps. 24 as bishop enters church or immediately after, used in Bishop Andrewes' Form (A D 1620) and frequently since.
   Delivery of Keys to Bishop
   Occasionally found in English 17th-century Consecrations, e.g., that of Peterhouse Chapel (A D 1633).
   Veni Creator
   New (it occurs in Modern Roman Rite)
   Placing Keys on Holy Table
   New. (so far as I am aware).
   The Passages of Scripture
   New. In the medieval rite there are no lections of Scripture at Consecration of churches except at the Mass, and in the English 17th century ones, none except for the Mattins and Holy Communion (which usually formed part of the Consecration).

The leaflet entitled *The Cathedral of Christ Liverpool – For the Use of* Clergy is the

Queen Mary signing the Deed of Consecration. Dwelly can be seen to the left by a lectern.

brief publication referred to in the *Church Times* to be used in all churches the Sunday before consecration. The final page is headed 'Notes upon the inner and spiritual meaning' and highlights twelve key elements in the service. The Bishop's perambulation of the building, The opening of the doors after the third knocking. The delivery of the keys and the Bishop's entrance. The Alpha and Omega inscription. The human soul drawing near to God alone and unattended. The hallowing accomplished. The rejoicings. Witness on stone and parchment. First sermon from the pulpit. The offerings of the people. The departing in the peace of God.

Frederick Dwelly was to achieve world-wide acclaim for the character and quality of his great services, but also for the character and quality of the service sheets themselves, the best of which are superb examples of design and typography. From the invitation cards onwards, through to November 1924 and the *Service of Records* and the *Book of Processions with Records and Deeds*, all the service papers have a distinct 'house' style. The actual *Form and Order of the Consecration of the Cathedral Church of Christ in Liverpool* is sixty four pages long, published by Humphrey Milford, Oxford University Press, and printed by J. A. Thompson and Co. Ltd. The paper was cream and the printing is in both red and black – three colours which became distinctive of the great Liverpool services over the next thirty years.

Architect's drawing of the only parts of the Cathedral which had been built by 1924.

Dwelly leading the Bishop down the steps from the Lady Chapel porch.

The Bishop had appointed Dwelly as *Ceremoniarius* for the services, a post which carried the responsibility not only of planning and writing the services, but also for conducting all the rehearsals, which he did with a stopwatch in his hand. Raven reported on the manner in which Dwelly literally ran up and down the Cathedral superintending the rehearsal of the various parts. At the service itself, he was calmly

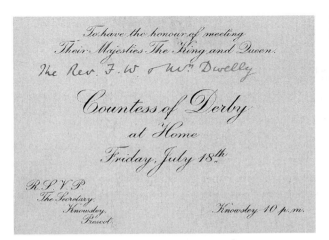

To have the honour of meeting
Their Majesties The King and Queen.

The Rev. F. W. & Mrs Dwelly

Countess of Derby

at Home

Friday, July 18th

R.S.V.P.
The Secretary,
Knowsley,
Prescot.   Knowsley 10 p.m.

Dwelly's invitation to
Knowsley.

present at every significant part clad in cassock, academic gown and preaching bands.

After what must have been the final full rehearsal, the Rev J. P. Baker, Vicar of Mossley Hill, wrote to Dwelly on 18 July:

Dear Old Dwelly,

Well done, old man, it was great! The service was wonderful, and considering the number of parsons who each knew the job better than you do, there were very few boss shotts!! I always think they are more difficult to manage than laymen at a ceremonial. Whatever happens the Bishop will 'make' the service. I thought him great in dignity, gesture and all-there-ness. I do love the man, and Liverpool will know him for the great soul he is before many years. – The place is beautiful for music, and if only we can get it run as the great mission house of the diocese, a spiritual force from the first, there are great days ahead. I am sorry those young chaps have not got the streets round them to care for. I want to see the very poor troop in un-afraid, and the place alive with the human touch (and fleas!).

A series of hour-long vigil services were held in the Lady Chapel starting at 6 p.m. and ending at 6 a.m. The service has all the marks of Dwelly's hand and was actually called *Acts of Devotion*. The congregations were composed of representatives of all the deaneries of the diocese, from Wigan at 6pm to West Derby at 5 am, but Dwelly had a prior engagement and could not be present with other members of his deanery. A letter was despatched from London by the 4.15pm post on 8 July summoning the Rev F. W. Dwelly and Mrs Dwelly to the Countess of Derby's At Home at Knowsley at 10 p.m. 'to have the honour of meeting Their Majesties The King and Queen'.

It may be that Dwelly felt highly honoured but too pressured with duties to make a positive response because he also received a short, hand-written letter from the Bishop:

My dear Dwelly,

Lord Derby is very anxious that you should come to Knowsley on Friday – he says you must be presented. I am awfully sorry for you, but I do agree with him. How can it be managed without killing you entirely?

Yours ever,

A.L.

This afternoon was gorgeous. I see the whole thing now.

Among all the official service papers and dozens and dozens of newspaper reports relating to the Consecration, the archive contains one wonderful piece of Dwelly scrawl on a rough piece of Cathedral-cream paper cut roughly down one edge from a book or larger sheet. It provides a brilliant insight into the real Fred Dwelly, boy-made-good from Chard:

My dear all of you

It is long past midnight – I am just in – but I cannot go to sleep without a word to you – when I was announced in the Presence Chamber Lord Derby said – Your Majesty – the creator of the service which you take part in tomorrow. I bowed low to the King and he said I am deeply interested in it. It must have been very hard work – to which I replied 'No great fun' and he laughed loud and repeated the same to Lord Derby and to the queen – what happened after that I cannot tell you only that we talked some time in a laughing fashion and then I talked to the queen but its all a dream to me – then the Bishop came and claimed me and took me to York and we had no end of a go – he was exceedingly gracious. Cantuar was as he always is wonderful.

I am full of sadness – I'd so like you to share this. Tomorrow – no today – its all done – the crowd at the Cathedral tonight was wonderful. Bert is most helpful –.

The final greeting is completely illegible.

There are numerous published reports of the main Consecration Service, the *Church Times* for 25 July being the most detailed. A detailed commentary is not necessary but the *Church Times'* critical assessment of the service is certainly appropriate for any account of the achievements of F. W. Dwelly:

I do not think any pen, however fluent, can give adequate description of the general effect of the Consecration service. It was overwhelming, bewildering, and awe-full in its solemnity and impressiveness. The bishop had prayed for – and had urged his people to pray for – the due and proper atmosphere. The prayers were undoubtedly answered. It was no spectacle in which the King and his people took part last Saturday afternoon. From first to last there was complete consciousness of the presence of the Holy Spirit of God.

But other things helped to provide the atmosphere. Sir Giles Scott has not merely provided for the Churchmen of Liverpool a majestic and magnificent building which by general acceptance must be accounted as one of the greatest buildings of the world, he has succeeded in the greater aim which, he tells us, he set before himself as paramount: he has provided a Temple of God which makes people want to pray ...

Then, too, the form and order of the service was an inspiration. I know something of the immense amount of care, thought and study which have been devoted to its compilation. It may perhaps not wholly escape criticism – few things do – but let no person be hasty in criticism who did not actually witness the ceremony of consecration! To provide a form which should adequately combine ancient and modern, East and West, was no light task. From Egbert downwards through the centuries the ancient forms of West and of East have been studied with care and with discrimination, and this Form and Order of the Cathedral Church of Liverpool may for all completeness challenge comparison with any in the past.

The music, it will have been noted, used at the Consecration service, was worthy of the occasion and was an immense help. Faux-bourdon and Descant were freely used, and with remarkable effect ...

As a spectacle, Saturday's Consecration service was, of course, wonderful, and the sight of the sanctuary when the last procession of clergy and dignitaries had passed to their places was undoubtedly striking. The fact, however, remains that the outstanding figure in the building was the Armenian bishop, who wore cope and mitre. Convocation robes have their use, their history and their beauty, but they do not 'go' with the architecture or the atmosphere of Liverpool Cathedral. The whole building and every stone of it are crying out for the ancient vestments of the Church, and I shall not be greatly surprised if the worshippers of the Cathedral before many years have passed are giving echo to the same cry. However, that is by the way.

The feature of the whole ceremony, concerning which the most favourable comment has universally been made, was the wonderful orderliness of it all. Those concerned in the various details of ritual and procedure might have been, for all appearances, regularly accustomed to them. Everything passed, or seemed to pass, as a piece of ordinary routine, so perfect was the whole presentment. But, as a matter of hard fact, many, many rehearsals had taken place in order to bring about the orderliness, and it is here that I think it right – and I am quite sure that I shall be giving expression to a general desire – to declare the immensity of the debt which the Cathedral committee, no less than the whole diocese, owes to the Rev. F. W. Dwelly, Vicar of Emmanuel Church, Southport. It is an open secret that it was he who very largely was responsible for the 'Form and Order' of the Consecration; it is he who has drawn up the forms of service which have been, as well as will be, used throughout the week; and it was he who, throughout those last weeks, has acted as Master of Ceremonies, and was, in fact, wholly responsible for the orderliness and the perfection of the service of Saturday last. If any person at all is entitled to take credit for the events of this week in Liverpool Cathedral, that person, above all others, is Mr Dwelly.

A portrait of Dwelly around the time he moved to the Cathedral.

CHAPTER SEVEN

Canon Dwelly

THE 19TH OF JULY 1924 produced great public adulation for one who was at that time simply a parish priest working in a little-known seaside town in the North West of England. However, the *Church Times* reporter made some highly pertinent comments, comments which might be considered again years later in Dwelly's ministry. The form and order of the service was praised highly, and Dwelly's skills in devising such special services were to be a central feature of his ministry for the rest of his life. His ability to use music effectively in worship was discernible from early days at Emmanuel and the establishment of the 'Great Choir'. On Consecration day, the thirty-six Liverpool choristers were joined by sixty further voices from Cathedrals of the Northern Province. Special music was composed for the occasion by Martin Shaw – a friend for the rest of his life. Liverpool Cathedral's need for something special in terms of robes might have been seen as something of a problem back in the twenties. In a decidedly Low-Church diocese, Liverpool Cathedral was not ready to adopt Cope and Chasuble, the ancient Eucharistic vestments of the church, because of their association with Roman and Anglo Catholicism. Though the clergy were not to wear special vestments appropriate to the building, the laity could be dressed in a style appropriate to the building and, with the eventual establishment of Dean and Chapter, the Cross Guild was formed, a company of former choristers who, in well-designed and colourful robes, acted as vergers and mace bearers in the services. They remain a uniquely Liverpool feature and are a result of Dwelly's practical imagination. The dignified orderliness of the first great service became a hallmark of Liverpool Cathedral liturgy. A vast building called for sensitive, imaginative and dramatic use of human movement. Even today, I have not seen such impressive ceremonial in any other English Cathedral and, again even today, the man responsible for this remarkable feature is acknowledged to be F. W. Dwelly.

While the services of the Octave were still in progress, letters began to flow in to Mr Dwelly, although he was not always correctly addressed, even by an Archbishop.

Bishopthorpe,
 York.
 July 22nd, 1924
 Dear Canon Dwelly,

 You must allow me to put on record as Archbishop of the Province my congratulations to you for your great share in the conception, and carrying out of the
Consecration Service on Saturday. I have already told you what I have felt about
it, and how deeply it impressed the King and Queen, and I am sure everyone who
was present. I have just been writing to the Bishop, and I have said to him that the
Service was one full of spiritual movement. The mind and soul were carried along
by the processions and ceremonies from point to point, and I saw no hitch in the
orderliness and silence and dignity with which all the various processions fulfilled
their place. It must have been a great joy to you to see your contribution to what
I may call true spiritual art embodied in the service, as it must have been in an
even greater degree to the Architect to see his vision embodied in the building. I
write hurriedly and most imperfectly, but I am just leaving for Bradford and
London, and I am reluctant to do so without sending you a word however inadequate of congratulation and gratitude.

 Yours sincerely, Cosmo Ebor

Lambeth Palace
 22nd July 1924
 My dear Dwelly,

 What a wonderful triumph for you personally among others the last few days
have been! The Forms for the Consecration and Dedication represent a sort of
Grey Book in excelsis, and were a joy to all who were fortunate enough to use
them. And what an immense amount of thought and work must have lain behind
them and all the arrangements and ordering of the whole thing. The Archbishop
has already written to the bishop and to the chairman of the Cathedral Committee
expressing something of his great joy and gratitude at all these wonderful happen-
ings, and has there mentioned appreciatively what he knows to be your part in
making them possible, and he has asked me just to let you know personally how
warmly he appreciates all you did – and not least the delicate care with which you
made so easy what might so easily have been for him rather a delicate and difficult
act. Unhappily His Grace was not too well on Saturday, but this did not mar his
appreciation of the whole proceedings.

 I shall have a chance I expect to see you when I am here in September.

 Yours sincerely,
 Mervyn Haigh

The Archbishop himself had written by hand to the Bishop on 21 July:

Such scenes as those of the last few days must be fruitful of abundant good. They
are a recognition on the largest scale of the whole community's sense of the

presence and place of the Lord God Omnipotent in the workaday affairs of men – mercantile, social, civic, political, artistic and never has such witness been more worthily formed than under those great arches on those stirring days ...

I am most truly and gratefully yours,

Randall Cantuar

I realise very fully how much we owe to Mr Dwelly in the whole matter for his cooperation and skill in all that was so admirably designed and effected.

Dwelly's letter from Albert Augustus on 27 July captures wonderfully the euphoria of the great days, as well as the Bishop's considerable praise for his younger colleague:

My Dear F.W.D.

After the praises of Kings, and the preference of Queens for your company, to that of any other, the unstinted admiration of both Archbishops ... I shall not attempt to be one who 'also ran' to quote the Earl of Derby.

I overheard you speaking of your mother and father to their Royal Majesties, and I resolved forthwith that one of the Royal copies of the Service must be given to them ... make it so, my boy.

Bless you for all you have been to me this week of modern Pentecost.

Tell your mother that the King said no service had ever before in his life made him realise that he had a religious heart.

I expect they will think, as I did that day, of Isaiah chapter LX.

Yours ever!

Albert Augustus

See that they have one of the first ten copies. You must have the pleasure of sending it from you.

After the rich archival resources of the Consecration period, the next couple of years are not recorded systematically and in such detail, but there is more than enough material to outline what Dwelly was doing. In the middle of the hectic months in preparation for consecration, on 23 May Dwelly received a letter from the Rev. G. A. Studdert-Kennedy offering him an exciting new challenge:

Would you like to go to America on the same stunt I have just returned from? Three months, all expenses paid and the most wonderful opportunity to bring the Message to the American people. If you would consider three months in America would you write to me at 4 The Sanctuary Westminster: I believe it would be well worth while.

Dwelly agreed to undertake the tour and was to spend nearly six weeks touring, lecturing and preaching in America in January, February and March 1925. Before that, however, on 1 December 1924 the newspapers carried the announcement of a new Canon at Liverpool and Chavasse, his former Bishop, wrote to him at once:

I am delighted to see in this morning's *Times* the announcement of your appointment to a residentiary canonry at Liverpool Cathedral. It is a fitting crown of the great services you have rendered to the Church in the Diocese, and will, I am sure, prove highly acceptable to Clergy and Laity alike. I am very thankful for you will be a positive and courageous champion for the Truth ... at a time when bold leadership is needed.

The following day, congratulations arrived from the Archbishop of Canterbury:

I rejoice to see that you are to have a fitting status in the Cathedral of Liverpool. We all owe you gratitude for your notable efforts in connection with the Cathedral and the ministry therein from its start onwards. May you go from strength.

The Archbishop's letter has been preserved in its original envelope addressed to Emmanuel Vicarage but then readdressed to Chard. It can be no coincidence that on the publication of such an exciting piece of news, Dwelly went home to Chard to tell his parents. The envelope had been readdressed in a hand later to become familiar in the Dwelly archive – that of Christine Wagstaffe. Mrs Rose Wagstaffe and her family were near neighbours and lived at 102 Cambridge Road. The family seems to have been heavily involved with the church and both sons and daughters were connected with the Galahads. Mrs Wagstaffe's letter is interesting in itself as the response of a parishioner to Dwelly's preferment, though of even greater significance in the light of Christine Wagstaffe's becoming Dwelly's personal secretary and close companion until his death. It was Christine's brother-in-law, Ralph Dawson, who was to write the official Dwelly biography shortly after his death.

My dear Canon,

This is to convey my most sincere and heartfelt wishes for your happiness. Of course we are all very sad at the thought that you will not be running in every now and again – how we shall miss you. Freda is crying in every corner but I don't feel as though we ever lose your comfort and friendship.

If you have brought happiness to any family during your time here you have to this. You have helped me to pull through – without your help and the thought of your faith in me, I feel convinced I should have gone under. In other words, you have made all the difference – and the children, in you, have had more than a father.

How can I thank you for keeping Chris. I think if she hadn't been going with you, I'd have been as miserable as everyone else – but as she is – its only a few extra miles between us, and I know your help and goodness will be ours always.

Ever your most grateful,

Rose Wagstaffe

One of the most significant letters of congratulation was written on the day of the announcement and came from Charles Raven, who was to be Dwelly's closest colleague for years to come – it was Dwelly and Charles Raven who more than any two other men created the worshipping life of the new Cathedral.

My very dear future colleague,

I am delighted that the decision has come so quickly and that we are to have you here in May. It is not only a tremendous joy that we shall be in closer touch, but a vast encouragement and relief. The past three months have pretty well worn me out: I've done 92 addresses etc on all sorts of unusual subjects since Oct 1st, and have months more of the same sort ahead. You know, I think, how lacking in initiative are all the staff except the bishop: they are dear delightful folks but very ordinary, and Liverpool at present demands more than the ordinary. So I've just had to go all out – and after last spring and Copec I'm running on a rather rackety engine. I hope I haven't trodden on the old men's toes or seemed to take too much on myself; but the risk had to be run. Now with you coming I can sing a sort of Nunc dimittis. You will bring exactly what we want – vision and executive power – and in directions that I can't touch. This means hope and security – just when I was beginning to feel a bit depressed.

You will be terribly missed in Southport: but will after all be in close touch with that part of the diocese. Liverpool will give you scope, and you know the conditions – that one can't handle the Cathedral as if it was a parish church.

Coop rang me up last night to say that he had just heard and to assure me that the diocese would be unanimous in welcoming you. My goodness, dear man, what dreams we may, please God, be able to realise. Anyway we have our opportunities. I am proud to feel that I had a small share in creating it.

Ever yours
Charles

Emmanuel Magazine for December 1924 informed the congregation of his preferment and of his forthcoming trip to America:

I am due to sail the first week in January and to visit thirty diocese in the U.S.A. I hope to be back in time to take the Holy Week Services myself ... It is estimated that whilst I am in America I shall speak in sixty-four places, so I shall need the prayers of those who believe in the message that I am sent to deliver. 'Reality in Prayer – public and private' as illustrated by some of the modern movements in the Church of England.

An article for the February magazine was written from America and gives some indication of how extraordinarily busy he was.

... I am grateful for your letters – so many that they give me a separate locker at the Post Office – and the understanding of saying, 'don't answer' – I couldn't possibly answer them. There is no time. This place is one constant whirl. I will give you my Itinerary as they call it here so that you can see for yourself that I need no rocking at night whether sleeping on a train or a sky scraper or in a shack.

I am so tired that I go off immediately I am alone ... Do you know, if I believed what is written in the newspapers about me, you would need to take me in hand seriously and reduce the swollen head of F.W.D. one travels by night and day, though most days are spent in speaking at conventions or conferences and Sundays preaching. I see by the programme that if my health continues good so that I can fulfil all my engagements, I shall have delivered my soul and mind in speech and sermon 137 times.

There are thirty-eight letters, mainly to Dwelly, in the American archive: they are diverse in character and length but they all indicate how busy he was, and reflect the vigour with which he engaged in the work. There are some brief notes about itinerary: 'Buffalo on Friday, Niagara Falls on Saturday morning, Toronto Saturday afternoon.' There are offers of accommodation when away from his main centre, the Berkeley Divinity School in Connecticut, and his hosts were determined to get the most out of his presence. In addition, there are a request to comment on a form of service, assistance in devising a Lenten service for official use in the diocese, enquiries over a list of books on prayer, material for use with celebration of Holy Communion and Choral Offices, an address on the Church and the stage, and an American edition of Acts of Devotion. Throughout his life, Dwelly was confronted by past friends and parishioners – even in America: 'When you first went to Cheltenham Parish Church my Mother and I used to attend the services and never shall I forget how much my dear Mother enjoyed meeting you.' There is the offer of a new publication, 'If you have thought of producing a book of your lectures.' There must also have been wide media coverage, for 'over the radio we heard your address'. 'Even though you have not been very long in this neighbourhood, the good that you have done has been of such a stimulating effect that we are all getting the advantage of it.'

There is only one extant quotation from an American sermon, preserved because he was asked for a manuscript of Sunday morning's sermon for the New York papers. Dwelly took up the suggestion of the theme of two Cathedrals – Liverpool and St John the Divine:

It is the honouring of God which is, in the end, the sacramental meaning of a Cathedral. God can be and indeed is honoured in the rich, though small expressions of life, but God of the infinitely small – so small that he enters the heart of a simple child which has responsiveness and through that child the Cathedral with a gift – the God of the infinitely small is also God of the breadth and length and depth and height of beauty, truth and goodness. We honour him when our imagination is pierced by the spirit of beauty as I believe is the mind of both great artists, Gilbert Scott and Cram.

We honour him when we lend all we are to rebuild those imaginations in terms of stone and wood and metal and glass. And in the honouring of him we grow into the largeness of his spirit of beauty and cultivate that sense of more than human appreciation which is so badly needed in the world today. It is pathetic to see people shut in to one crannie of life however beautiful that crannie may be. We may not rest content until we consecrate our larger faculties for sharing the lovely and cooperating in the lives of truth.

It is this sense of something bigger than ourselves which the world needs today. A sense that when cultivated will develop in us a power to get away from our calculating selves by a quickened response to the all entrancing.

Your Cathedral will help you to this if you give yourselves wholly to the principle of its consecration and take an adequate share in the building. But let not those who are mere extroverts think they can judge what the building of a Cathedral means. The extrovert can only judge by personal likes and dislikes without knowing the underlying principles. For him there is no tremendous in life. Afraid of his own thoughts, and timid in the mighty movements of the unknown quality within him, he is limited by the calculations he can understand and at the best merely builds a mausoleum where none but he and his one or two shall dwell mummified.

But the man who has passed beyond individualism, the man who has discovered the fulcrum of his personality, will build for future generations a place large enough to be a place of unity sufficiently lofty that there is no sense of limitation for the growing soul. When there is nothing that is not of the best and where everything suggests the compelling power of that intimate revealing other one who loves to redeem man so that all may be free to reach up to the highest in the lovely and the true as well as the good.

The vicar's achievements in America, in 164 addresses, would seem to have dominated the PCC meeting the day after his return to Southport. The chairman, Mr J. E. Jarratt, informed the meeting of the five areas Dwelly had most concerned himself with during his visit: the enquiry into the preparations for an international conference on prison reform; the international student movement's preparations for the 1928 Conference in Chicago; the establishment of diocesan liturgical enrichment commissions; the alcohol reform acts; and the establishment of an American Board of Vision and Courage in relation to black people.

In the newspaper report of the council meeting Dwelly declared that 'he had never had greater and more generous hospitality, but he had never been worked so hard and unmercifully. The state of the church, as he came across it, was one of efficiency beyond anything he had dreamed possible. In the educational world the same efficiency prevailed, but one was impressed with the fact that their methods and their ends were vastly different to ours. The motive which they set themselves was to make the next generation more fit for big business, and the god of big business dominated every other issue in the church and in the educational world.' Two problems in American life impressed him most strongly: 'The first was the colour problem, but the second and greater was the wealth problem. The possession of so much wealth by so few ...' There is no evidence to suggest that Dwelly ever again undertook such a lecture tour and all of his massive energies seemed to have been focussed around his work in Liverpool Cathedral.

On Saturday 2 May 1925, in the presence of a large congregation at Evensong, Frederick William Dwelly was installed by Albert Augustus as 'Canon of Liverpool, Cermoniarius' with the words:

> It appertaineth to the Office of Canon to be the counsellor and adviser of the bishop in Holy things as well within as without the Chapter; to be a student of sacred learning, and of all such matters as tend to establish and confirm the truth of the Gospel and the discipline of the Church, to be instant in prayer for God's blessing upon our labours and those of all who are fellow-workers with God, especially for those of our Chapter; to maintain brotherly love and hospitality so far as in him lies; to be zealous for the beauty and service of this our illustrious Cathedral Church of Christ in Liverpool; to take his part in the daily offering of the devotions allotted to the Stall, and to remember all who minister in this Diocese together with the Benefactors of this Holy place.

J. P. Baker, Vicar of Mossley Hill, had written to Dwelly on 30 November 1924 to congratulate him on the canonry, particularly with regard to his future cooperation with Charles Raven.

> I am so thankful you are to go to the Cathedral to help Raven whilst there is time – before things had deadened down into a ghastly lost opportunity. Now I am happy about things. You and Raven will be brothers, and others will come to your aid in the course of nature. You will try first to correct that barbarian sub-dean into a Christian attitude towards those poor lay folk who happen not to agree with him.

The close friendship and professional cooperation of Dwelly and Raven were responsible for significant features in the life of the new Cathedral. Their work together is reported on and assessed by Frederick Dillistone's biography of Raven, in which he wrote:

> [It was] a friendship which was to become one of the most treasured possessions of his life. Though Fred Dwelly and Charles Raven were to pass through many harrowing experiences during the next twenty-five years, when loyalties in other directions were strained to the limit, their intimate regard for and affection towards one another were never broken.

Raven held a canonry from early 1924, before Dwelly's appearance, and he had two special responsibilities, in both of which Dwelly came to play a significant part. Post-ordination training is now, of course, considered an essential part of preparation for full priesthood in the church. Liverpool was the first diocese in the country to set up formal continuing education for its young priests, who attended sessions at the Cathedral on Tuesday mornings, and most of the teaching was in the hands of Raven and Dwelly. They had a strong influence during this crucial period of minis-terial growth on such figures as John Tiarks, future bishop of Chelmsford, Douglas Harrison, future Dean of Bristol, and Michael Ramsey, future Archbishop of Canterbury.

Their styles as preachers and lecturers differed hugely. Raven was highly dramatic and scholarly and, on occasions, devastatingly critical, while Dwelly 'talked in a heart-to-heart manner about pastoral and devotional ministry.'

As far as the laity was concerned, the Raven/Dwelly influence was felt most strongly at 'the 8.30'. These late Sunday evening services were started by Raven in the summer of 1924 and became so popular that they drew in people from all over the Diocese. They were set after the time of parochial Evensong so as not to draw people away from their parishes. The service itself began with half an hour of organ music played as the congregation assembled and then was very simple in form with an address, often by Raven or Dwelly, at the centre. A range of significant public figures from both inside the Church and beyond were invited to speak. The Cathedral really was being developed as an important centre for the whole commu-nity and not just as a bastion of Anglicanism. Dillistone gives a graphic account of the behaviour of the two regular preachers:

… what held the congregation together was undoubtedly the double influence of two strangely disparate personalities. Dwelly would lie flat on one of the great oak tables in a darkened vestry before going in to preach; Raven would pace up and down, almost physically sick, rehearsing his words and gestures like an actor. Dwelly captured the audience by his sheer informality of approach, talking to them as his friends for whom he really cared, about important matters which they had not perhaps sufficiently taken into account. Raven captivated them by his looks, his gestures, his command of his subject, perhaps most of all by his ability to relate the great themes of the New Testament to personal needs and duties.

As far as I can tell from the records, the 8.30 continued until the outbreak of the Second World War, when there is a typescript of the Sermon Dwelly preached on the day that war was declared.

Dwelly had such a breadth of interests and involvements that it is not possible to communicate all his activities in a simple chronological line. As we know, it was Dwelly who persuaded Percy Dearmer into becoming an active supporter of the Life and Liberty Movement and, at one point, it was hoped that the organisation might take the opportunity to produce a new hymn book. This was not to be, but Songs of Praise was published in 1925 and adopted by Albert Augustus as the new hymn book for the new Cathedral. Dearmer's dissatisfaction with English hymnody had been voiced while Dwelly was still a student when the old edition of Hymns Ancient and Modern dominated the Church of England. As early as 1903, Dearmer and a group of friends were planning to produce a small hymn book for supplementary use alongside Ancient and Modern. By the following year, their ideas had extended and clarified and Ralph Vaughan Williams had been recruited to the team as musical editor, with Dearmer as editor of the text. The book was a considerable step forward in terms of quality. As a result of conversations with Vaughan Williams, Dearmer appointed Martin Shaw as Choir Master and Organist at St Mary's Primrose Hill and new high standards in hymnody were set at that church. As Shaw was later to write,

> Our musical policy, never put into words but mutually understood and agreed upon, was that the music should be chosen on its own merits. The obvious thing to do, it might be thought, yet I really believe S. Mary's Primrose Hill was the only church in London where, for instance, the popular weak Victorian hymn tune was never heard. The usual argument is – you must give people what they like. Percy said – 'you must give people what is good and they will come to like it!' It was right through and through, spiritually and morally of course, and it was also 'business', for congregations filled the church.

Although not intended as a 'party' book, *English Hymnal* became associated in the minds of many people with the Anglo-Catholic wing of the church, but Dwelly recognised Dearmer's abilities in the field of hymnody and declared: 'When the differences of "church before Party" happened, PD took the line that we can sing people into putting Church before Party even if we cannot teach it. He maintained that the religion of the people is the religion of hymns – we must have Songs of the Spirit.'

With Vaughan Williams and Martin Shaw as musical editors and Dearmer as text editor, assisted by a small group of people including Dwelly, *Songs of Praise* was conceived. Although *Ancient and Modern* had been chosen as the book for Liverpool Cathedral, Dwelly was asked to enquire whether Albert Augustus might be won over to adopting the results of the new initiative and cancelling the order for *Ancient and Modern*. This he did, and Dwelly's wrote that 'with his amazing power of response, he gambled on cancelling the book for *Songs of the Spirit* and won.' At a later stage the title was changed to *Songs of Praise*. The book became influential, partly because it was adopted for use by many schools. The preface to the original edition was forthright in its declaration:

> ... the present generation desires to enter into the heritage of noble religious verse which is ours. That heritage is ours by right of the great poetry in which the English tongue is supreme, by right also of the magnificent prose which since Coverdale and Cranmer has formed the substance of our Christian worship, though it was never adequately matched by the hymns in common use. Our English hymns, indeed, few of which are earlier than Dr Watts and most of which were the product of the Victorian era, have not been altogether worthy of the English Bible and the English Prayer Book; and the bulk of the tunes to which they were sung illustrated a period of British music which the musicians of today are anxious to forget ...

In his biography of Mervyn Haigh, at that time chaplain to Randall Davidson, Archbishop of Canterbury, F. R. Barry wrote of a group of friends who were staunch in their support of the liberal character of *Songs of Praise* – people such as Haigh, Dearmer, Harold Anson, Leslie Hunter, 'that erratic genius Fred Dwelly' and H. R. L. (Dick) Sheppard. The new hymn book 'stood for what that group of friends stood for. Its aim was to offer congregations – who take their theology mainly from the hymns – a virile, outward-looking presentation of the Christian faith for the new age, freed from some of the weak, mawkish sentiments which had crept into nineteenth century hymn books. It was meant, too, to appeal as widely as possible, reaching out from the inner circle of things ...' In my youth, the book was referred to by some as 'the golfers' hymn book' and it certainly contained some words and ideas closer to Humanism than to Christianity, but, as Barry judged, 'it matched the hour, and at that time and period it served its purpose. It proved to be exactly what was needed in the Christian church in the late twenties.'

At the time of his appointment to the Canonry at Liverpool, Dwelly had revealed his involvement in liturgical reform and hymnody. He had the confidence to organise events on a large scale, he was highly energetic, greatly in demand as a preacher, concerned for the importance of music and human movement within worship, he possessed great personal charm, he was intensely loyal to his friends and he had strong professional and fraternal relations with many of the foremost figures of the Church. The Cathedral itself was extremely busy in the years between Consecration and the formal establishment of Dean and Chapter in 1931, but Dwelly still found time to assist in the devising of some highly significant services elsewhere in the country. Anyone capable of devising the Liverpool consecration services was going to be in demand by his clerical friends.

There is an intriguing letter in the archives from Old Palace, Canterbury, Nov 2 – no year is given though 1928 would seem likely.

My beloved Dwelly,
    Ever so many thanks for that, your latest and most brilliant effort – I set it down in front of the A at his desk and made him go right throughout, to the accompaniment of my commentary of praise in the best Grey Book style! He was really impressed and added 'It's such splendid language too.' ...
    So does the light radiate – and Liverpool lead the way in interpreting the Gospel and revising all Revised Prayer Books and claiming for religion like another Hildebrand – compared to which even such cathedral building is bagatelle.
    Love and power to you.
    MH

On 4 December 1928, Cosmo Gordon Lang succeeded Randall Davidson as Archbishop of Canterbury at an installation service in Canterbury Cathedral. The Dean, George Bell, future Bishop of Chichester, was a friend of Dwelly over many years and in terms of imaginative invention they were kindred spirits. We know that

Bell consulted the Bishop of Truro and the Dean of Wells over some fundamental modifications to the service – putting the enthronement in the hands of the Dean and Chapter rather than the Archdeacon and moving the marble chair of St Augustine from the Corona to a platform at the east end of the nave. The Archbishop's role in the world-wide Anglican Church was being emphasised. In Lang's own words, 'The Dean … had taken infinite pains about all the arrangements. He had given full play to his vivid imagination in order to make the ceremony symbolic not only in ecclesiastical life, but of the national life, including the Arts. Hence the series of independent representative processions, admirably marshalled. Never certainly had any previous Archbishop been enthroned on a scale of such colourful and symbolic magnificence.'

Recognition for the success of the service is given in Lang's biography to the Bishop of Truro, the Dean of Wells, Percy Dearmer and Fred Dwelly, although the letters to Dwelly after the event would suggest that Dwelly's role had been of paramount importance, not only in devising and writing the service, but also in the rehearsal and running of the great national event.

> The Deanery
>   Canterbury.
>   5 December 1928
>   My dear Dwelly,
>   I hardly know how to thank you – I could not thank you sufficiently for all you did to make yesterday's service so marvellous. It would have been very different, and very much less impressive in all sorts of ways without you and your brain and your art and imagination, and your outstanding executive and organising capacity. Indeed you made the whole difference both in composition of the service, and its most thrilling moments, and in the arrangement of all the details of the ceremony – plan, marshalling, processions, robing, bringing the greater chapter in and so much class that I cannot fault it! Thank you a thousand times. And you were so magnificent to work with – for everyone else. The whole Church owes you a great debt: I rejoice that you and I were so brought together, and worked so radiantly for so noble an occasion. The opportunity was a wonderful one – and thanks to you wonderfully used. It was a work of the whole Church of Christ …
>   Let's work together again before long.
>   Yours ever gratefully,
>   G. K. A. Bell

Bell's handwriting is difficult to decipher but his excitement, admiration and gratitude are overflowing and the letter so resembles those Dwelly received after his first great Liverpool service. Lang himself wasted no time in sending his thanks – fortunately the letter was typed.

> My dear Canon Dwelly,
>   I must send you a word of special thanks for the invaluable help which you gave

to the Dean and Chapter in the arrangements for the memorable Service yesterday. I heard from many quarters that the movement of the various Processions went without the slightest hitch and with great dramatic silence and solemnity. It was plain that a master hand had been at work. That this great drama should have been presented with such moving solemnity and without any kind of interruption is, I am sure, greatly due to you, and I have my own debt of gratitude because the smoothness of the whole great proceeding contributed much to my own peace and quietness of mind. With much gratitude.

Yours sincerely,
Cosmo Cantuar

Reports of the success of the service must have been reported to Albert Augustus, who wrote to Bell on 6 December:

My dear Bell,
You and Canterbury are very welcome indeed so far as Liverpool is concerned for our contribution to your great day, and I am sure that Dwelly enjoyed bringing it. He is indeed a genius and you can now measure our good fortune here. To whom much is given – . We never grudge his services elsewhere. It is not only that he is one of the few people I know who can make persons walk straight, and that he has a sense of fitness in liturgical form, and nearly always in language; but he is full of the spirit of worship and never allows me to forget that highest significance of what we are doing.

But he did not do it all himself – and certainly he does not think so. Heartiest congratulations on the whole thing and on your great part in it. My wife was very grateful for the ticket – I have seen neither her nor D but I am looking forward eagerly to their account.

Dwelly's comment to Bell was typical of him: 'Oh but it was fun playing with all the spirits of the past and bringing out of the treasures things new and old.'

One might light heartedly surmise that if Dwelly had been operating fifty years later he might have been nicknamed Rent-a-Precentor because even from the limited papers in the archive, Dwelly was greatly in demand to help colleagues elsewhere in the country to formulate impressive services. Even before he left Canterbury after Lang's enthronement, he received a telegram from the Bishop of Croydon anxious for his assistance: 'Greatly need your help service of Worship new Archbishop. Croydon. January. Could we meet in London before you return.'

Correspondence continued with Bell at Canterbury and he wrote on 30 April 1929 telling the news of his preferment as Bishop of Chichester. One sentence is of particular interest: 'I saw the PM and told him my various "ploys" – which made him say "You want an active man there!" How happy I should be if such a one as you were to come!' However, this was not to be and the Deanery at Canterbury was offered to Dick Sheppard, an appointment which pleased Dwelly, and Bell who wrote again on 17 May:

I leave now with a much easier mind, and more happiness. I'm very pleased indeed about Dick. This is only an exchange of chum with you. Are you coming on June 11? It would be very nice if you would; and I hear you are most kindly looking at the Consecration Service. Have you the Chelmsford Enthronement Form? I hear that was excellent – and your handiwork. I want the Chichester to be good too!!

May brought Dwelly a series of highly significant letters, one of which on the first of the month was from Lambeth Palace and marked Confidential.

My dear Canon Dwelly,
I have been asked to be responsible for the drawing up of a form of service for the Special Thanksgiving in which the King will take part on some Sunday later in the summer. You have given so much time and thought in these recent years to the drawing up of Special Services for special occasions that I would be grateful to have some hints or suggestions from you ...
Would you be so kind as to put your expert mind upon this most important but most difficult matter? I must try to get help from many sources and I naturally turn to you. I would be very grateful if you could give me some suggestions as soon as possible as it is desired that the matter should be well in hand by the middle of the month.
Yours very sincerely,
Cosmo Cantuar.

The letter also gave fuller details about the occasion of the service to be held in Westminster Abbey and broadcast throughout the country. Before the event, the Form of Service would be sent to the Dominions 'so that the whole Empire can take part.'
While Dwelly was dealing with this demanding and exciting request from the head of the world-wide Anglican Communion, he received a letter from 10 Downing Street dated 9 May.

Dear Sir,
I am desired by the First Lord of the Treasury to write to you with reference to the living of St Edmund the King, Lombard Street. The living which is vacant by the death of Rev. G. A. Studdert-Kennedy is in many ways of special importance and, after the most careful consideration, the PM has come to the conclusion that he cannot better serve the interests of the church as a whole by offering to submit your name to His Majesty for appointment to it.

Dwelly replied immediately, promising to give his decision 'in the course of a few days'. There is no evidence available to give any idea of Dwelly's response to the offer but we know that he was in the middle of work on the King's Recovery Service for the Archbishop. Dwelly's proposals were written on 15 May. A carbon copy of the letter remains in the archive but a significant quantity of material was enclosed with the letter – 'copies of the background that we have for such services, with copies of the prayers they used in case you may wish to refer to them. Also a draft suggested Litany of Deliverance ...' Some further quotation from the letter is justified as it reveals something of Dwelly's planning thoughts ahead of a special service. The archive is full of magnificent published special services, some with pencilled comments in Dwelly's hand, but there is little in writing to explain the principles on which he was working.

I am sorry to have been so long in forwarding these suggestions to your Grace – a love of pruning my stuff is the reason, and even now could do much more polishing with advantage.

(a) To retain a connecting link with the earlier forms of thanksgiving for a King's recovery.

(b) To develop the same along the lines of your own teaching of 'hallowing grace', thus bringing the mode of approach to God in harmony with our age,

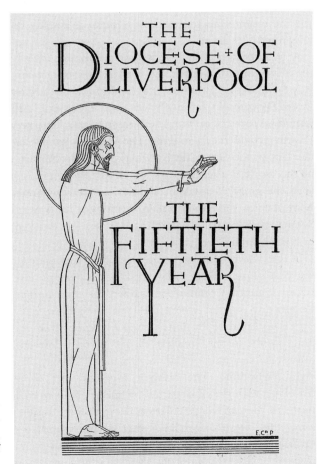

Edward Carter Preston's design for the fiftieth anniversary of the diocese. The figure is stylistically reminiscent of the Carter Preston stone figures which are such important features of the Cathedral.

(c) To acknowledge before God that synthesis of the ways of healing which our age is learning to appropriate and to do so in a way which will not be entirely unacceptable both to the medical profession and to our praying folk, and that without missing the glory of the transcendent.

(d) That the healing of the King is due in some measure to the martyrs of science and therefore a mention of them comes in the Prayers before the Blessing.

(e) To slightly adapt one of the ancient blessings so that the Broadcast listeners may be conscious that you have not forgotten those 'scattered upon a thousand hills'. Some people will come to give thanks: others will listen to give thanks.

Twenty years previously, Dwelly had been an unknown assistant curate in an insignificant church in the Lake District. Now he was the praise of deans, bishops and archbishops, rapidly establishing himself as one of the leading liturgists of his day and in line for an important Crown appointment. The demands on his energies that were being sought across the country were as nothing compared to the range and scale of work which he was undertaking for Liverpool Cathedral at more or less the same time. His tremendous efforts were justly rewarded when in 1928 he was appointed Vice-Dean.

At Windermere, Cheltenham and Southport, Dwelly had been deeply involved in the Boy Scout Movement and retained his contacts for many years. In 1929, the first Boy Scout World Jamboree was held in Arrow Park over the Mersey on the Wirral, in the Diocese of Chester. It was to be Liverpool Cathedral which hosted the great Jamboree services on Sunday 11 August 1929. One service would not suffice and so Dwelly provided at 3.00 p.m. 'The People's Service of Thanksgiving and Prayer for the Gift of the Scout Ideal'; at 4.45 p.m. 'The Service of Welcome to the Scouts of all the World' – a service with lots of stirring hymn singing including 'Mine eyes have seen the glory' 'Jerusalem' and Martin Shaw's 'Pioneers'. The Bishop preached at both of these services and then at 8.30 p.m., at a 'Service for Parents and Friends of Scouts', the Chaplain of the First Windermere Sea Scouts preached – his name was, of course, Fred Dwelly.

In 1930 was celebrated the Jubilee of the foundation of Liverpool Diocese and also the year of a Lambeth Conference when bishops and archbishops from the world-wide Anglican Communion gather for their ten-yearly meetings. There is no evidence to suggest where the idea came from, but there is ample evidence that over two hundred Bishops visited Liverpool from July 12 to 14, and all the planning, down to the smallest details of transport and accommodation, carry the unmistakable stamp of Canon 'Organiser' Dwelly. The service book alone is forty-eight pages long. The bishops, together with other members of their families travelling with them, departed by special train from Euston at 2.25 p.m. From the moment they arrived at Allerton Station on the southern outskirts of the city at 6.08 p.m., they were driven in a fleet of one hundred and ninety cars, first to the Cathedral, then to the Town Hall for dinner and then to the homes of their (mainly clerical) hosts throughout the Diocese. The Cathedral service was on Sunday at 3.00

p.m., but most of the distinguished visitors preached at a morning or evening service somewhere in the diocese. It required almost military precision to ensure that the whole weekend was not a disaster, and everything right up until the final moments before the service was planned carefully, including the management traffic problems arising from the annual Parade of the Orange Lodge on their traditional marching day, 14 July.

In his speech at the Town Hall Dinner, Albert Augustus conveyed forcibly to his colleagues the vitality and freshness of Cathedral and Diocese. A couple of years later, Dwelly was to use one of the Bishop's phrases from the speech as the title for a great service for members of the free-churches of Liverpool. It is also interesting to note that the host at the dinner was the Lord Mayor of Liverpool, Mr Lawrence Holt, one of the foremost Unitarians in Liverpool who was to become a great friend and supporter of Dwelly.

You will join us in the Cathedral tomorrow in giving thanks for the fifty years' work, and to answer the call of the jubilee for the proclaiming of liberty, not to do what we like, not liberty to try things because they are new, but liberty to enter on adventures and to make experiments in which newness of life may find expression; in other words, liberty to grow.

The service which Dwelly had designed for the following afternoon gave expression to this admirable aspect of liberty: here was no modified Choral Evensong, no experiment for the sake of experiment, but a carefully researched and excellently performed piece of liturgy. On the surface, Dwelly might have been seen as the great showman creating spectacle in 'God's Dwelly House' as some called the Cathedral in later years, but in reality his processions and thoughtfully prepared, imaginative rituals were profoundly expressive and in the vanguard of twentieth century development of Cathedral worship.

The *Church Times* correspondent wrote at length about the service, which he found meaningful, impressive, beautifully performed, and he declared it to be 'the most memorable service held in Liverpool'. The performance of the music and the creative way in which it was employed produced favourable comment, as did the overall influence of the Cathedral and its worship on the whole Diocese.

The Service Book was prepared by Canon F. W. Dwelly, Ceremoniarius of the Cathedral, and he is to be heartily congratulated on having prepared such a splendid setting for the thanksgiving. And the service itself showed how things were advancing ...

In fact, the ceremonial of Liverpool Cathedral ... is most elaborate, and makes one thankful for the dignified simplicity of our Western Rite. And the improved demeanour of the clergy! I noticed one section leave the church, and there was hardly one who did not bow to the altar. Whatever else our Cathedral may have done, it has uplifted the standard of worship among ordinary church folk ...

Finally, an ungrudging tribute must be paid to the way every detail was thought out. Each person knew his place and duty. There was not a hitch from beginning to end. The 'stage management' was perfect.

In terms of design, shade of paper and typography, the Service Book itself was superb and did far more than simply provide the words of the hymns and prayers so that the congregation could participate. The spacious layout highlighted the different phases of the service and led the worshippers to an understanding of the whole experience.

In everything, the hand of Dwelly the artist was to be observed, and the great services also brought together the artistry of a range of people. Through his work for *Songs of Praise* Dwelly had come to know such people as Ralph Vaughan Williams, Martin Shaw and Poet Laureate, John Masefield. Having met and worked with them, the persuasive Canon Dwelly was soon calling upon his new friends to help him to enrich the worship at the Cathedral. That part of the archive holding materials from some of the artists is both fascinating and infuriating because in most instances they did not bother to date their letters. The first editions of the pieces of music are dated and we have such pieces as Vaughan Williams' 'Te Deum in G', 1928 (with minor amendments in red ink from the hand of the composer), which was 'Composed for Liverpool Cathedral and are dedicated to Albert, Bishop of Liverpool.' Shaw's setting of 'The Easter Anthems' was dedicated 'To the inspirer, F.W.D.' And the full score was for trumpets, timpani, tubular bells, cellos, double-basses and organ.

The Martin Shaw letter sent with 'The Easter Anthems' is, for him, remarkably formal and legible.

My dear Freddy,
   Here's the Easter Anthem – I hope it's something near what you want. All the choir responses at the beginning should go briskly. Of course it ends really with 'even so in Christ shall all be made alive' and any attempt to make the Gloria a big thing would be anticlimax so I have just given it simply. I would very much like to come to the last rehearsal and performance. I'll pay my fare if you can get me put up I'm too hard up for hotels.
   You will see I have done two trumpet foreshadowing fanfares before the great words each time – first 'Christ is risen from the dead' and last 'In Christ shall all be made alive.'

On 9 February 1930 there was a major Cathedral service which brought together the skills of Shaw and Masefield. The purpose of the service was explained at the beginning of the lavish service book, *Kinship with the Sea*.

The purpose of this service is to offer to Almighty God our thankful remembrance of the life and work of all who follow the calling of the sea, and the spirit in which their work is done.
   To that spirit of disciplined adventure we owe the existence of this Port. Our

prosperity depends on it. As we cherish the best in it, so shall we best serve our country. As we share it, so shall nation be brought nearer to nation in mutual understanding and the common service of mankind.

And it is the gift of God.

Today we ask that He may preserve and strengthen it in all seafarers, make it manifest in the whole life of our city, and use it for the welfare of this country and the peace of all the world.

Dwelly required and commissioned something originally called a masque – words by Masefield and music by Shaw – to form part of the service straight after the sermon. One of Shaw's scribbled notes gives some notion of the choral resources required:

My plan (and Masefield's I imagine)
    Merchants: 4 groups of men (Armstrong's lot)
    Sailors: Cathedral Choirmen (? or another body of men)
    All: Full Cathedral choir Men and Boys. Contains choral writing (four-part mainly) and climaxes, so must be sung by singers.

    I have got a fine contralto and closed with her – Miss Constance Willis is her name.

    It is most important that I should come down to Liverpool. The Merchants chants will be deadly unless done in a certain way and if they get them started and fixed in a dull and wrong rhythm it will kill the show.

Freddy
    You now (with this MSS) have everything for your end ie Merchants, Sailors and All.

    I am sending you in a day or so (or bringing on Saturday) one complete score for conductor and organist.

    I am anxiously awaiting word and fare money for Saturday.

Finally a hasty scrawl in thick blue pencil:

This is the full score. Everything. Anxiously awaiting instructions about Saturday – Please send money for fare as I have reached limit of overdraft and can't draw cheques.

A more formal, statement from Shaw published in *Up to Now* in 1929 presents an interesting insight into the way a musician responded to Dwelly:

The most wonderful experience of this sort that I have ever had was at Liverpool recently. That arch-designer, Canon Dwelly, dropped in at my house casually one afternoon and asked me to compose a wedding anthem for the first wedding that would ever take place in Liverpool Cathedral, and named a date a few days ahead. Such is his way. He also suggested that I should pay a visit to Liverpool and preach in the cathedral, for the consecration of which I had composed all the special music. Though, as I have said, I feel in a pulpit like a fish out of water, such is Dwelly's hypnotic persuasiveness that I feebly consented . . .

There is no one who can 'bring it off' like Dwelly . . .

On the Sunday morning Dwelly took me all round the cathedral from on high, and I had the unique experience of hearing my own anthem, splendidly sung by Goss-Custard and his fine choir, float up to me. They also sang my 'Pioneers', which Dwelly told me was always now chosen for ordinations. Who but Dwelly would have thought of Walt Whitman's being sung at an ordination.

Some time in 1929 or 1930, Dwelly made the acquaintance of another artist with whom he worked for the rest of his life: Edward Carter Preston. Albert Augustus wrote of him early in 1931: 'Carter Preston who is the finest kind of agnostic wandered into the Cathedral on Christmas Day and said to Dwelly afterwards, "You came very near to the ineffable". He is a kind of prophet like Blake and lives very high.' Carter Preston is best known in the Cathedral for a large number of life-size stone statues, but from evidence in the archives it would appear that his first work for the Cathedral was the design of a little commemorative brochure in 1930 for the Jubilee Service. There were only two hundred and fifty copies printed and they were numbered and signed by the artist. The publication is illustrated with four striking woodcuts, the first of many Carter Preston was to produce for other service sheets and booklets. The design and print for the title page and for messages from Bishop and Lord Mayor are very fine. Even before the formal foundation of Dean and Chapter, Dwelly had secured the services of a man whose art would enhance the appearance of all of the special services literature for which Dwelly became responsible.

It can be hard to comprehend quite how far ahead of his time Dwelly really was. By 1930, Liverpool Cathedral, with Fred Dwelly as Vice-Dean, Charles Raven as Canon Chancellor, and Albert Augustus David as Bishop, had more than come of age and the time was right for the official formation of the Dean and Chapter.

CHAPTER EIGHT

Dean of Liverpool

I n AN AGE BEFORE FAX MACHINES, email and the mobile phone, Dwelly was
a frequent sender and receiver of telegrams. At 10 a.m. on 2 July 1931 a fourteen-
word message was despatched from London and received at the Lodge Lane Office
in Liverpool, just a short bike ride from the Dwelly residence. The message might
almost have been in code and could have meant very little in the telegraph office.

Dwelly 6 Grove Park Liverpool
   He bids me set my mind at rest
   Bishop

In the archives this salmon-pink telegram has been preserved alongside another
piece of almost illegible Dwelly writing which explained the significance of the
earlier, enigmatic message.

2 July – 1931 –
   At about 11.30 – a telegram came and Chris read it to me from the Bishop saying
Ramsey Mac has set his mind at rest – this means that I am to be Dean of Liverpool
– so that the desire of a life came true – I know I'm not big enough for it but I am
grateful to God and my first wish is that Mother and Father should know for it is
to them I owe my desire to please God my love for Church and nature and they
would be so proud. Few men get the whole desire of their life and so great a priv-
ilege – none could be more grateful. Now for morning prayer and prayer habit in
the freedom of the gift which God has given to the world through love – it is that
I must develop for it is his gift.
   The words that come to me as I kneel down and pray shall be my resolve.
   This shall be my rest for ever
   Here will I dwell for I have a delight therein
   He shall be my son and I will be to them a father.

There could be no public rejoicing at the news in the telegram and Dwelly had to
wait until 13 July for a confidential letter from Downing Street.

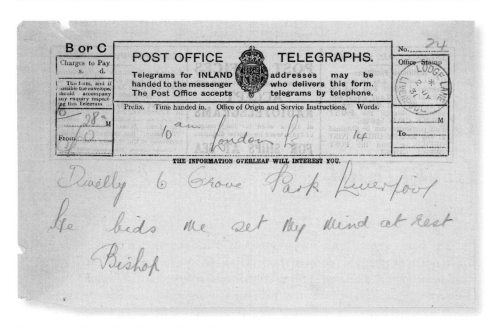

The telegram from the Bishop with its coded message.

Dear Canon Dwelly,

The Order in Council creating the Deanery of Liverpool received His Majesty's approval on 29th June, and it is now my duty to submit a name to the King in this connection.

After the most careful consideration, I have come to the conclusion that I cannot better serve the interests of the church than by offering to you the appointment to this Deanery. On hearing from you that you will be willing to accept this offer, I shall be happy to submit your name to the King.

Until His Majesty's approval has been obtained, I have to ask that you will treat this offer as confidential.

Yours very sincerely,

Ramsey MacDonald

The news was released to the press in time for the *Liverpool Post and Mercury* to carry the news on 21 July. The initial stipend was to be £1,500 a year until such time that the Maintenance Fund was sufficient to provide the full stipend of £2,000. He received in addition £100 as annual housing allowance until the provision of a deanery house. For whatever reason, no deanery was ever provided and, together with the Cathedral itself, 6 Grove Park was to be his home until his death. It was a decent late nineteenth-century detached house in a road of similar properties on the line between the densely packed houses of Toxteth and the trees and open spaces of Sefton Park. The house still stands but in a rather run-down condition.

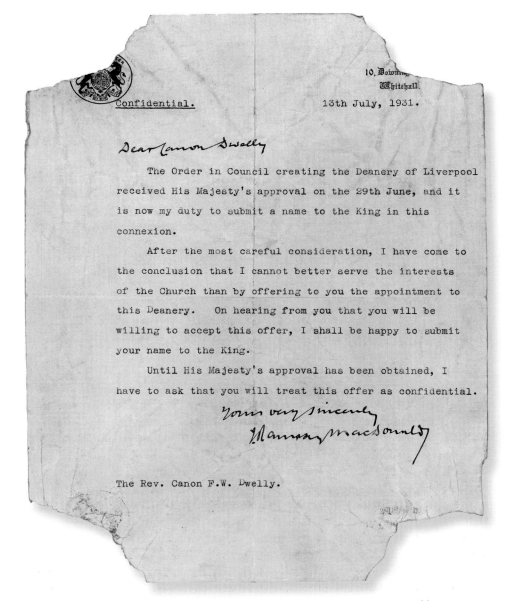

Confidential.

10, Downing,
Whitehall.

13th July, 1931.

Dear Canon Dwelly

      The Order in Council creating the Deanery of Liverpool
received His Majesty's approval on the 29th June, and it
is now my duty to submit a name to the King in this
connexion.

      After the most careful consideration, I have come to
the conclusion that I cannot better serve the interests
of the Church than by offering to you the appointment to
this Deanery. On hearing from you that you will be
willing to accept this offer, I shall be happy to submit
your name to the King.

      Until His Majesty's approval has been obtained, I
have to ask that you will treat this offer as confidential.

Yours very sincerely,
J. Ramsay MacDonald

The Rev. Canon F.W. Dwelly.

All that remains of the letter of appointment from Prime Minister Ramsay MacDonald.

    I have no way of knowing how many letters of congratulation Dwelly received on
the publication of his news, but dozens remain in the archives – each one with a
large tick on it in one of the many Dwelly coloured pencils. It is the range of letters
which is so significant. A. F. S. Harding wrote from Whitby that 'It seems a very long
way back to the old days at Queens' and so few of my contemporaries has risen in

fame.' From Shoelands House, Seale, Surrey: 'Dearest Dwelly, Of course we all knew you were to be Dean, and the only possible first Dean; but, oh, I am so glad it has all gone through. Thank God for Liverpool. We never meet but I love you just as ever. I am such an asthmatic crock now that I can hardly move or talk, Your loving, Dick' [H. R. L. Sheppard] From one of his near neighbours in Grove Park, 'Very many congratulations on this opportunity to make your genial self of even greater value to all than ever. Bernard Chavasse' There are wonderfully cheery letters from parishioners, like Mrs Kathleen Little who heard the news from a shop-keeper when she was out buying some fish in Windermere. Even his home town remembered him: 'Chard is very proud of you, and how delighted your dear little mother would have been. Grace Chaffey.'

It does not take much imagination to realise that the services associated with the establishment of the Dean and Chapter would be well-researched, imaginative and splendid. Despite all the time needed for planning and preparations, the Cathedral services continued throughout a very busy summer with a number of significant special events, including such diverse services as South Division Liverpool Brownies, the Anniversary of the Consecration, the Dedication of the Chavasse Memorial, Celebration for the Royal Lancashire Agricultural Society, Special Musical Service, and Celebrations of the Centenary of the British Association for the Advancement of Science, with sermons by Rt Hon. J. C. Smuts, Sir Oliver Lodge and the Bishop of Birmingham.

The Service Book for the service at which the Dean was installed on Sunday 4 October had a beautifully designed front cover, the work of Edward Carter Preston, and ran to thirty-two pages in length. Research similar to that undertaken in 1924 preceded the planning of the service and was published in the press by the Bishop at the end of September. 'By careful selection of material from manuscripts we have been enabled to follow a true line of development from the day when the King Edward the Confessor attended the foundation ceremony of the Cathedral; at Exeter. We have drawn particularly from manuscripts that give a reference to what was done at Canterbury, Lincoln, Exeter, Salisbury, Worcester, Evesham and Hereford.'

The service was no hollow reconstruction of the rituals of a bygone age, as the Dean of Chichester was at pains to explain in the press: 'All were marked by fresh-ness and originality. Yet in no part was there any feeling of the merely theatrical. The "stunt" impulse was absent because those who were responsible for the worship had drawn from ancient wells, but had used their draughts as living water to fertilise the plant of sincere conviction. They had something they passionately wanted to say.' He went on to comment on what was to become the traditional vesture of the Cathedral services. From the inception of the Diocese, it had been distinctly Low Church in churchmanship and consequently in dress. The chasuble and cope, stan-dard clerical dress in the majority of English Cathedrals, were never seen, but Dwelly's artistic eye saw the need for splendid vestments to enrich the ceremonial,

Light streams through the east window as Canon Charles Raven stands at the chancel steps in October 1931 at the establishment of the Dean and Chapter.

and so he dressed the laity in what he felt was appropriate to the building and its ceremonial. Dwelly knew where to go for assistance over vestments and turned to his old friend Percy Dearmer, whose *The Parson's Handbook* had become the definitive word on dress and ceremonial. Nan Dearmer was later to report, 'Percy preached in the Cathedral and took part in consultations with Canon Dwelly over dress and ceremonial. The Dean tells me the distinctive vergers' gowns and many cloaks warn on processional occasions were all devised with Percy's help and advice.'

The Dean of Chichester was alert to the toning and contrasting shades of the fabrics: '... the Bishop wore his scarlet chimere and not a cope. But for the other members of the Cathedral body the eye of an artist had chosen a habit that blends aptly with the red stone and light oak of the building. Canons and singing men and boys wear a cassock of dull red, and over it surplices of unbleached holland; the canons having in addition, almuces of black stuff edged with grey fur, and lined with dull red, forming a hood behind. something was needed to break the clash between this scheme of scarlet and black and white of the bishop and his chaplains. The solution was found in the gorgeous green gowns of the vergers ...' The garments referred to are unique to Liverpool Cathedral and some of the actual gowns worn at the Foundation service were renewed as recently as 1998. The team of men and boys who wear them is also unique and largely the result of Dwelly's thinking.

Even in its unfinished, early days, the Cathedral provided a vast space for human movement and the performance of the liturgy. For due significance to be placed on people and their ceremonial movements, a substantial team of crucifers, mace bearers, vergers and collectors was required – a team of at least twenty was not unusual. By a stroke of genius, Dwelly recruited such a team from his former choristers. Having devoted years of their lives as trebles in the Cathedral choir, voice-break and retirement was not an easy experience and Dwelly found work for them and created a tremendous sense of belonging in an organisation to be known as the Cross Guild.

The ceremonial for the Foundation Service was splendid and commented upon favourably by everyone and, alongside this, so was the music with Edgar Robinson as Choral Conductor and Henry Goss Custard as Organist. An anonymous music

Service paper designed by Edward Carter Preston and featuring the Liverpool Cathedral double cross crest.

critic was perceptive in his comments and had a clear understanding of music in worship. 'Since this Cathedral was first opened it has developed ... an acute and increasing perception of the value and usage of music in all its services ... One would say the key note was the balance preserved between music intended to heighten and increase the devotional aspect of the service and music intended to inspire and uplift a congregation.' It might have been a surprise to see 'O come, all ye faithful' as part

East window, reredos and high altar, Liverpool Cathedral.

The Carter Preston design for the cover of a published letter from Francis Neilson to 'You who set forth the beauty of worship in music and in movement in Liverpool Cathedral'.

of a service in October but it was perfectly appropriate, as were the second and third verses of 'Jesus Christ is risen today'. There is always the danger that a cathedral service can take on the feel of a concert of splendid musical pieces interspersed with prayers and a sermon, but, although the Cathedral used a considerable number of choir pieces for the services, everything formed part of a worshipping whole with every piece for the service contributing in a unique way at its particular point in the service.

The first part of the Palestrina music – an adaptation of 'Come Holy Ghost' – was quite exquisitely sung. The softly echoing supplicatory phrases, culminating in a single boy's voice, produced an effect of extreme beauty.

Dr Martin Shaw's anthem (John Masefield's specially composed words 'They buried him and the soldiers slept') was very well sung. As a *piece d'occasion* it has more value than most efforts of its kind, largely I think, because Mr. Shaw has relied rather more than is customary in 'special' anthems upon simplicity and dignity with a sparing use of fortissimo resources of the choir. They are not afraid of innovations at the Cathedral. They are willing to install a hidden battery of drums and trumpets, and, have secured them, to pursue their use to a logical conclusion, not only with the organ, but on their own in fanfares and flourishes.

Dwelly, and no doubt such people as Charles Raven and the Bishop, were anxious that the new foundation was to be genuinely in touch with people of 'wisdom and experience' and the College of Counsel was conceived, with the first members being announced on the service paper: the Earl of Crawford and Balcarres, Rt Hon. General Smuts, Rt Rev. George Bell, Sir Stanford Downing, Sir Frederick Radcliffe, Dr John Masefield, Professor Conwy Lloyd Morgan, Professor John Myers, Mr Francis Carolus Eeles, Mr Martin Shaw. This body was to meet once a year but they also formed a group of influential people who could be called upon for advice and support.

There was a wide cross section of city and diocese present at the service, together with former Dwelly parishioners from Windermere, Cheltenham and Southport. A contingent of the 1st Windermere Sea Scouts was part of the Dean's Procession and actually led him from the Chapter House up into the Chancel for the second part of the service.

Any major Cathedral service was reported on extensively in the thirties and 'Commentator' in the *Liverpool Daily Post and Mercury* pointed to the significance of a new and great cathedral: 'It is mainly through its services that Liverpool Cathedral exerts an influence far beyond the boundaries of the diocese. Many who have never been inside the Cathedral, or even seen it from afar, know of its influence in this regard. To those who live in the city or the diocese, especially to those who often walk in the House of God, or stay to worship there, the building itself is the first influence. How many thousands have already been moved to adoration within its walls no man can tell. But, with all its wonder of strength and beauty, the building by itself would not long keep this power over the hearts of men. The most beautiful Cathedral in the world is cold and lifeless unless the Spirit of God acting through the spirits of living men fill it with the warmth and power of love.'

The *Church of England Newspaper* in November carried an article (following on from the *Post and Mercury* comments) on the new Chapter, and seems to be an apt summing up of the character and potential of the new Cathedral and its leaders:

Its success is due to the intimacy and friendship of the new Dean and Canon Raven, who together have laid themselves out to meet the need which the Cathedral so eminently fulfils.

The conditions of the twentieth century make necessary a new spirit among men, and it falls to such as the first Dean of Liverpool to be seeking ever to attune the presentation of the faith of our forefathers to the peculiar needs of the time. Liverpool Cathedral is thus destined, for some years to come, not merely to be the Mother Church of the Liverpool Diocese, but also continue as the 'research' Cathedral of the Anglican Communion.

As well as the members of the Principal Chapter, the list of Canons Theologian appointed in 1931 includes some powerfully influential people who were undoubtedly capable of that research for the future: Very Rev. W. R. Matthews, Rev. Professor L. W. Grensted, Rev. E. E. Raven and the Rev. Francis Underhill.

Many references have been made to the freshness, excellence and meaningfulness of the services in the Cathedral, as devised by Dwelly, and the archive has sufficient material for the reader to gain a clear insight into the Easter services which became nationally famous through broadcasting during the nineteen thirties. One newspaper correspondent had known of the high quality of Liverpool liturgical experiments but he made his first visit to a service on Easter Sunday 1932 and was hugely impressed:

Here is a development of Anglican Cathedral worship which deserves the closest study and the warmest sympathy of all churchmen, whatever their school of thought. No one who is dissatisfied with the traditional worship of our Cathedrals

Edgar Robinson with the choristers in 1932. Ronald Woan is on the second row in the middle.

and larger parish churches can afford to ignore the experiments of Liverpool. The word experiment, however, is barely adequate to describe what has practically become a tradition, for the principles governing the ordering of the rites and ceremonies appear, at least to the visitor, to have become already firmly rooted in the minds of those who take part in them and of the congregations which assist at them.

Another journalist, this time from the *Church of England Newspaper* in 1931 had been equally enthusiastic in response and interestingly places the main Cathedral Service in the context of the *Book of Common Prayer*. What he has to say fits so well with what we know of Dwelly's work on liturgical reform and is the clearest indication as to his stance: the traditional is not rejected; instead it is used meaningfully within the context of fresh material which highlights, rather than draws away from, the old words. 'Is it adequate for a great Festival? I mean the *Prayer Book* or the *Revised Prayer Book*. I had for a long time felt that the answer must be given in the negative, but I made up my mind to attend service at Liverpool Cathedral for the Easter Festival. C.E.N. Readers may be interested in my experience. I found the services were almost continuous from 5.45 am, the first communion, until 9.30 p.m., when the late evening hour of worship ended. *The Prayer Book* was strictly adhered to at 5.45, 7.00. 9.15 (a Choral Eucharist with music by Byrd); 10, Morning Prayer ... and 5.00 Evening Prayer ... but at 11 a.m. and 3.00 p.m. the Liturgical Easter Anthem, the

A view over the rooftops of
Liverpool in the 1930s.

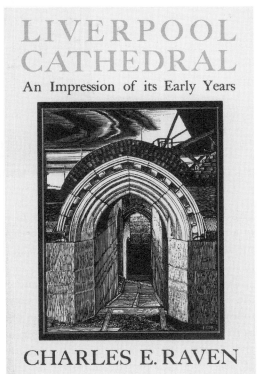

Front cover of Charles Raven's book with
a woodcut by Edward Carter Preston.

A Carter Preston woodcut
typical of much of his work
included in service papers
during the 1930s.

Lessons and *Prayer Book* prayers were used with an entirely unfamiliar background
of a strong devotional preparation and a rich final act of adoration. At the heart of
the service was the familiar *Book of Common Prayer* which had a fuller value because
of this preparation.'

The 1932 Service was similar in form and content to that of the previous year but
the Service paper of that year gives a short factual introduction to what was to
follow: 'The Festival of Easter calls for an offering of worship so wide and manifold
as to justify the provision of a form of service added this day to Holy Communion
and Morning Prayer. It begins with a selection from various sources of suggestions
of which we may prepare ourselves for that which is prepared for us. Then in a

Lambeth Palace S.E.
29th October 1931.

Dear Dean,

I have received your letter of October 25th. May I appoint
Wednesday, November 25th, at 12.30 here for the ceremony of conferring
a Lambeth D.D.Degree upon you?   I am asking my Registrar to give you
full information as to details and requirements, etc.   The custom is
that the recipient of such a Degree wears the Hood of the University to
which the Archbishop belongs — in this case Oxford— which you would
provide and bring with you.   It would be for you to decide whether you
wished on this occasion, as you may well on other occasions hereafter, to
wear the ordinary D.D. black and scarlet gown.

You may probably wish to invite some of your friends to be present
at the ceremony which is held in the Library at Lambeth. If so, they would
be very welcome.   I hope that you and Mrs.Dwelly will lunch with me after
the ceremony, and if any of your colleagues at Liverpool or any representatives of the Cathedral will be here please let me know so that I may invite
them also.

Yours very sincerely,

Cosmo Cantuar:

The Very Rev.

The Dean of Liverpool.

Letter from the Archhishop of Canterbury, October 1931.

procession from East to West, moving to the Resurrection Hymn, is brought an
ancient threefold Easter Blessing answered by the Hallelujah Chorus. Then follow
readings from the Epistle and Gospel, with the Easter Anthem between them,
leading up to the "Te Deum", the Creed, and collects. After an Anthem, written for
the Cathedral by John Masefield and Martin Shaw, come our now familiar

Intercessions, set to music by Palestrina; the Sermon, with Hymns before and after; a reminiscence of the Eucharist Thanksgiving, and, when the final blessing has been given, a Hymn sung by the Congregation only as the Dean's company leaves the Choir.'

The 1932 correspondent was delighted to find the worship free from 'that distressing air of novelty (in the bad sense of the term) which causes the word "stunt" to rise to the lips.' Instead,

> They are a legitimate development; continuity with the main stream of Catholic liturgy is immediately perceived; they are rooted in Holy Scripture and the old service books ...

If this element of continuity is apparent in the rites, it is also present in the cere-monial, though here again its details were unfamiliar. The obvious practical intent of all comings and goings within the choir and presbytery, and the baseness of ceremony for the sake of ceremony, could not be missed. The great sweeping movements of the various processions, the stately pacings to and fro of the groups of clergy and other ministers as they went about their business, the precision of every movement which somehow did not create an air of self-conscious formality, the almost austere restraint governing the whole – all these belong to an order of things which has characterised the purest stream of Catholic ceremonial, and they are lessons which all who have the ordering of public worship should study dili-gently.

When people complain that ceremonial distracts them and robs them of interior quiet, one should not always put this down as a Puritan objection. Perhaps it is the aim and spirit of the ceremonial which is at fault. That some ceremonial, though unfamiliar, can have a quite opposite effect and positively deepen one's sense of recollection and make the heart ready for prayer in an almost magical way, was the experience of one stranger to Liverpool on Easter Day, and appar-ently also of the majority of the congregations who came to worship. 'Let not him who seeks cease until he finds, finding he shall wonder, wondering he shall enter the kingdom and having entered the kingdom he shall rest.' The worshipper who heard the choir sing these words, as the Bishop entered and knelt before the High Altar, was enabled by all that was going on to go through that very experience. The quiet golden reds of the choir men's cassocks, the soft greens and purples of vergers' gowns and chanters' mantles – all this helped to deepen the sense of peace and tranquillity so precious but so rarely attainable at great Church functions.

And the music. When reports of great services at Liverpool Cathedral are spread abroad, it is not usually the music which is specially commented upon. Yet it can be said with deliberation that the Cathedral possesses an absolutely first-class choir, ably directed by a musician of exceptional competence and sensibility. Too often is the worshipper sadly disappointed during a visit to some large church or cathe-dral where it is reported that 'the music is so beautiful'. Even if this is true in the abstract, Church music is too seldom quite unliturgical, being a mere performance more or less unrelated to the devotional direction of the service and the 'note' of the fast or feast celebrated. Very often, too, what is called beautiful music is merely intricate music or even loud music. The music at Liverpool Cathedral was strictly liturgical in character and sung with an understanding and skill far above the average. They sang such good things, too – Bach, Palestrina, Byrd, Handel, Vaughan Williams, Martin Shaw all had their share, in addition to the composers of the well-known Easter hymns. The cathedral also is fortunate in its music director, who is responsible for much arrangement and adaptation of old music to meet the special liturgical needs of the carefully planned rites. A most rare and pleasing feature of the singing was the light and shade in volume of sound. Easter Day is commonly regarded as an excuse for an immense noise and little else besides. Here we knelt quietly and were led up to our more vociferous praise by the gentle invitation of the choir singing pianissimo 'O come let us worship ... in His presence is fullness of joy,' passing on to those exquisite words of the Rosy sequence, 'With Mary in the morning gloom I seek for Jesus in the tomb' in the proper plainsong melody.

I am not aware of any research which might have been undertaken in the field of Cathedral Worship which has examined Easter Day services across the cathedrals of England in the 1930s, so care must be taken over any claims made for the exceptional

Dean Dwelly and Bishop David with the future King George VI.

character and quality of a Dwelly service. Though the Easter Morning service was broadcast every year by the BBC, it would be wrong to suggest that every listener was attracted to Dwelly's work. The Bishop was to receive at least one letter which has found its way into the archives and must be quoted.

Dear Sir,

I put on my dressing gown to come down this morning and listen to your Service but a more uninspiring affair I have never had the agony of listening to. If you cater for hysterical anaemic females, or if you are an agent for the Roman Catholic community you are doubtless a success, only the latter do it much better.

Do you or your clergy imagine that educated men are to be attracted by all the maudlin hypocritical make-believe rubbish you inflicted on us? If yours is a Church of England for God's sake let us have a Church of England Service; and if you do not know what that means go and listen at Ely Cathedral or St Paul's or almost any other decent place.

We men are not to be taken in by all this shrieking and shouting and thumping on the organ, it only gets on our nerves.

The only thing in the whole show was the Collection Hymn, 'The whole bright world rejoices now', this was, to be just, inspiring, but all the rest was so much 'tripe'. As for the sermon, you have an excellent delivery; and if only you had read sufficiently to have something fresh to tell us it would have been worth hearing: however, you did curtail it to about five minutes, and a sermon I listened to tonight by a young Welsh Baptist who was once a miner but now an M.A. of London University helped to strike a balance on the day.

I am a member of the Church of England, once a solo boy, and my son was in Westminster Abbey choir, but I am bound to say that the clergy know neither how to read nor to preach, such an art as elocution they have never heard of; and after the tomfoolery at your place this morning – well it has affected my nerves, and I hope the B.B.C. will never broadcast you again. I am sending them a copy of this letter in order that they may have a view from the man in the street. Do ask your clergy to try to be men, at any rate while carrying out their duties in your church.

Believe me, in disgust.

Yours truly,

H. E. Granger

The Bishop placed the letter in the archives: the BBC broadcast again the following year.

It is illuminating to read what the Rev. Colin Dunlop, a future Dean, thought of services in which he participated in Liverpool Cathedral on Whitsunday 1932. He was full of praise for much that he experienced and yet had some pertinent criticisms to make of the Eucharist:

You know how greatly I enjoyed my visit to you this Whitsuntide and how grateful I am to you for all your kindness. It was to be a never-to-be-forgotten weekend. Before coming I rather wondered whether I should like the services as much as I liked them at my first visit when everything was so novel. I am bound to say that this time I liked them even more and was better able to appreciate the details which go to make up the whole, which at first visit are swallowed up in the general impression. The music in particular seemed to me to be superb and so truly liturgical, in that it never swamped the devotional aim of the service but always, both in its character and quality, assisted worship, without blurring the liturgical outlines of the service. The only thing that I felt was unsuitable was the chanting of the Psalms to Anglican chants. In conjunction with music of the calibre of Causton, Holst, Palestrina, Bach they seemed terribly thin and bourgeois. They fall between two stools not being congregational or simple, and not interesting enough to listen to ... There is no doubt in my mind that the whole colour scheme of your service has been amazingly enriched and simplified (both) by the unbleached linen of the surplices. I had no idea how it would look when you mentioned the possibility last year. To start off with, the unbleached material makes the garments hang far better, and the sight of the clergy and choir entering the Cathedral is extraordinarily beautiful. And it makes both the robes of the ministers and the prevailing colours of the Cathedral fabric and furniture all of a piece, all of the same ordering of colouring ...

Dunlop was more adversely critical of the Eucharist and his comments were unlikely to have come as a surprise to Dwelly and the Chapter. Raven informed us that there had been a long period of experiment to make a Choral Eucharist the main Sunday service, but it had not won the support of the Diocese in which 'Choral Eucharist plainly does not appeal'.

The Sung Eucharist was, I thought, the service which least embodied the excellencies which one has come to associate with Liverpool Cathedral worship. I know you will forgive me when I say that it seemed to be conventional in the bad sense.

He goes on to highlight specific areas where he felt improvement would be possible before summing up the current situation.

I like your aim to return to the simplicity of the 5th- and 6th-century ceremonial. It is a good basis on which to start reconstruction, what we now call especially Roman is usually a foreign addition to the early simplicity and practicality of ceremonial.

His final point relating to the position of the High Altar was to become relevant when the whole Cathedral was completed:

I could not help wondering what a celebration would be like in your finished Cathedral. I believe it would be a great step forward for the High Altar to be set up in the Central Space under a baldacchino, raised on a number of steps leading up from all sides. Then at a celebration the people would be gathered all round the Family Table, and this would devotionally be a great gain. The present High

Altar could be still kept as the Chapter Altar, but for all great diocesan occasions the Altar under the choir arch would be the central focus. The celebrant could stand facing west as he did sometimes in the great Basilicas ...

Before 1931, the Cathedral had been led by its Bishop, as acting-Dean, and a body of Provisional Canons to which Raven was appointed in 1924 and Dwelly a year later. By statute, Dwelly become Dean in 1931, but in attempting to understand the man and his role it is essential to consider the fundamental beliefs and methods of operation of that Provisional Chapter. Posterity has been well served by Charles Raven in a short essay, *Liverpool Cathedral: An Impression of its Early Years*, published in 1933 and written just after he left Liverpool to become a Canon of Ely Cathedral, and Regius Professor of Divinity at Cambridge. Any serious student of the period and of the Cathedral must read the long-out-of-print thirty-five pages in full because it is such an important assessment of the very nature of the Cathedral ministry and the men who guided its early years. So much that Raven has to say relates strongly to much that has already been high-lighted in the aims and achievements of Dwelly's career. Raven was the ideal person to have undertaken the account in that he had been part of the Cathedral community for eight years, but his recent appointment to Cambridge and Ely gave him sufficient distance from the people and the issues to be able to write dispassionately.

Raven declared that he was not intending to write a detailed history of the Cathedral but rather he was attempting to 'express and interpret the spirit in which the shaping of the Cathedral's life was undertaken, and the lines along which growth took place'. He intended to concentrate upon the ways in which the Bishop and his Chapter began to clarify their ideas about 'the function of a cathedral in relation to the world of the twentieth century'. The book is succinct and clearly shaped, almost in the manner of a high quality public lecture in three sections: A The possibility of a creative adventure; B The general lines to be followed; and C The actual results attained.

The challenge of a creative adventure was of paramount importance to the minds of the first provisional chapter and in keeping with everything we have observed about Dwelly's ministry in the church.

By common consent the supreme task of the church at this time is to interpret its inheritance of doctrine, cultus, and organisation so as to satisfy the minds, meet the spiritual needs, and adjust itself to the environment of the twentieth century. The changes in outlook, temper, and social structure characteristic of the past hundred years have been so vast and so rapid as to make it well-nigh impossible for institutions to keep pace with them. In politics, in education, and perhaps most noticeably in religion there is a real danger that traditional equipment may become out of touch with present realities and incapable of dealing with present requirements.

There had been excitement in Liverpool at the prospect of a new cathedral, unimpeded by ancient statutes and ready for 'fresh and creative vision'. Scott had designed a splendid fabric which called for innovative artistry in the presentation of religion. 'Moreover, a great modern city, cosmopolitan, industrial, adventurous, had built a Cathedral. That Cathedral must develop a life worthy of the community and of the age that had produced it. The eternal revelation in Christ must be presented in terms that can be understood by the people of today. Its theology must be a real interpretation of God to minds thinking along lines of modern knowledge: its cere-monial, its music, its services must enable modern folk to experience worship: its organisation must display the aspiration after fellowship and the ability of the church to rise above legal and mechanical relationships.'

Raven's admiration for the leadership style of the Bishop was clear. A new cathe-dral demanded risk and experiment which could only take place within the right atmosphere of mutual respect. 'The Bishop set himself from the first to create an atmosphere of affection and trust in which every member of the Chapter could put forward suggestions without fear and see them tried and fail without grievance, and by which loyalty and frankness came to be not only natural but inevitable.' To those who know the Chapter story of the middle and later thirties, the statement takes on even greater significance. Everything indicates that in the early years, before the formal foundation of Chapter, atmosphere and relationships within the group were admirable: what happened later was lamentable and Cathedral and Diocese suffered long-lasting damage. 'It is worth recording that though there was often strong disagreement there was never a sense of grievance or a breach of friendliness ...' A few years were to bring charges of open dishonesty and public flouting of trust.

The theological basis for the whole life of the Cathedral was clearly of paramount importance. Liverpool as a diocese had experienced the extremes of sectarianism and the Diocese had carried a distinctly evangelical label – not many years before a parish priest was actually imprisoned for ritualism. Raven claims Chapter's freedom from any one label while accepting the relevance of three. 'Catholic in the sense alike of maintaining the universality and continuity of the Christian revelation and of insisting upon the prime importance of corporate fellowship, the beloved commu-nity, and the sacramental principle; Evangelical in proclaiming the need for radical change from self to God, the fullness of salvation and of abundant life in Christ, and the supreme duty of evangelism; Modernist in acknowledging the unity of truth, the necessity of perpetual growth and consequent restatement, and the freedom to prove all things.' The Chapter was not without firm convictions and a sense of direc-tion, 'Experience convinced the Chapter that it is in the Johanine concepts, summarised by the words light, life, and love, that our age finds its appropriate understanding of the Gospel.'

From the start, the Cathedral was seen within the Diocese as a place of learning and education. A Cathedral School of Divinity was established and followed soon after by a joint Board of Divinity involving Anglicans and Free Churchmen. Courses were held catering for many levels and 'some two thousand students were enrolled for each winter session'. 'This work sprang directly out of the life of the Cathedral and as the inevitable consequence of its primary conviction.' In Liverpool, theology was alive and vibrant and 'to such a theology creeds and traditions are finger-posts, not boundary fences; faith is not static but dynamic and adventurous'. To keep theology developing and in touch with many aspects of everyday living, the members of the College of Counsel were selected.

The section devoted to the services and ceremonial of the Cathedral is of particular interest as far as Dwelly is concerned and Raven referred back to the Consecration Service which foreshadowed so many services which were to follow and was judged by Raven to have been 'a new expression of public worship'. 'What was needed was a service which, while fulfilling all that past experience could suggest, would possess a coherence, a rhythm, an appropriateness of its own for the circumstances of today. Such a service must be the work not of a liturgical expert (if this means a student of past precedents) but of a creative artist who perceived what the ceremony signified, knew how to interpret its significance in apposite technique, and could enable the congregation to experience and share in the dramatic movement of the whole.'

In liturgy as in so much else in the Cathedral life, experiment was entered upon wholeheartedly:

> If religion was life at its highest, then worship could not be the repetition of a familiar routine: it must contain discovery and inspiration, must reveal new possibilities of communion and new insight into the ways of the Spirit.
>
> So the conviction gradually became clear that every great service must be in the highest sense a work of art. As such it presupposes a threefold capacity in those responsible for it. There must be first a clear perception of the intention of the whole – what is the good news that God would reveal at Easter or Christmas to a congregation of seafarers or doctors or university students? Then there must be a careful consideration of the elements which are essential to the expression of the good news: every details must contribute in due proportion and at its proper place in the unfolding of the intention. Thirdly, if the whole is to make its impression, it must be ordered and rendered that without distraction the worshipper becomes immediately sensitive to its significance, is caught up into its movement, and experiences as a direct intuition the revelation which it is designed to unfold.

Raven emphasised strongly that the Cathedral was not attempting to draw people away from their parish churches and all the societies and events they coordinate: 'Hence its services aimed rather at inspiration than at edification, at arousing desire more than satisfying it, at attracting outsiders more than ministering to a regular congregation.' The 8.30 service was set late in the day so as not to conflict with services in the parishes, and that popular service began to answer a specific need. 'Its effect has been to create a very large but quite informal fellowship, to provide a rich supply of learners and workers, to draw into the life of the church masses of young people otherwise spiritually homeless and lonely, and to provide parishes with new workers. The service was designed for these folk – for young men and women working in shops and offices, living in lodgings, and strangers in the place; but it has made for itself a much larger circle, particularly in the undergraduate and school-teacher class.'

From the start, the Cathedral Chapter was anxious to establish sound working relations with the city, the Diocese and the wider Church. There was always a danger that a cathedral might attract its own closed congregation, but Liverpool was to be the Cathedral of the whole community. Looking outwards, all the Chapter members took seriously their responsibility to identify with specific aspects of the life of the city. At the same time, Chapter was anxious to create right working relations with the Diocese and its parishes and not to be seen as 'the great shrine'. They realised there was much welcome work that they could undertake through classes for newly ordained clergy, so groups – or colleges, as they were called – with a variety of interests were established at the Cathedral, and parishes were encouraged to make pilgrimages to the Cathedral where the incumbent would assist in services attended by groups of his own parishioners.

The establishment of a corporate life was essential for any new cathedral: 'Friendship, genuine, free, and sensitive, was the necessary condition for effective and creative collaboration.' The Bishop had provided a maxim round which they could establish all their enterprises: 'We can do our work, if we care enough about it, and don't care who gets the credit.' The new statutes were built upon the principles of friendship and corporate responsibility. 'It was clear from the first that the Cathedral was to be governed by love and not by law; that its welfare depended upon the mutual loyalty of its officers; and that to appeal from the spirit of the constitution to its letter would in effect be a breach of fellowship and betrayal of trust.'

From his ancient house within the precincts of Ely Cathedral, the former Canon Chancellor of Liverpool attempted to sum up his thoughts on the Liverpool experiment: 'The Cathedral has developed a clear and coherent life of its own, characterised by a definite theological outlook, by services and an order fully in harmony with that outlook and expressing it in terms of worship, by an acknowledged and intimate connection with the many-sided activities of its civic, social, and religious environment, and by a type of government relying wholly upon fellowship, loyalty, and corporate effort.

It is evident that such results can only be maintained if their nature is plainly understood by all parties responsible for the welfare of the Cathedral. If there is to be freedom to create, there will also be opportunity to obstruct. If reliance is to be placed upon friendship, disloyalty to it can always make havoc: if right personal relationships are regarded as the essential preliminary to right policies, the capacity for team work is a primary qualification in the making of appointments. To many such an ideal will seem impracticable, at its best precarious, and at its worst calamitous.'

One of the many photographs of the Dean with his dogs.

CHAPTER NINE

Precarious and calamatous

'LAMBETH PALACE
16th October 1931
My dear Dean,

It would give me great pleasure if I could mark my sense of the value of your services to the Church, particularly in regard to its worship and the dignity of your position as the first Dean of the legally constituted Chapter of Liverpool Cathedral, by conferring upon you in accordance with my Statutory right the Degree of Doctor of Divinity. I know that this would give great pleasure to many of your friends in the Cathedral and the Diocese of Liverpool, and I hope it may be agreeable to you ...

Yours very sincerely,

Cosmo Cantuar.'

The black and scarlet robe worn by Dwelly when the degree was conferred upon him in the Library at Lambeth on Thursday 26th November hangs in a cupboard in the Cathedral archive room. Rarely can an appointment to a deanery have been accompanied by such public, private, and official acclaim. By 1936, the 'Summary of Disputes, The Bishop and the Dean and Chapter of Liverpool Cathedral', ran to nineteen typed pages. Indeed, some of these 'Disputes' became notorious in the Diocese and in the Church of England at large.

The heart of the problem seems to lie in the dramatic deterioration of the relationships between Bishop and Dean, a deterioration commented upon later in 1969 by W. R. Matthews, Dean of St Paul's, who had been a Canon Theologian in Liverpool in the 1930s. 'This troublesome circumstance was the disagreement, or rather the almost intolerable tension, between Dr David, the Bishop of Liverpool, and Mr Dwelly, who had just been appointed the first Dean of the unfinished Cathedral, to the building and establishment of which both had given devoted leadership. I admired and loved both these men and was naturally embarrassed because each would talk freely to me, while for years they were not on speaking terms with each other. I know it is almost unbelievable, but I must repeat that to this day I do not know the cause of this quarrel or what it was about. One fact, however, was only too evident – that the disagreement of these two good men was a weakness in the Cathedral's witness to the Christian faith and, if only they had been able to go forward in brotherly unity as in old days, the Church and the City of Liverpool would have had reason to be thankful for the Cathedral even more than it has now.'

The readers of this biography will have established a picture of the very warmest cooperation and friendship built up between Dwelly and Albert Augustus over nearly nine years. In addition, Dwelly's brilliance with children must have helped to establish many strong friendships amongst the members of the Cathedral community. Many years later, Mary Raven, daughter of Charles wrote: 'My first memory of Dean Dwelly was when he arrived on our doorstep our first Christmas with a sack (literally) full of presents for myself and my three siblings – he hadn't met us before but he loved children and knew we were strangers to the city – I think he was a sad man who greatly regretted having no children of his own.' Mrs Diana Luck was daughter of the Bishop and wrote recently, 'I can give you all my vivid memories of that very colourful character who played such a prominent part in all our lives. When I was about nine I invited him to be my Godfather – my own having died – and he carried out his duties with tremendous flair – he was always full of ideas and fun and used to take my brothers and myself to so many interesting expeditions.'

That brother, Patrick David, has written,

... as children we adored him – like a favourite uncle. With his interest in youth work and adventure training he had a way with young people. On holiday in the Lake district I remember climbing Helvellyn with him in a snowstorm when I was sickening for the measles and being encouraged 'Mountaineers don't give up'. I was about nine. On the same holiday in his car 'Would you like the steering wheel or the accelerator?' Naturally I chose the accelerator! One really could do that sort of thing in those days! And then suddenly, having been a frequent visitor to our house in Liverpool, he stopped coming. At the time we gathered that he and our father had fallen out but we were too young to understand what it was all about. But we missed him a lot.

Whether or not there was one single issue over which Bishop and Dean disagreed so profoundly as to destroy their friendship and professional relationship, I have not been able to discover, though soon after the establishment of the Dean and Chapter there began a series of ongoing disagreements which were to be a blemish on Cathedral and Diocese for years to come. There might be a danger here of giving undue prominence to what became known as the Unitarian controversy, simply because it generated such massive local and then national interest. The very beginning could not have been simpler or more uncontentious. A wide range of speakers from both inside and outside the Anglican Church had been invited to preach at the 8.30. A letter was written from Great Stones, Headington, Oxford on 29 May 1933,

The tower rises dramatically above the nineteenth-century houses in Great George Square.

from Dr L. P. Jacks, a leading Unitarian scholar, agreeing to deliver three sermons: 4 June – The Holy Ghost; 11 June – The Holy Catholic Church; 18 June – Death. The delivery of these sermons seemed to have passed without any critical voice being raised.

Almost two months earlier, on 20 March, Dwelly had invited the Rev Lawrence Redfern, Minister of Ullet Road Unitarian Church in Liverpool, to 'preach the sermon at the Autumn Assize Service'. The Unitarians were at that time an influential body of people who had done a great deal to improve social conditions, and such families as Rathbone and Holt were associated with the work at Ullet Road Chapel, one of the most important Unitarian Chapels in the country, famous now for its Burne Jones windows. Redfern was clearly deeply moved by the Dean's invitation:

> Your very kind letter this morning quite bowls me over. You do me a great honour in asking me to preach the sermon at the Autumn Assize Service and I am delighted to accept your invitation to do so.
>
> I appreciate it not merely for personal reasons but as a gesture of friendliness towards my people who have never been in love with the dissidence of dissent, but long to march with the great Christian host, of which our Cathedral is such a magnificent symbol.

Further explanation of the background of the subsequent controversy was given by Redfern in an article in *The Inquirer* and cited by Alec Ellis in *Lawrence Redfern – A Memoir*:

> In 1929 Sir Sydney Jones was appointed High Sheriff of Lancashire and he invited me to be his Chaplain. At the opening of the Assizes in the three Assize towns of Lancaster, Liverpool and Manchester, where the justices of assize attend morning service at the cathedral or parish church, it is customary for the Chaplain or the High Sheriff to preach the sermon. But for the reasons that we can surmise, this tradition was not followed during my year of office, though I usually read one of the lessons. In Liverpool, however, there is good reason to believe that the Dean was greatly disturbed by this departure from the normal practice, and was anxious to make good an omission which set aside the declared ideal of the cathedral, which in the words of Canon Charles Raven (as he then was), 'should be above all sectional and divisive influences, and able to unite us all in whatever works for the true service of God and man ... a centre of unity where all can sink their divisions in sole adoration of Him in whom is neither Jew nor Greek'.

Alec Ellis has judged the sermon to be 'entirely non-controversial' and concerned with a desire for sound leadership through the troubled post-war conditions. 'There are no great new things to do. Peace, happiness, prosperity – the Kingdom of Christ depends for its fulfilment as it has for all the centuries of Christian history upon the old familiar laws of justice, mercy and truth as between man and his fellow-men.'

At no time in the furore which followed the service on 22 October was there any adverse criticism of Redfern or anything that he had said; the complaint was that he was a Unitarian. The first public awareness of what was to follow came in a letter in the *Liverpool Daily Post* on 25 October from Rev. Roger Markham, the Rector of Aughton, under the heading '"Catholic Faith" at stake'. 'To speak plainly Unitarianism is a heresy which strikes at the very foundation of the Christian Faith by denying in any real sense the Incarnation of the Son of God ... I believe that many of those who subscribed to build our Cathedral – and they were not as some people seem to think, confined to the citizens of Liverpool – would have hesitated to give their money had they supposed that this, the Mother Church of the diocese, would be used as a place where those who did not hold the Catholic Faith, or indeed any form of the Christian religion, would be invited to air their views.' I do not know whether Mr Markham was part of that small band of people who gain satisfaction out of writing letters of complaint to the newspapers but even his first letter shows how ready he was with his adverse comments in more than one direction: '... Mr Redfern's sermon contained a great deal more of Christian morality than did that of the Bishop of Birmingham, who seemed to think that the propagation of the human race should be conducted on the principles of a stud farm.'

For the rest of October and into November the local papers ran a sequence of letters, at least three from Markham. Not all the letters were so antagonistic, as two on 27 October indicate: 'Surely it is a very helpful sign, in these days, when two religious bodies are broad-minded enough to combine in a common purpose.' 'The intolerance and bigotry shown by "Churchman" is amazing. It is common knowledge that the cost of the building of Liverpool cathedral has been subscribed to by practically all classes and creeds ...' 'Knowing that a previous request for a Unitarian minister to preach in the Cathedral had been refused, many welcomed the innovation last Sunday as a sign of hope for the future, but evidently the old spirit of intolerance still persists.'

Suddenly, the criticism relating to the invitation to one preacher has been broadened: 'I would support the Rev. R. F. Markham's protest against much that is being introduced into the services of the Liverpool Cathedral. Though I may belong to another school of thought than that to which he does, yet, with him and many others, I am distressed to find truth often ignored, if not denied, and the Scriptures mutilated, misquoted, and misapplied in these services. It is as if the composer of the forms of service had quite a different scheme of doctrine in his mind to that of the Christian scriptures, picked out from them only that which suited his ideas, and altered them to agree with his opinions.'

So then, the invitation to a Unitarian was attacked from both Catholic and Evangelical wings of the church, and J. B. Lancelot, Senior Diocesan Canon, was anxious to distance himself from the invitation: '... the Diocesan Canons ... have no sort of jurisdiction within the Cathedral, and, therefore, cannot be blamed in any way for the new departure which must have aroused misgivings ...' On 8 November the

Editor brought the correspondence to an end. Local people had publicly expressed their opinions, some openly and charitably, others more entrenched and dogmatic; as far as the Cathedral archives are concerned, opinions were fairly evenly divided.

Whatever may have been spoken or written on the matter by Dwelly or the Bishop, nothing remains in the archive, but Raven's *Liverpool Cathedral* was published in the autumn of 1933. Whether or not the piece was generated because of the controversy this writer has, at this moment, no way of knowing.

More than a few in Liverpool must have been relieved when the public bickering in the press came to an end and the Cathedral and its company could take up its work out of the glare of media publicity , although this was not to be as a result of the intervention of Lord Hugh Cecil and the national press: 'Lord Hugh Cecil has sent to the Archbishop of York a petition for the citation of the Bishop of Liverpool "in respect of certain offences against laws ecclesiastical"; and to the Bishop of Liverpool a memorial making "certain complaints and charges" against the Dean of Liverpool.' The paper quotes in full Cecil's letter and the petition and memorial. Only the briefest extracts are fitting in this context:

The Bishop had informed Cecil of the relevant details in a letter of 20 November and added a strong justification:

> The principle upon which I have acted is based on our Lord's words, 'He that is not against us is with us.' We are not to exclude a man from fellowship and cooperation because he has not attained the full truth or found his place among Jesus' nearest friends. With him there should be fellowship within the limits of affirmations, though not of his denials. He has truth enough to make him active for Christ. It is a warning against an evil temper of exclusiveness destined to work much mischief in His Church.

The central demand of the petition reads,

> I ... hereby humbly pray, petition and request that your Grace will be pleased to cite to appear before your Grace as Metropolitan of the Province of York or before the Episcopal Synod of the said Province ... the Right Reverend Father in God, Albert Augustus by Divine Permission Lord Bishop of Liverpool in order that he may there answer this complaint and charge against him ...

The memorial to the Bishop in respect of Dwelly's actions is a lengthy legal statement, at the heart of which is the demand:

> I therefore charge the said Dean with having offended against the laws ecclesiastical in the matters aforesaid, and particularly against the canons of the year 1603, and modified in the year 1865 ... And I further charge the said Dean that, contrary to the laws ecclesiastical, he has, by his action in the matters aforesaid, encouraged men to hold heretical opinions inconsistent with faith in the Incarnation of Our Lord Jesus Christ and in His Deity, or at the best to think lightly of the error of such heretical opinions.

The whole sequence of incidents reveals much about the characters of, and relations between, Dwelly and the Bishop. Albert Augustus had been placed in an invidious position by at least one of Dwelly's actions, but, in public at least, he took a very balanced attitude, as can be seen in the January 1934 edition of the *Liverpool Review*: 'A Unitarian Minister preached at the Assize Service in October. He had been invited by the Dean. The Bishop, who had not been consulted, disapproved of such invitation, and the Dean undertook that it should not be repeated. Another Unitarian gave three addresses at the 8.30 non-liturgical service on Sunday evenings with the Bishop's full concurrence.' The differences between the occasions are clear: the Sunday morning service was a 'regular' *Prayer Book* service, while the Sunday evenings were 'specials' – occasions when a wide variety of speakers were welcomed.

The *Liverpool Echo* for 5 January reported that the Bishop did not intend to proceed against the Dean, and quoted his letter to Lord Cecil:

... the Dean has accepted my ruling and expressed his regret that he, having treated the Assize Service as a 'special' service, invited a non-licensed preacher thereat without consulting me. Thus my only difference with the Dean has been removed and will not arise again.

In regard to the 8.30 p.m. and other 'special' services he and I fully agreed that in view of the sacred call to a larger unity it is of the highest importance to maintain the liberty we have claimed, and, as seems expedient, to exercise it. I am not prepared to admit that such liberty is contrary to Canon Law. The other ground on which you ask me to condemn the Dean, namely, that 'he has encouraged men to hold heretical opinions' suggests that he had invited Unitarians to uphold their faith in the Cathedral against ours. No preacher invited here has ever transgressed the honourable understanding not to question Anglican doctrine, nor should we in any case invite one whom we could not trust to restrict himself to common ground.

In view of this explanation, you will not be surprised to learn that I do not propose to proceed against the Dean.

The Bishop was completely open about his attitude to the problems and his sermon at the 8.30 on 7 January was reported in the *Daily Post*. The whole piece is sensitive and balanced; while giving full support for credal statements of doctrine and dogma, he saw the dangers inherent in clinging exclusively to them: '... it is very necessary that we should take clear account of the dangers to which the use of words in the expression of our faith exposes us. Religious history amply demonstrates the evils that flow from the misuse of formulae, and similar evidence is not wanting now.' The Bishop boldly went on to state his intentions and those of the Cathedral:

We intend to go on teaching not only our own faith, but also the traditional expression of our faith, and we will defend it when it is attacked. But we will not behave to other men of other confessions as if they were always on the point of attacking ours. Until they attack it we will not regard them as our enemies, and therefore enemies of truth.

When we are forced to defend the truth enshrined in our creed, let it be in quietness and confidence; not in fear, as if it were something fragile and precarious, dependent for its safety upon our little victories over one another; not in anger, as though every man who questions the letter is thereby denying the spirit within. And when the difference concerns the Person of our Lord, let us specially remember that words can but faintly and faultily describe what He is.

A lengthy, carping and angry letter from Lord Cecil to the Bishop appeared in the *Daily Post* on 9 January. It is not insignificant that the letter was received by the Editor before the Bishop, the true recipient, had received his copy. The letter is aggressive and some of the arguments have moved beyond obvious good sense, becoming personally abusive. Albert Augustus's reply of 10 January is far more balanced and wisely brings the trial by newspaper to an end: 'You have stated your case against me. I suggest that we suspend our argument till it has been brought to a formal issue.'

Unfortunately, because of the Bishop's ill health he was unable to be present at the meeting of the Upper House of the Northern Convocation and the matter remained unresolved until the June meetings. Then Hensley Henson, Bishop of Durham, placed the motion before the house that 'Accordingly, this House is of opinion that, in the exercise of discretion approved in 1922 with regard to invitations to preachers at special services, the bishop should not extend such invitations to any person who does not hold, or who belongs to a denomination which does not hold, the "common Christian faith" in Jesus Christ as "Very God of Very God, Who for us men and for our salvation came down from heaven and was made man".' To be outvoted by all his fellow Bishops from the Northern Province was a painful rebuke to Albert Augustus, but that same day he wrote most graciously to Temple: 'You and I had very difficult parts to play today. I wish I could think that I have handled mine in anything like the same spirit that you showed. Nothing could have been fairer than your summing up. You will not expect me to agree with all of it, but I haven't often admired you more, and in what you said I have nothing to complain of.' Albert Augustus informed his Diocese of the decision in the *Liverpool Review*: 'The Upper House has decided that invitations to give addresses at special services must be restricted by the conditions that govern invitations to Nonconformists to preach at regular services of the church. As I have already said, I shall conform to this decision. In making it, however, the House found itself (reluctantly, I think) compelled to declare by implication that Unitarians are not for that purpose to be reckoned as "members of the Christian communion". In this exclusion I do not, and shall never acquiesce. On the debate itself, I would make a first and final comment: it was largely a defence of a Christian doctrine which nobody had attacked.'

The Bishop had suffered a considerable humiliation at the hands of his fellow Bishops but, though the vote had gone against his wishes, he remained firm in his convictions and determined to restate his case against the exclusion of groups from Christian fellowship because of their unwillingness to subscribe to a literal

Dramatic view looking upwards across the chancel to one of the organ cases.

interpretation of certain credal statements. I do not know the month of publication, but shortly after the York Convocation, Oxford University Press published *Who Are Christians? An Inquiry into Spiritual Relationships within the Christian Fellowship* by the Bishop of Liverpool. It was a twenty-three page pamphlet, carefully planned and argued, in which Albert Augustus expressed his abhorrence at the excluding tendencies of credal statements which 'make doctrine a ring-fence instead of which it ought to be a sign-post. We use it to exclude rather than to direct'.

He placed the origins of the Christian Creeds, particularly the Nicaean, into their historical context, within the intellectual and philosophical framework of the age in which they were formulated, and indicated how such statements were subject to all the shifts of meaning which are an inevitable feature of language. 'Yet there are still Christians who seem to assume that every religious idea can be defined in words. Our Lord gives us no warrant for this assumption. Indeed, it may be safely assented that in the theological sense He Himself gave us no definition at all. He revealed truth in pictures offered to our imagination. He enshrined truth in stories.'

The irony within the main conclusions is painful and intense. Dwelly and the Bishop were really so close over the essence of their personal beliefs on this matter and yet something in both of them sets them in sharp public conflict.

What keeps us spiritually asunder, breaking our vital unity, is not some point originally in dispute, but the spirit of the mutual attitude engendered when men insist in pursuing controversies in terms that belong to a bygone age. The differences themselves, essential as they seemed at the time of severance, have lost much of their significance. They will be settled, if ever, not by the old methods, but in the solvent of a new temper, springing from real obedience to the great command-ment of Christ. 'By this shall all men know that you are disciples, if you have love one to another.' Here is the distinguishing mark of the Christian.

What the public observed throughout the whole controversy was not love and mutual respect from both sides but frequent bitter animosity. My feelings are that Dwelly was right in his desire to offer the Cathedral pulpit to an eminent Unitarian but that by refusing to confine these invitations to 'special' services in the first instance he put back the ecumenical cause many years. To have moved more care-fully in full cooperation with his Bishop would not have been to deny his personal convictions but rather to have shown more practical and political common sense.

Unfortunately, the Unitarian Controversy was not at an end. I do not know how much correspondence Dwelly sent or received between October 1933 and June 1934 but a substantial number of letters to Dwelly are preserved in the archives. One of the earliest is from Vere Cotton, a highly significant member of the Cathedral community and a member of the Executive Committee:

> I'm very sorry to see from today's *Post* that Hugh Cecil seems determined to go on with his outrageous action. You and I may not always see eye to eye on every topic which arrives but in this case I'm most wholeheartedly in agreement with what you did, and so I'm sure will be the great bulk of public opinion.

The letter goes on to indicate that if Bishop and Dean are to incur heavy legal costs, many of their supporters would wish to make a financial contribution.

As is typical of the Dwelly papers, there are letters from people who knew him long ago. Jim Welch, a London solicitor, wrote 'in the name of old times', having known Dwelly in the days in Chard. A. F. Eveleigh wrote in similar vein: 'My Dear Fred, I hope you will pardon me for addressing you on such familiar terms, but you were just Fred to me when we were boys together'. Herbert Perrett, another solic-itor, probably not known by Dwelly wrote, 'we have been refreshed by what seemed like a breath of fresh air into organised Christianity'. From a friend, 'whatever happens you will have us all with you'. Dwelly must have been very heartened by a chatty letter from someone whom he had known as a little girl in Southport:

> I'm an awful mutt really, I always feel the same when I hear of a friend having trouble – I want to tell them I love them and then I suppose I feel that they will let me help them in some way – someday. I know a married woman should be dignified etc. but just at the moment I feel very like a queer little girl kneeling at your feet in the study tickling your sock while you read 'Saul' to me.

Rev. Colin Dunlop wrote from the British Embassy in Baghdad, 'This is only the merest line to tell you how much I have been thinking of you during all this long public controversy ... I do feel for you very deeply and long for the end of it all.' Twelve members of staff from Manchester High School for Girls sent a donation of thirty shillings 'as a tribute to you and a tribute to your brothers of the Free Churches'.

Some letters are more worrying. One from Sir Frederick Radcliffe to Vere Cotton declared, 'It was gross stupidity of the Dean to invite Redfern to preach at a liturgical service of the regular kind'. Some of Dwelly's thoughts are revealed in a letter to him from his old friend Rev F. H. Gillingham from Blackheath. The letter suggests that Dwelly was contemplating writing to every Church of England clergyman to see where they stood on the matter. 'If you are "persuaded" that the thing to do is to find out how many parsons of the Church of England are with you in this Cecil business, then I suppose it is no good saying anything, because I know you well enough to realise if "you are persuaded" you will carry it out. But if you are not quite persuaded, think round it once more.' Dick Sheppard, with his usual outspoken zest, offers great support: 'Now, dearest Dwelly, I am sure you have raised the next real and live issue that will decide the question as to whether the Church is to become a little devotional clique of correctly balanced people, or the larger, braver, more Christian Church.' Had his proactive line been followed I do not know what might have happened. 'Now my little proposal, merely for your consideration is that 1. You should find out when Bill Temple is to pronounce. 2. Get a little group together under your chairmanship. 3. To meet anyhow after Easter to discuss not what you did but what those who are wholeheartedly with you do (or say) next – if anything. 4. That ten days before Will Temple pronounces we should hold a great meeting, say, at Albert Hall (Liverpool too excited for it to be held there) and to say respectfully, firmly, and without threats that on this matter the church's "larger heart and kindlier mind" we are not prepared to compromise ...' It is interesting to note that in the same letter Sheppard indicates that Dean Inge would be a weighty supporter, and he is almost strident in his published support in *The Quiver*:

> If Lord Hugh Cecil must go on the war-path in this particular way, may I offer him my own heretical scalp, should he consider it worthwhile, for his mediaeval museum? I should indeed by glad to be labelled Jonathan in the exhibits and placed alongside Dr. David.
>
> Let Lord Hugh do the thing thoroughly and not pick out two heretics only. What are the Bishop of Liverpool and his Dean among so many? I, too, in my time, have invited Dr. Jacks (I do not know Mr Redfern's work) to preach both in St Martin-in-the-Fields and, worse, much worse no doubt, in Canterbury Cathedral.

The Rev. 'Pat' McCormick in the *St Martin's Review* takes unequivocal issue with Cecil: 'We dissent passionately from the latest issue he has thought it right to advance.'

Before the Jacks and Redfern furore, Charles Raven had left Liverpool for

Cambridge and Ely but continued to identify strongly with Dwelly and his problems. He was still in regular contact with the Cathedral and at the time of the controversy wrote a number of letters to Dwelly – unfortunately most are undated or only partially dated. Raven's astute mind discerned strategies which he wanted his friend to adopt; whether such strategies could do much to repair relations between Bishop and Dean are very uncertain. We have to remember that throughout, despite being himself under severe censure, the Bishop supported his Dean in public and carried the blame himself. Raven was, no doubt, right to draw attention to some of the points that had been made at the Church Congress in Southport in 1926 but people in high office might well have felt threatened.

> I believe if we link up the present issue with the Church Congress we are (a) doing something which is historically true (b) making the whole church (Cosmo, Bill Temple and all of the speakers at Southport) responsible for our action, (c) pinning David and the diocese down to support us. If you print this, then we can if necessary refer to Temple's speech at Southport and say 'how on earth can you now condemn David when at the Church Congress you said exactly what you are now condemning him for doing'.

Another letter, also written early in January 1934, takes the case further:

> I have just reread the chief speeches at Southport. William Temple's might have been written for our special purpose. Spirit is fellowship – many movements outside the Church show it – we must respect, support and share in such movements – we must not exploit or condemn them – only in the whole church will the fellowship with the whole Christ be revealed. We could reprint his speech as a pamphlet: personally I should do so: it leaves him completely and irrevocably committed. You might I think seriously think of reprinting this speech as justification for our action. In any case it is amazingly strong support for us.

And in a third letter:

> You and I are not likely to forget the guidance given to us both at the time of the Consecration and at the Church Congress – particularly in the speech of the present Archbishop of York. We were told of the greatness of our opportunity, of the need both for continuity and for experiment, and especially of the duty of encouraging fellowship between our Church and all movements of the Spirit among men of good will. We were warned not to expect agreement or assume superiority, but to give generous recognition to the worth of others and generous co-operation if they were ready to work with us.
>
> Guided by our Bishop we have tried to be faithful both to the maintenance of our Anglican heritage in the *Book of Common Prayer*, the rubrics and canons, and to our special opportunities as a new Cathedral in a great and grievously divided community. Time after time you have helped us to establish links with doctors, scientists, artists, musicians and men of affairs. Few events have been in my

Plaster model of one of the Carter Preston figures which are such important features in the Cathedral.

experience more obviously right than such occasions as that on which General Smuts and Sir Oliver Lodge preached to us; and those occasions have been very many. They have, I believe, not only been rich in spiritual power for ourselves, but have given new status and influence to the Church of England, going far to justify its claim to be indeed the Church of the nation and not of a sect.

Yet another letter written in the first week of January is alarming and revealed that Dwelly had invited Jacks to preach again at the Cathedral – diplomatically a disastrous decision but a strong example of Dwelly's strength of purpose and unwavering loyalty to his friends. From the report in Raven's letter, Dr Jacks' responses revealed a wisdom and good sense lacking in Dwelly on this matter:

As regards preaching for you, he urges that you get the Bishop's authority and then put your invitation in writing. He feels (1) that such a course will stiffen David (2) that he himself cannot at this juncture appear to act with the Dean against the Bishop. He is right. If you can get David's assent, you will immensely strengthen our case: if you act without it, you will be exposed to criticism as rebellious and impatient. We (or you) may have to defy the Bishop later: you must not run the risk of doing so yet.

The York Convocation was certainly not

the final word in the controversy, and Dwelly and Raven, probably on even terms, were responsible for the next outburst of complaint. On Sunday 17 June, Canon Davey, the Canon in Residence for that day, read aloud from the pulpit in the Cathedral a letter from Dwelly and Raven to Dr L. P. Jacks, and also the letter written by Jacks in reply. Both letters are restrained yet powerful expressions of passionately held views. In view of the Bishop's unwillingness to discipline Dwelly over the Redfern sermon and the invidious position in which he was to find himself at York, it was surely wrong that the Bishop was not even informed that the letters were to be read publicly from the Cathedral pulpit. The Bishop, rightly, found it necessary to inform all Liverpool Incumbents about the matter in a 'not for publication' memorandum in September:

> ... without my knowledge, a so-called apology to Dr. Jacks, signed by the Dean and addressed from the Cathedral, was read in place of the usual address, I have one final word. The apology was sent to me on 16th June as part of a projected pamphlet. I approved parts of it, but was not told, nor had I any idea, that it was to be delivered instead of a sermon. It is not legitimate to use any pulpit for private or personal purpose. I have directed the Dean accordingly.

The letters are important expressions of significant ideas: they had to be written, but their method of communication was surely wrong, deeply discourteous to the Bishop and, in the short term as least, damaging to Cathedral and Diocesan relations.

Raven's hand in the letter was clear enough – stylistically very similar to his *Liverpool Cathedral* publication of the previous year – but an undated single page of a letter to Dwelly clarifies the case:

> As regards my share in the business – I'm afraid, my dear, I've only made things more difficult for you. As regards the Jacks letter, if it would make things in any way easier for you to lay the chief responsibility on me, please don't hesitate to do so. No one has tackled me about it. If they did, I should say 'The Dean and I discussed the whole position at very great length, and agreed that some sort of explanation to Jacks was essential. Then I produced a draft, the Dean saw, corrected, and revised it. It was then submitted to one or two others. In its final shape it represents an agreed statement from those who signed it. The reading of it in the Cathedral was by the Dean's decision: he is solely responsible with the officiant at the service for what is done at it: I think he was entirely within his rights in what he did'.

In many of his letters, on a variety of matters, Raven does reveal a certain intolerance, a determination to pursue his ideas even though conflict would be inevitable. While admitting the 'safety' of his own position as a Cambridge professor, his letter does express his anxiety over Dwelly's immediate future:

> I'm afraid I've been largely responsible for getting you into this mess. I don't want you to bear odium which should properly fall on me. Don't go and worry about

shielding me. All that I really care about is that you should continue your work at Liverpool and that your adversaries should be confounded and brought to naught. So feel quite free to plan your defence on the lines that will secure the continuance of your leadership in the Cathedral.

My love and trust and joy.

Charles

If they force you to resign it will break my heart. That I simply couldn't bear. So for God's sake don't let them.

The Raven–Dwelly letter in the first sentence expresses 'our deep sense of regret and remorse' but the bulk of the letter goes way beyond any personal apology into a strongly worded statement as to the whole character of the new Cathedral in Liverpool. The attack on Temple and the Bishops in the second paragraph was bound to arouse personal hurt and anger.

Anyone who reads your sermons and has appreciated your teaching will feel that this issue has been indeed a conflict between the spirit and the letter of discipleship, and those who note the contrast between the Archbishop's utterances on this occasion and his speeches in former years, and notably at the Church Congress in Southport in 1927, will have his faith in the value of episcopacy and of institutionalised religion rudely shaken.

Although much which follows is in more temperate language, the anti-Episcopal charge at the start could not but antagonise.

The letter goes on to outline in a restrained manner the dangers inherent in demanding strict credal conformity, both in the past and the present:

... while we recognise the right of any society to impose tests upon its members, and are not inclined to dispute the value for ourselves of the traditional creeds, we must make it plain that the attempt to foreclose the present inquiries by reference to ancient formulae seems a method damaging to intellectual honesty and hard to reconcile with any belief in a progressive revelation or any true concept of the nature of God's dealings with mankind.

The letter proceeds by placing the new Cathedral in the intellectual tradition of F. D. Maurice, Charles Kingsley and F. J. A. Hort and by stressing that what they have been attempting to do of late is clearly and simply in line with the spirit which was the guiding force for the Cathedral from the time of its consecration when

most representative leaders of the Church of England united to assure us that a great opportunity lay before us and a great responsibility upon us, that the Cathedral built with the goodwill of a modern industrial city must strive to rise above narrow and sectional interests, and that in a day of fresh beginnings our loyalty to the Anglican Communion should express itself in a reverent and courageous adventuring. Not less plainly was this advice emphasised by both the present

Archbishops at the Church Congress held three years after the consecration in our diocese. By that time the general and programme of our Cathedral had been settled. Our Special Services and our invitation to preachers of other denominations were a matter of common knowledge. Our doctrinal position was fully explained at the Congress by our Bishop and members of our Chapter.

The letter does far more than apologise to Jacks. It is used as an opportunity to reiterate the passionately held views of Dwelly and Raven and to express their determination to stay with their principles:

> In these days when the future of civilisation is obscure, when man's confidence in the security of his conventional standards is crumbling, when crude superstitions have been revived and Christian faith and ethics are being challenged, those of us who stand for the religious interpretation of life, those of us who draw inspiration from the Gospel of Jesus, should surely declare our unity. To quibble about ancient formularies, to appeal to outworn precedents, to refuse all movement as dangerous and all change as disloyal is to deny the faith, to betray the cause, to reject the opportunity ... We cannot and will not go back upon the road along which you have helped to lead us.

Dr Jacks in his reply is courteous, deeply charitable towards his hosts, but outspoken and prophetic: 'The general effect of your letter, on my own mind, is to confirm a long-held conviction that unless the churches of Christendom are able to transcend their institutional selfishness, their corporate self-seeking and uncharitable relations among themselves, learning to help rather than to hinder one another, and to bear one another's burdens instead of increasing them; unless, that is, they are willing to put religion before Church policy, the days of organised Christianity are most assuredly numbered.'

Jacks' image at the opening of one paragraph would not have been lost on anyone in possession of a basic knowledge of church history:

> In placing the interests of religion first, and the interests of church policy second, you have lit a candle in the Church of England that will not easily be put out. The light of it will have a far penetration both in time and in space. It will be seen and welcomed by an immense multitude of Christians, not professedly Unitarians, but no more bound by the Creed of Nicaea than they, whom the Bishop of Durham's resolution, if taken seriously, would render outcast from the Visible Church ... I am deeply sensible of the difficult position in which you are placed by the Bishop of Durham's resolution. If, henceforward, you are to be restricted, in your choice of Cathedral preachers from outsiders, to Nonconformists whose membership of the Visible church is guaranteed by unequivocal acceptance of the Creed of Nicaea, I am afraid you will find the area of selection not very large to begin with and continually diminishing as time goes on; you may even encounter doubtful cases among eminent members of the Church of England.

Surely out of courtesy to his Bishop, who since 1924 had treated him with admiration and warm friendship, Dwelly ought to have spoken face to face with him before the letters were read from the pulpit as part of a service. In the same way, he ought to have consulted with the Bishop before inviting Redfern to preach at the Assize Service: he did not do so. It is highly unlikely that Dwelly did not know that the Bishop had refused to invite Redfern to preach at the Assize Service in 1924. It is not surprising that the Bishop felt it necessary to defend himself in his Memorandum to Incumbents in September 1934 and to attempt to quell feelings of unease in the Diocese: 'My correspondence and interviews revealed not only strong feeling about a particular event, but also a certain dissatisfaction with the Cathedral generally in its relation to the Diocese.' I believe time has proved that Dwelly was right in all his inclinations, which were central to the Unitarian Controversy. He fearlessly stated his beliefs but his actions, at least at the time, were counterproductive within the Diocese and cannot have helped to maintain sound relations with his Diocesan Bishop.

Papers from the archives of the Bishop indicate that there was serious disagreement between some of the members of the Principal Chapter. Charles Raven's position as Canon Chancellor had been taken by Canon J. S. Bezzant, a colleague who was no longer trusted by Dwelly and Raven. As Raven wrote to the Bishop, 'as to Bezzant I'm afraid that the Dean and I both regard him as so clearly concerned with Hugh Cecil's attack (you know, I suppose, that he was one of those who got the rural deaneries to protest) that we would rather not involve him in our action'. Bezzant showed his public disapproval of the reading of the double apology to the Unitarian ministers from the Cathedral pulpit by writing to *The Times* on 23 June:

> ... Neither the letter to Dr Jacks nor the reading of it together with his reply, nor any other reference to the subject, was in any way authorised by the Dean and Chapter as the body corporate to whom the administration of the Cathedral and the initial responsibility for what is done in it, by Statute belong ... Meanwhile, though of course Professor Raven has every right to express and publish his opinions about the general aspects of the controversy it should be pointed out that it is now two years since he resigned the offices which he formerly held in this Cathedral. He has now no responsibility for its administration and no authority to speak in its name: his connection with us is purely honorary.

Within days, Raven's reply was published in *The Times*: 'by Statute and by a usage the eight thirty and other special services are under the sole authority of the Dean: for their conduct the Chapter's concern has never been asked or required.'

The Bishop wrote to *The Times* on 26 June:

> This controversy has developed on lines which give me much anxiety. It was right and proper that the Dean should apologise to Dr Jacks and Mr Redfern, whose replies showed an admirable spirit. But three unfortunate mistakes were made. The letters of apology controvert the York decision; they give the impression that the Chapter desire to carry the argument against it; and one of them was read at

a Cathedral service. I would ask that all who have been moved either to support or to oppose us will suffer the original incident to rest, together with the judgement pronounced upon it, and, if they would turn their minds to the larger issue which I have tried to set forth in my pamphlet, *Who Are Christians?*

Dwelly interpreted the letter as an open attack upon himself and wrote that same day to the Bishop:

I have just read, with not a little surprise, your letter in today's *Times*. Why, in view of such a letter, did you bother to ask me for my frank opinion upon your Review article? The Review does not matter in the light of your letter in *The Times*. The great weight of your personality is now definitely against the Dean and opposed to his judgement, I do not complain, though I could have wished to know it direct from my friend instead of through the newspapers. Your disapproval has now widest possible publicity – we can never catch it – those who with me have followed you with the best we could give know now how fully we must make clear our only convictions ourselves. As for me now I know the true position. Now every one knows. There can no longer be any doubt. So away F.W. to the wise men for guidance and that without delay. I must pull myself together and look (not indeed to my laurels) for a place where the sole of my feet can rest secure and having found it I must lay claim to it and that publicly in the Cathedral.

The exact order of events may be uncertain, but we do know that the Bishop indicated that the Dean ought to resign. The Dean had sought legal advice before writing a long letter to the Bishop on 27 June:

Thank you for your letter of six o'clock on Tuesday morning. I much value being told your whole mind on the subject. Before you proceed with your own plans collect all the evidence and see that the Cathedral is now none the less right ahead of any other Cathedral as you may see from the facts. You are wrong in doubting – I have no fears and I know all the facts – you have told me nothing new except that you think I ought to resign. I am not going to resign from the causes you set out as they do not cover the facts.

I sincerely hope you will not think of resigning. You have got the love of those who are suffering and even those who entirely disagree with your latest action are already and whole heartedly with you when you want us and until then we shall be united and grow stronger in quietness and confidence. I shall discover wherein we can find security until you want me and in that security I shall gather all as a hen gathers her chickens. I beseech you not to resign. Your life's mission has been to release mankind from fear. God has blessed you beyond that of any other in our day by giving you constant difficulty wherewith to sharpen your service tools. Those that be with you are more than those against you.

The difficulties between you and me are not difficulties of purpose or spirit but of method and as you yourself are often saying methods must be changed. As I love your family and because I know you were never so near the dawn of your desire I beseech you to hold the thought of resignation.

The authority on Albert Augustus is John Peart-Binns who shrewdly subtitled his chapter in *Four Bishops of Liverpool* 'the Liberal Autocrat'. In his writing he is clear in his admiration for many of the Bishop's attributes and achievements but he finds fault in both Dwelly and the Bishop. Peart-Binns takes his readers back to attitudes prevalent at the time of Consecration in 1924 when one of the services of the Octave was arranged for 'Free Churchmen' and began with some words from Psalm 133: 'Behold, how good and joyful a thing it is: brethren, to dwell together in unity!' In his welcome to the congregation, the bishop was forthright in his words: 'at the consecration of our Cathedral, yours and mine ... And now our Cathedral is open to all. A home in the heart of the diocese for every child of the Church ... A sanctuary in the midst of the people for all who seek righteousness, comfort and peace ... Here may charity abound, and the full unity of the church be celebrated.' The greatest irony, which must have been particularly painful to many at the time of the controversy, was that the sermon to the Free Churchmen was preached by the Bishop of Durham, Hensley Henson! Part of that sermon was reported in *Liverpool Courier* for 28 July, 1924: 'Your presence here is profoundly significant. That it should be possible for the Bishop to say with such fitness that this Cathedral is "yours and mine", is of the happiest augury. Only a united church, led by the spirit of truth, will gain audience. Primary responsibility rests with us, Anglican and Free Churchmen.'

Peart-Binns has admiration for both Bishop and Dean and is not unaware of their shortcomings. He certainly casts doubt on the choice of Dwelly as Dean:

> In the appointment of the Dean, David allowed his affection to override intellect where intellect should have won. One wonders if Raven not Dwelly should have been Dean. Raven was a star. Raven would have split any diocese as a Bishop in six months; but he would have made a first-rate and distinguished Dean and, though doubtful, that restless spirit might even have been content with that Office.
>
> David's relations with Dwelly were founded in great affection, and all worked well so long as that intimate relationship lasted and Dwelly was eager to carry out what were really David's decisions. But, intellectually, and in all personal matters, they had little in common; and when the intimate relationship broke there was no longer common ground.

The situation is well summed up towards the end of the essay: 'It was a time when there was a galloping animus between Dwelly and David, with fault on each side. David would not "let go" of the Cathedral, failing to accept that he was no longer Dean as well as Bishop. Dwelly had an inflated sense of his own place ... Once Raven had left, Dwelly tended to regard the Principal Chapter as his curates ... and the General Chapter as David's mob, the corporate choice and voice of the Bishop, and ... no possible use to him as Dean.' It might well be argued that the split between Cathedral and Diocese which developed in the 1930s has still not been mended.

CHAPTER TEN

'What has happened ...?'

T HE UNITARIAN CONTROVERSY, following the sermons by Redfern and Jacks, troubled the Cathedral world of 1933, and the Raven-Dwelly public reply fanned the flames of anger and hurt in the summer of 1934. By December of that year the newspapers were publishing news of what appeared to be even greater conflict between Bishop and Dean, and under the headline 'What has happened at Liverpool Cathedral?' the *Church of England Newspaper* commented, 'Early this year came the lamentable controversy arising out of the invitation to a Unitarian to preach in the Cathedral. Now we have the far more disastrous dispute in which the Dean is charged with causing "grave scandal" by refusing to execute the mandate of the Bishop to install two archdeacons.'

Dr David had been invited to attend the Victoria centenary celebrations in Australia and on 27 September 1934, the eve of his departure, the Bishop was present at a service in the Cathedral during which five Diocesan canons were installed, together with two new archdeacons, C. F. Twitchett, Archdeacon of Liverpool, and J. P. Baker as Archdeacon of Warrington. The service was announced briefly in the *Daily Post* without any suggestion that serious dispute might surround part of the service.

By the time of the Bishop's return from Australia in December, the media had taken up the story that the Dean had refused to act upon the Bishop's mandate to install the two archdeacons and that the archdeacons had subsequently instituted charges against the Dean. The *Church Times* correspondent reported the scandal in the city: 'On Thursday, the city was covered with placards: "Another Cathedral Sensation!" "Archdeacons prosecute Dean", etc. So we knew we were in for it.' The *Liverpool Echo* highlighted the seriousness of the charge: 'Such an action is said to be without precedent since the Reformation.' The lead-up to the case seemed to provide more newsworthy material than the case itself, and was reported lengthily and verbatim in a number of papers, but summarised in a balanced manner in the *Church Times*. The case was heard in the large hall in Church House before His Honour Judge Dowdall, Chancellor of the Diocese, and four Diocesan incumbents nominated by the Bishop on the telephone from Australia.

The Archdeacons' counsel [Mr H. Gamon] detailed the events antecedent to September 27. He charged the Dean with creating grave scandal by refusing to execute the mandate of the Bishop to install the Archdeacons. Mr. H. B. Vaisey, K.C., for the Dean, said that the charge could not stand. The mandate was only received by the Bishop at noon on September 27, and only received by the Dean ten minutes before the Cathedral service began. As the Chapter Canons were already in their place in choir, it was impossible for them to examine the document. Besides, it was not addressed to the Dean and Chapter at all, but to The Very Rev. The Dean and Canons of the Cathedral Church of Christ. In such circumstances, there was no mandate.

The Chancellor held that this technical objection was important, and would retire with the Commissioners to consider it. We all saw, from a legal standpoint, the force of Mr. Vaisey's contention, and so were not surprised when, in a few minutes, the Commissioners returned, and the Chancellor announced: 'I have advised the Commissioners, as a matter of law, that the Dean and Chapter were not served in proper time. They accept that view. Therefore they would report that there are not sufficient prima facie grounds for instituting further proceedings.' So ends the dispute. And we are all asking why the Church of England alone washes its dirty linen in public.

Dwelly was not taken by surprise that the two Archdeacons were to be installed at the service and a legal report declared that 'the Bishop was requested on more than one occasion by the Dean to make formal request to the Principal Chapter to assign stalls in the Cathedral for the said Archdeacons ... The Bishop asserted that no formal request was necessary and that his simple word given to the Dean was sufficient ...'

The Archdeacons, not the Bishop, issued the request for the commission. Cyril Twitchett has entered the folklore of the Diocese as being determined to exert the full powers of his office and even, on occasions, overreaching his powers.

To the layman it must have appeared then, as now, that the dispute arose from legal technicalities, and indeed a filing box of legal documents in the archives gives support to this view, including the nineteen-page '1936. The Bishop and the Dean and Chapter of Liverpool. Summary of Disputes', comprising seven areas of dispute.

In their conclusions, the lawyers asserted that the heart of the problem lay not in the intentions of the principal participants but in the Cathedral's Statutes under which all had to operate:

A great many, if not all, of the difficulties which have arisen between the Lord Bishop of Liverpool and the Dean and Chapter and its general members may have been avoided if the Statutes governing the said Cathedral had dealt more clearly and definitely with the various functions of the Bishop as (1) the Head of the Diocese (2) the Visitor and (3) Ordinary.

In their preliminary statement, Counsel were clearly supportive of the Dean and Chapter and saw in the Bishop's actions the recourse to litigation:

Upon every occasion when difficulties had arisen the practice of the Dean and Chapter has been first to raise the matter with the Bishop; and, only when they have failed to receive satisfaction, have they sought the advice of Learned Counsel versed in Ecclesiastical Law. This advice they have communicated in its entirety to the Bishop in every instance between the Bishop and the Principal Chapter or any of its members. The Bishop had not welcomed the advice so tendered and has refused to recognise the authority or even that the propriety of any interpretation of the Statutes other than his own, which interpretation he has required to be accepted uncritically by members of the Principal Chapter. The Bishop had indeed declared in writing that if there were any dispute between himself and a Canon over the interpretation of a Statute, the Bishop's interpretation must be accepted.

When Charles Raven's seat on Chapter became vacant, the Bishop, as was his right, appointed Canon J. S. Bezzant as the new Chancellor. To Chapter's annoyance, the Bishop proceeded to outline the work and duties of the Chancellor and, in Counsel's words, 'to all intents and purposes to regard him as an officer not of the Principal Chapter but as directly associated with the Bishop and responsible directly to him'.

The Bishop appeared to have taken a similar line over the work of Canon Davey and matters became seriously contentious in 1934 and 1935. The Bishop then sought the support of the members of the new General Chapter over the matter; he seemed to be determined to use the General Chapter to exert his wishes and interpretations upon the Principal Chapter. The Chapter Minutes are fierce in support of their rights and in condemnation of the Bishop's actions:

24 April 1936

Canon Bezzant proposed the following resolution namely: a special meeting of the General Chapter having been called for 29 April 1936, and whereas the agenda for that meeting as circulated by the Bishop reveals that its purpose is to pass a resolution constituting a formal censure upon the Principal Chapter or certain of its members, it be resolved:

That the General Chapter as constituted by Statute exists to afford advice and council to the Bishop, at his request, on matters pertaining to the Cathedral and the Diocese. To make statutory use of this purely advisory body as an instrument for so censuring a member or members of the Principal Chapter is entirely ultra vires. The General Chapter has no status to adjudicate on matters of difference between the Bishop and any members of the Principal Chapter concerning the conduct of the Cathedral and its services, which are matters of discipline, for dealing with which, other statutory provision is made. They are cognisable by the Bishop in his capacities as Ordinary and Visitor, as regulated by the law and not otherwise.

Overall responsibility for services in the Cathedral became another area of contention

and Chapter Minutes and Counsel's summary of a dispute drew attention to disagreement over the arrangements for the Couriers Service. There are no details in the
archives to illustrate the nature of the difficulties which arose for the service planned
for 29 February 1936 but the Chapter Minutes are determined in tone:

> The Chapter would direct the Bishop's attention to the letter from the Dean to
> the Bishop, dated January 10, in which there is no refusal on the part of the Dean,
> but a counter suggestion, which in their judgement indicates a spirit of helpful-
> ness, and certainly not of refusal. They cannot find in the correspondence any trace
> of the Dean's alleged purpose to substitute for what had already been agreed upon
> an arrangement of his own. On the contrary, the agreement in the Dean's letter
> and enclosure to the Bishop, dated February 12, repeats the Dean's desire to be
> helpful, and points out 'I have arranged, as we agreed, the details of the task
> through the Cathedral's stewards'. The letter to the Bishop dated February 16
> further asserts the Dean's willingness to carry through the Bishop's service 'I will
> myself supervise, and the whole body and will, as always, be glad to co-operate'.
> Under these circumstances the Principal Chapter is convinced that the issue of the
> memorandum would create a totally false impression [and] would again reiterate
> their request that, in order to avoid difficulties of this nature, the Bishop should
> communicate in writing with the Principal Chapter upon all matters of this kind.

Though not mentioned in the summary disputes, another matter caused extremely
bad feeling between the Bishop and the Principal Chapter. When he was appointed
a Canon Theologian in 1930, Canon Edward Raven was called upon to take part in
the continued educational training of the junior clergy. This work was part of the
Cathedral's work in post-ordination classes under the immediate supervision of the
Canon Chancellor and the general superintendence of the Dean. In the summer of
1935 the Bishop received letters of complaint from a few of the diocesan clergy. In July
of the same year the Bishop wrote to the Chapter Clerk to complain:

> My dear Alderson Smith,
>   Canon Edward Raven has on more than one occasion visited assistant curates in
> the diocese under my authority, but not during the last three years. In the last
> week of June I discovered that he was engaged in a new series of visits. He told
> the curates that he had been asked by me to do so. Upon inquiring I found that
> he had received his instructions from Canon Davey acting as Vice Dean in the
> absence of the Dean. Canon Davey writes: 'I further requested him (Canon Raven)
> to refer directly to the Vice Dean in all matters arising out of his task as a Canon
> Theologian.' All this was arranged without any reference to myself, and I have had
> many letters from incumbents protesting against the whole proceedings. Canon
> Davey refers me to you.
>   Will you kindly ascertain from the Dean and Chapter at their next meeting and
> let me know whether they think it right and proper that the Dean or Vice Dean
> should arrange for confidential visits to the clergy and reports thereon to an officer

of the Cathedral without consultation with the Bishop and even without his knowledge?

The contents of this letter put both Canon Edward Raven and all the members of the Principal Chapter in a very bad light. When the matter was raised at the July Chapter meeting it was resolved that all correspondence arising out of the complaint should be inserted in the Minutes. The letter from Raven to the Bishop written in Cambridge on July 17 vigorously defended his actions and the actions of the Chapter:

... I am sorry, my Lord, but I cannot possibly allow myself to be excused at the cost of what I know to be an undeserved attack on Canon Davey. Canon Davey has acted towards me throughout with perfect propriety in the way that I am sure you would have desired him to have done. He made me free of the Cathedral; he did his utmost to facilitate my work; and the statement quoted in your letter against him was said, and was perfectly understood by me to have been said, simply to assure me of the support of the Cathedral officials in my work generally. It was precisely the same courtesy as I have received from whichever official was selected to look after my comfort before. As I told you in my last letter I never for one moment imagined – nor I am positive did Canon Davey – that it was intended to refer to my interviews or to my questions regarding the propriety of my work. That this is so, is clearly proved by the fact that at no time did I dream of applying to Canon Davey for help in a very complicated position I was faced with. Unless you have told him, he does not even now know what that problem was. You were responsible for my job and any question about that obviously concerned you – and it is with you I have dealt throughout. Canon Davey's remark referred to such matters as preaching etc and my means of getting in to touch with members of the class ie matters in which the Cathedral organisation could and should properly give me their assistance. He never said one word to contravene the instructions I received in the first place from yourself. It was a courteous pledge of help such as one would hope for from one's colleagues in greater authority than oneself.

So far as all this trouble is concerned I cannot, my Lord, accept the statement that it was due in any way to Canon Davey. He did not even know I was coming until I replied to his telegram on or about June 15. I wrote to the Dean about the end of February suggesting June 20 for my arrival. About the end of May I wrote again to Canon Bezzant, the man immediately concerned with the Cathedral classes, reminding him I was coming as usual. He was away and did not get my letter till he returned about the middle of June. He then passed it on to Canon Davey who wired to ask me the date of my arrival and to tell me he would deal with my programme ie my general arrangements.

Canon Bezzant took up the matter himself directly with the Bishop in a letter written on July 30:

My Dear Bishop,

After our last Chapter Meeting I was very surprised to read, in a copy of a letter sent to you by certain incumbents, a statement to the effect that you knew nothing about Canon Edward Raven's visit and the work he proposed to do until just before complaints reached you. You must surely have forgotten the conversation we had on Trinity Sunday evening, after the eight-thirty service, when I came to your house at your request. I then told you that Edward Raven had written to the Dean and to me; but I had been asked to see Edward Raven in Cambridge and had done so; that he proposed to come and do the job he had done in former years; that he had written me a letter asking me to make arrangements and that, as Davey was supervising the work of the Post Ordination classes, I had handed the letter to him. And I most distinctly remember you saying, as I walked down the steps of your house, that it must all be changed before another year. When I read your statement referred to above, I felt bound to say that I had told you on Trinity Sunday.

The inference that can be drawn from all of this clerical wrangling must be that senior clergy in the Diocese were unable to trust each other. There was the most serious breakdown of communication between the Bishop and the Principal Chapter. So many years have passed since this time of bitterness and legal struggle that the full picture may never be known, but what is clear is that there was an apparent inability to resolve the personal conflicts. Dean Dillistone's comment that the Bishop found it hard 'to keep his hands off the Cathedral' may well have been true. From 1923 until 1931 he had been both Bishop and Dean. Though there had originally been the warmest of friendship between Dwelly and David, this relationship broke down totally and nothing could be resolved between two strong-minded men who refused even to talk to each other.

Up to the 1930s, it was not difficult to produce a chronological narrative of the development of Dwelly's ministry, but from 1931 onwards, although individual themes can be related separately, those themes were densely woven one with another and so much was happening at the same time. Some of the legal wrangles might seem to indicate an irascible, uncharitable side to the new Dean, maybe a certain pettiness, maybe a lack of loyalty to a Bishop who had been his friend. However, the archive materials give evidence of another person in the Dwelly saga whose story sheds a very different light on the Dean.

In 1931 a young Oxford graduate, Joseph McCulloch, was ordained Deacon to serve his title at St Nicholas Church, Blundellsands, an affluent parish near the coast, north of the city. There are more letters to Dwelly from McCulloch in the archives than from any other single person. His life and career is of little significance as far as the Cathedral is concerned but the McCulloch papers shed light on Dwelly as the patient supporter and friend, able to discern the worth of someone, even without evidence on which to base that judgement.

Joseph McCulloch was born in a dock-side parish in Toxteth, not far from the Cathedral, in 1908. He came from a working class background and from a young age was taken to worship at St John's, Toxteth Park, a Church strongly influenced by the Oxford Movement. Worship at St John's became a deeply formative experience in his young life, changing 'a drab life with one that is colourful and poetic'.

He went up to Exeter College, Oxford, and after graduation, returned to Mersey-side as a Deacon in Blundellsands and, as part of his post ordination training, encountered Raven and Dwelly at weekly sessions in the Cathedral. During that first year, he wrote a novel, *Charming Manners*, under the pseudonym John Michaelhouse. The real name of the author came to light and some members of the parish as well as some members of the Diocese were determined that the young man should have no future as a priest in the Church. As Dillistone was to report in his biography of Raven,

> The novel was in the nature of a satire on suburbia and it was not hard to imagine the possible identities of some of its characters; it seemed all too evident that they were members of the parish in which the author himself was serving his curacy! The effect was sensational not only in the parish but also in the diocese at large. There were cries of indignation from laity and clergy alike and McCulloch's whole future was in jeopardy. As he had not yet been ordained priest, the Bishop was strongly urged to exercise discipline by refusing to allow him to pursue this higher office within the sacred ministry. And although it appears that in personal ways the Bishop did everything in his power to help the man under attack, it would have scandalised large sections of the diocese if he had admitted him to the priesthood.

The immediate outcome was that McCulloch quietly left the Diocese. As Dwelly and Raven were both determined that he should not be lost to the service of the

Church, Dwelly went to great lengths to help him, simply showing him that he cared and that he was willing to extend to him the marks of true friendship whatever the circumstances.

The affair did not appear to have caused any disagreement between Bishop and Dean, and indeed the Bishop showed considerable kindness and concern for the unfortunate young Deacon. In a hand-written letter of 6 August 1932 he had to break the difficult news that he would be unable to ordain him Priest at Michaelmas.

> Your Vicar writes most kindly, but it is clear that he is not entirely satisfied with your work so far. I think that the root of the trouble is that you rely far too much on your own judgement as to what to do and how to do it, and are unwilling to face unpalatable facts and distasteful criticism, and are therefore going your own way. You have not yet grasped that you are pledged to a discipline for which others as well as your self are responsible. I am also very much disappointed to hear that you are in arear with the repayments of the money we lent you. On such a stipend as yours these instalments should have been an effective first charge. Moreover I am not satisfied with your progress in study. I abolished the exam for priest's orders in the belief that I could trust my Deacons to give their mornings to reading. I do not see how you can possibly have done so while writing (or even finishing) a novel. You ought to have waited. I think you need work in a parish where the obvious tasks are nearer and harder. I suggest that you should with our help find one as soon as possible.

Both Raven and Dwelly were in correspondence with the Bishop over the matter and there was no sense of animosity in their letters. On 17 October Raven wrote that

> It was a great pity that the book was not shown to any of us until it was in page proof. I told J.M. at once that it was in my judgement sensuous, and that it would certainly be criticised as immoral – though I should not agree with such a verdict. He could easily have removed the passages that gave offence if we had seen it in time. The comments that I made to him upon it agreed almost exactly with yours. I have also told him to keep quiet: he must give the trouble time to abate and avoid publicity and the temptation to retaliate. But of course like all such folks he dramatises his own experiences, and has not the wisdom to be patient.

It may well have been Dwelly's idea that, to escape from the Diocese and avoid the publicity, the young man might return to his old college in Oxford and engage in some serious reading. Joseph clearly had financial problems and from official receipts in the Cathedral archives we know that the Dean gave at least two sums of money to help relieve severe financial strain. The receipts are not dated but one is for the sum of forty pounds and the other for seventy pounds. Seventy pounds was the sum owed to the Liverpool Diocesan Board of Finance, who issued a receipt for that amount on the tenth of October. That Dwelly was trying to help the young man was known by several eminent churchmen, including William Temple,

Archbishop of York. Dwelly was almost certainly engaged in considerable correspondence on Joseph's behalf and eventually the plans began to bear fruit. The Bishop of Southwark, Richard Parsons, was invited to help and wrote in confidence to Dwelly on 29 of November, 'The novel itself gives me the impression of having been written by a man who does not really understand the Church, and gives no indication of the work of a man deeply conscious of a vocation to the ministry.' The Bishop was certain that the young man's work should be closely and firmly guided by an experienced priest and in a letter to the Dean on 10 December he announced that Joseph would be placed with the Reverend F. H. Gillingham at St Margaret's Church, Lee, Blackheath. This same letter reveals that Dwelly had offered to find the money for the young deacon's stipend himself:

> With regard to his stipend. Gillingham would greatly prefer that he should be paid as one of the curates on his staff from the parochial funds. This is possible owing to the fact that another curate that he was expecting about this time has fallen through. However at Trinity he might, unless his senior Curate is in the interval promoted, find some difficulty in continuing to pay McCulloch, in which case he will let me know, and I will turn to you for the wherewithal which you so kindly promised. I agree with Gillingham that it would be better for McCulloch that he should feel that he was earning his pay in the ordinary manner from the place in which he worked ... If, without inflicting hardship on any one else, it were possible for you to provide from the source of which you proposed to pay McCulloch, some sum for our Diocesan Fund for assisting with grants to the stipends all of assistant clergy, I do not pretend that this would not help ...

During December, McCulloch was writing almost daily to the Dean and in a postscript on 21 December he wrote: 'By the way, Sir, at last I am brought to admit that it is only with the greatest difficulty I am steering my frail bark between the Scylla of penury and the Charybdis of financial obligation.' A letter of 26 December indicated that the Dean had responded positively and the expression of thanks might well indicate that such requests had been made more than once: 'As always your kindness came when it was most needed.'

By 12 February 1933 Joseph had declared his love for Betty Gillingham, the Rector's twenty-one-year-old daughter, and his letters are full of schemes for future publications. To my eyes, the letters remain the product of a slightly arrogant young man, ready to set pen to paper on a variety of subjects and often ready to indulge in scathing criticism of his fellow curates, parishioners and people with far more experience than he had. Despite his criticism of people and systems, McCulloch's devotion to Dwelly was evident in every letter, the tone of some verging on adoration. A letter of 15 March 1933 has some comments to make on the Liverpool post-ordination work but it also reveals much about the overconfident young Deacon.

> At the moment, I have a strange hankering after academic pretension. I want to

read hard in the realm of Theology. The snag is, I can't get hold of a theological library. There isn't one available nearer than Oxford. And this place Blackheath is an intellectual quagmire. There isn't a soul who can stir his mind to much activity, and apart from Betty, whose interests are entirely bound up with the representation of art in its various forms but who is willing to talk with me about religion, freedom, style or what I will, there is not one soul I can converse with to any purpose. So you may picture the pitiful spectacle of myself grubbing about trying to keep my mind alive without much reading. The Bishop's exam doesn't provide enough. Why must I read Dean Church's *Oxford Movement* again in order to write answers to questions in June? There is only one book that in the whole of the year which is new to me and that is a work on Barthianism ... My sympathies quite honestly are with the Liverpool Post-ordination course. Constant contact with live minds like those of Canon and Raven and Canon Davey kept me reading widely last year. Possibly after I am priested I may be allowed to compare the two systems in the Church Press. I shouldn't think any one else has the unique position of having been a deacon twice, so to speak. And I should think I might be qualified to give a judgement. If you want live clergy, I think to give them a weekly intellectual stimulus is far better than to set them a number of books, which vary in their value according to the mental capacity of the reader. My fellow Curate and Deacon, for instance, has the mind of a good Rugger player ... The difficulties at Liverpool was the poor level of the younger clergy. Undoubtedly in the Southwark Diocese they are very, very much better. Culturally and intellectually they are more capable of benefiting from the Liverpool system, whereas the Liverpool newly ordained would be better under this Southwark system of Deacons examinations. Arthur would be of great value to these fresh young men from Oxford and Cambridge. But the board schools cramped broad cast mind all over the young Liverpool clergy with their clichés and their moulded opinions and their scant culture!!

By the autumn of 1934, Joseph and Betty Gillingham were married and installed in a flat at 33 Buckingham Gate, SW1, and Joseph was assistant curate to Canon F. R. Barry at St John's, Smith Square, Westminster. F. H. Gillingham had seen improvement in Joseph's progress into the priesthood but, even as his father-in-law, he still had misgivings which were voiced in a letter to Dwelly in January 1935:

Joseph and Betty seem very happy and if happiness and sympatheticness are the two essential for wedded happiness then I think they have achieved it. I am – in the light of that – getting over my disappointment for such it undoubtedly was – I thought Betty might have done so much better – but there again is that worldly ambition which I have condemned over-long. That Joseph has improved enormously is clear to all and I hope one day will completely abandoned the husks of intellectual gymnastics for the more substantial kernel of true evangelism. He has much, very much to thank you for – you paid a heavy price for befriending him and so have I – it may be that we shall both be paid in full ...

McCulloch settled into his new parish, and when Canon Barry was away for six months in Australia, his young curate felt that he was doing excellent work, despite

> the encumbrance of a curate who appears to be in a perpetual coma. Tonight we showed signs of the beginning to move. I started with twenty-nine – I think we had a couple of hundred this evening. We must have a queue before Barry comes back in February – everything was hopeless – choir, organist, parish organisations – also the usual C. of E. accoutrements.

He continued to write and his over-eager pen was encouraged when he was invited to give a twenty-minute talk on the BBC. The Bishop of Southwark must have tried to dissuade him from publication, but the young man remained totally confident in his ambition, as he explained in an undated letter to Dwelly:

> It is my own fault that he is now so anxious that I do not publish anything I write. He visualises it as both rash and immature, with neither deep religious experience or clear thought behind it. The difficulty is not lessened by my broadcast in which I had to make many sweeping statements without adequate support or workmanlike constructiveness to justify them. My onslaught on the Prayer Book and on Theology was naturally unacceptable to the Bishop as neither a comprehensive or mature revaluation of all the real problem.

Few of Dwelly's letters to McCulloch have survived, but one of them was clear in its intentions of making the young man start to think more critically about his work, and ensuring that all material intended for publication be submitted first to Canon Barry. On his return from Australia, Barry was forthright in expressing his own opinions of his young curate in a confidential letter to Dwelly in March 1935:

I say that McCulloch is a worry – he clouds my work in anxiety instead of relieving it, and I don't know what to do with him. He's smashed up my P M Parish group! Partly I think because of his terrible facility for being rude to people. And now there's another book coming out, which will put the lid on it! I'm going to have a heart to heart with him on Wednesday – but I wish I knew where it would end? Is there any chance of getting him offered something else? I don't believe he'd be too bad in the small suburban parish; but he's hopeless with working class and so dreadfully hard for other people to work with. If you can keep him away I would be thankful! Of course he has qualities, and he is splendidly loyal to me; but I don't see any future for him here, or for me if he stops much more longer! But don't give me away to him will you?

In a second letter two days later there is a report of Barry's meeting with McCulloch in which there was an admission that 'he'd queered his own pitch here too badly to cut any further ice and wanted to go. I couldn't disagree with him – so now he's in search of a country parish where he can stand up on his own feet and make good – which I believe he may, for he's sound and humble of heart if only he can learn to control his tongue and get the better of his patronising exhibitionism.'

To everyone's relief the Dean and Chapter of Westminster were patrons of the small rural parish of Turweston, Brackley, Northamptonshire, and he was instituted in September 1935. On the twenty-fifth of the month, F. H. Gillingham wrote to Dwelly to report happily on the institution service and expressing confidence for the future. We may never know fully what Dwelly did for the troublesome young priest but Gillingham wrote strongly: 'I think they have been very lucky, and everything has turned out very favourably for them, although you have paid a heavy price for it, and I have not got off absolutely scathless. However, it must be some kind of comfort to you to know that you steered these people through very troubled waters into a quiet haven.'

In his own hand at the end of the letter Gillingham gave evidence that Dwelly's earlier offer of financial help to fund the curacy at Blackheath had, at least in part, been taken up and that the payments were in arrears:

My treasurer reminds me from time to time that I owe him £120. He means I'm afraid you do. I don't wish to press you in the matter in the least if it is incon-venient for you – as most undoubtedly it would be for me. Then I won't press it – I only remind you 'cos you yourself suggested a year's grace. It's beastly even having to mention it – and I could not do it in person; but now can blush unseen behind a letter.

Dwelly's generous offer was at that time a financial embarrassment and he had to hope that 'your worthy Treasurer would stay his execution a little longer – not for long, but until I find out how much my own legal costs in our late troubles amount to.'

McCulloch signed almost all of his letters to Dwelly 'Yours ever, Joseph' but he wrote what was for him an unusually short letter ending 'Yours sincerely, Joseph McCulloch'. It was written from Turweston on 3 December 1935, and the contents might suggest that Dwelly had also given regular direct help to Joseph:

Forgive my bothering you again, as you know, the occasion demands it. Would you be so good as to tell me if the arrangement which was come to still stands? I am of course worried for fear it falls through. I'm not losing faith, Sir, but would be glad of the assurance that you will not fail me. I don't know whether perhaps you would like all the receipts for the £70 on this occasion, or whether you will send me the cheque informally as you have usually done.

Dwelly's own legal expenses over the turbulent years in the first half of the 1930s must have been considerable and yet he was giving the most generous financial support, directly and indirectly through Gillingham, to a young man whose qualities as a priest were, to say the least, highly uncertain. His sense of loyalty is beyond question. His ability to judge character may be a little more suspect, though it must be remembered that in later years McCulloch became Rector of St Mary, Warwick, and then of St Mary Le Bow. It is particularly sad that in two of his autobiographical books there is minimal reference to the tremendous support he received from the Dean of Liverpool.

In the spring of 1936, the publishing firm Michael Joseph gave notice of the appearance of a new novel in May: *Limping Sway* by Joseph McCulloch. In the words of the publisher's blurb,

An ancient cathedral, a peaceful close, a colony of clerics and their families. Although a hundred years have gone on since Trollope sat down to write of this familiar English scene, the cathedral close still provides a background for the clash of human temperaments. In Godminster, where the twelfth-century Cathedral endures among the thriving industries of a modern age, Bishop and Dean and Archdeacon's wife are involved in antagonism, hatred and officialdom – in all the tragic-comedy which may be found wherever men and women are bound together in the services of an institution such as the Church. Fiona and Gillian, the Dean's two lovely daughters, inevitably scandalise Archdeacon Gunter's wife. Mrs. Gunter, a Mrs. Proudie in a modern setting, lives only for vengeance – a vengeance which has far-reaching consequences, destroying the career of Fiona's lover and bringing strange tragedy to the Close.

To read *Limping Sway* more than sixty years after its publication is to understand something of the hurt and anger which the novel generated. It is not a story about Liverpool Cathedral, but important elements relating to some of the main characters are immediately recognisable even now. McCulloch must have thought that by setting his novel around the Cathedral and close of medieval Godminster he was creating an entirely fresh, fictional world, but he was wrong and his main characters are so clearly based on actual people. Bishop Henry Manning Trevor was described as being 'able, gifted, distinguished, at the age of sixty three on his consecration to the See of Godminster, he had gained a reputation for elegance of appearance, wintry charm, excellence of scholarship and harmlessly libertarian scholarship. He had that nice facility of mind which discriminates between theory and practice. An advocate in theory of greater religious freedom, he was in practice a careful conserver of existing limitations. His adroit conservative modernism had earned him an ancient diocese, and his ability to run a certain distance with the hare while still consorting with the majority of the hounds might yet earn him a good deal more.' It is difficult not to see this as a biased and uncharitable presentation of Albert Augustus David, and if Trevor is a representation of David, Rupert Baring is a recognisable Frederick Dwelly. 'Baring, ten years his junior, had come from the neighbouring diocese of Midchester where he had been a canon in the Cathedral. His appearance was unimpressive – of medium height (Trevor could give him four or five inches), irregular features, no particular attractiveness. But his eyes were disquieting – disturbingly penetrating – the eyes of a man who had no fear even perhaps of that greatest of clerical pitfalls, indiscretion, the unwisdom of too much honesty. Trevor had heard that his new Dean was a man of great artistic gifts rather than of intellectual abilities.' And 'For a year they found collaboration possible – a new regime was instituted – many innovations were made at the Cathedral and Godminster heard a new gospel of freedom. Unfortunately, the concord of Bishop with Dean could not last long, and over a tea at the Older Universities Club, where they had met in London during a session of the Church Assembly, they came very near to quarrelling over the trifling matter of a ritualistic clergyman, whom the Bishop wished to discipline and whom the Dean defended according to his view of freedom.' The Dean's wife was conveniently removed: 'Actually, there was no Mrs. Baring. Nobody in Godminster knew who she had been, but it was generally understood that she had died after the birth of her second child.'

It has been reported to the writer that Christine Wagstaffe saw more than a little of herself in Fiona Baring who had 'managed her father's household for the last two years. She had arrived at the Deanery, not quite eighteen, but perfectly capable of managing three servants, a gardener and a gardener's boy; she soon acquired the art of driving a car, though that was not done too openly; and she was more than a match for the stream of callers who for the most part called once but never again.' There are a number of people still alive who remember the daunting aspect of Chris Wagstaffe and the way in which she supported and protected Dwelly right to his death.

Even some of the minor characters are recognisably real people. Ralph Dawson, Chris Wagstaffe's brother-in-law, was a close devotee of Dwelly but he was also the Bishop's Chaplain or, as McCulloch was to put it, 'Hugh was the Bishop's Chaplain but the Dean's disciple.' I do not know enough about the real Archdeacon Twitchett to know whether his presence lies behind Archdeacon Gunter – described by the novelist as 'an unimaginative mediocrity'. Mrs Gunter was the daughter of the previous Bishop and she did not approve of the current worshippers and services in the Cathedral where 'instead of the sparse but extremely proper congregation which had come to the Cathedral on Sundays in pre-Baring days, now the Sunday Services were crowded out with hoi polloi of Godminster – who ought to have been attending their own parish churches or lying abed (as was their former wont). And as for the services themselves, one might as well go to a music hall as Godminster Cathedral these days. The processional acrobatics and dressings up and mummerie and nonsense which went on there – really, at times she could not believe her eyes.'

Other small details are also reminiscent of actuality. Godminster Cathedral held an 8.45 p.m. Sunday Service – instead of an 8.30 – and the Dean was involved in litigation, 'a lawsuit brought against the Dean of the Cathedral by two members of the Chapter.'

Before I read *Limping Sway* in the Reading Room of Cambridge University Library, I hoped that I might discern details that I did not know about Liverpool Cathedral and its Dean. I was looking for revelation in the wrong direction. I now think that the significance lies in the way in which some senior clergy felt that they could never trust Dwelly again if he allied himself with Trevelyan, the McCulloch figure of the novel. Dwelly's support for McCulloch must have been known beyond the boundaries of the Liverpool Diocese and the grapevine would quickly have spread the news of this second novel from the controversial young priest.

The first communication from McCulloch to Dwelly after the publication is undated but was almost certainly written early in May. 'Betty has just come back from London with the most unhappy news she could ever bring – that I have hurt the man I love the most. I am too stunned yet to understand it – please give me time. One thing that I say – that till this moment I was ignorant that the book could be interpreted thus. I wrote it without a thought of Liverpool in my mind – until now it had not occurred to me or to Betty that Godminster and its inhabitants were anything but our own creation.' Betty Gillingham wrote to Dwelly on 9 June that 'It was a terrible heartbreaking conversation we had on the telephone over a month ago, and I was too stunned by the sound of your voice to be coherent. I have felt chilled in heart ever since.' McCulloch in both his excursions into novel writing seemed to have been totally unaware that much of his so called fiction was actually extremely close to reality. F. H. Gillingham was conscious of the damage which the novel caused and the way Dwelly's standing in the church had suffered. Gillingham's letter of 10 August 1936 deserves to be quoted almost in its entirety.

My Darlings,

Let me warn you at the outset this letter is going to hurt you – I would do anything to spare you pain but for your own souls good I must write in the following strain painful though it is to me to. It's about that unfortunate book. I met the Dean today – at his request and he is a very sad and disappointed and hurt man. I know what he means to both of you Joseph especially – he ought to be held in high honour for he has saved Joseph's life. I don't believe that either of you would knowingly pain him but Joseph you have unwittingly done it and in a very marked way: so much so that he is inclined to think that Albert Liverpool was right and he himself was wrong about your priesthood.

He has had many blows and knocks from high officials but all these have attacked his policy and not his person – He could answer back but Canterbury, York, Liverpool, Oxford and in directly Southwark have now all attacked him. Why? Because they see in your book intimate and secret things which they have said to be him – he passed them on to you and you have published them in some cases almost verbatim. He has written to each and said 'I must acknowledge the justice of your attack' – he passed them on to you in confidence never dreaming they would be divulged. Result. Cantuar has actually withdrawn confidential work with which he had already entrusted him – as his confidence in him has been shaken.

I told you that I recognised the Dean and the Bishop of Liverpool in your story, but I was not behind the scenes as you were – the Dean says all that took place is vividly described and he sees not only himself and the Bishop but Bezzant, Ralph Dawson etc. York said to him 'Whose story has he described if not yours?' Result that the Dean will never give you his confidence again until you have given him some very definite evidence – not in words – but in action spread over many years of your changed attitude towards not only other people and things but to yourself as well. You wrote in your book that the characters were not from life you also have told the Dean by letter that you never meant to or thought you were describing actualities and past events in which he and others were intimately and painfully concerned – he believes you are speaking the truth and are sincere but he says that makes it all the more serious because it is clear that you don't know yourself and until you know yourself you can't begin to start on any one or anything else. He also tells me – and that I never knew it or if I did I had forgotten it – that Southwark had a letter in writing from you in which you say solemnly that you won't publish anything for five years – if that is true Joseph my dear boy – how can you break it so glibly and frequently. I know your answer will be I offered the book to the Dean to read and he refused. I told him that but his version was this I won't read it – I must leave that to you thinking that would be more than enough to check you.

Well now what's to be done? You haven't many if any friends amongst the hier-archy – and you have forfeited the Dean's intimacy pro tem at any rate – among the lesser fry – I am left and I will – I must always be a friend because amongst other reasons you'd belong to me and there is Christopher Michael.

You must write to the Dean and – tell him you have received this letter – send it to him if you like because he hasn't seen it and ask his advice what to do and if he tells you – act on it – for its no use asking advice if you won't take it and you are not too good at taking it.

You cannot look for any favours from Canterbury, York, Oxford, Liverpool – all

except York are old men and seven or eight years should see them through fortunately – people nowadays forget quickly – let's hope they will have the clock which
was set back at Blundellsands is set back further than ever now and it can only be
put forward slowly and gradually.

There seems no doubt that events in Liverpool were close to the heart of the book;
as much is admitted by Betty in a distraught letter to Dwelly on 17 September.

Joseph sought only to serve you, Mr Dean, – I can swear to that. It was his great
desire to write a book that would completely vindicate your way of life and he has
most bitterly failed, and the cost of the failure cannot even be paid by us, ourselves
– that is the really bitter thing. But his motive at least was not evil.

Some level of working relationship was re-established: Chris Wagstaffe was
Godmother to Christopher McCulloch, and a small number of letters from
McCulloch written during the 1940s are preserved in the archives. The final letter,
written on 24 June 1955, is addressed to someone called James.

I was just about to send you this publication for your interest, when I read in the
Church Times (somewhat obscurely placed!) that F.W.D. is to retire in the Autumn.
When you gave me that most pleasurable lunch in Cambridge a few months ago,
we mentioned this contingency, and you thought that, faute de mieux, I might be
F.W.D.'s Elisha. I doubt if the mantle will be allowed to fall – it will probably be
wrapped up with moth balls and stowed away. But it is a job at which I would
dearly love to have a crack, and it would be sad if mere mediocrity – good but
unimaginative – should be installed in his room. I wonder if there are any wheels
which might be set in motion, or avenues explored.

McCulloch committed the error of thinking that he was writing pure fiction when
much of his material was factual and he was aware of the danger. On 12 September
1936 he wrote to Dwelly:

When I sat down to write it, I found my own experiences powerfully coloured
what I put on paper and I set to work ruthlessly to destroy whatever might
obtrude of my own experience on the imaginative work I was trying to write.

His ruthless attempts were not adequate, however, and his arrogance in the same
letter reveals to me just how little he understood himself and his abilities: 'I have
always wanted to follow in Trollope's footsteps, though I am willing to admit that I
have neither the stature not the maturity yet to do it adequately.' The biographer
who tries to disentangle fact from fiction would be even more at fault than poor,
young McCulloch, though the pages of Limping Sway will almost certainly reveal
some truths about life in and around Liverpool Cathedral. Wherever the truth might
lie, it is certain that Dwelly's relationship with his Bishop must have been even more
antagonistic after the McCulloch affair.

CHAPTER ELEVEN

Cathedral community

'SIRS, – In the illustrious House of Old Sarum; in 1215, like as in that of Canterbury, Lincoln, the Worcester and other our Cathedrals, there were joined in the Fellowship of the Chapter others also, peaceable men and furnished with ability, whose wise counsel found for the people new and living paths of the manifold grace of the Spirit; are you ready so to be joined to the Fellowship of our Chapter of Liverpool?' These words were spoken by Charles Raven at the service establishing the Dean and Chapter in 1931. The rubric in the service paper speaks of 'The College of Counsel, so that others from beyond the borders of the diocese may hither bring their contributions of wisdom and experience, to the end that contact with the wider operations of the Spirit shall in every generation be established and maintained.' By the twentieth century, the ancient cathedrals of England had long-established communities, including those who worked in the cathedral, those who worshipped there, and those whose experiences might be drawn upon by the Dean and Chapter whenever the need arose. Liverpool, a twentieth century institution without ancient traditions, was in need of a body of people drawn from varying walks of life who might offer their advice and support to this newly established cathedral.

The names of the first members of the College were listed in the service paper: the Earl of Crawford and Balcarres, the Right Hon. General Smuts, the Right Rev. George Bell, Sir Stanford Downing, Sir Frederick Morton Radcliffe, Dr John Masefield, Professor Conwy Lloyd Morgan, Professor John Linton Myres, Mr Francis Carolus Eeles, and Mr Martin Shaw.

It is unfortunate that few papers from the College of Counsel have been retained in the Cathedral archives. The influence of such men as Masefield and Shaw on the material used in some of the great services has already been examined. Correspondence from some of the other members of the Counsel suggests that they took their role seriously and did not see it as being confined to infrequent formal meetings. It had been the intention to meet once a year and a short report appeared after the meeting held at the Oxford and Cambridge Club in London in November 1932:

There was a discussion on the life and work of the Cathedral both in its connection with the diocese and also in respect of the unique situation that had grown up as required in relation to the Church of England as a whole. It was recognised that Liverpool Cathedral had become a national possession, that it stood for something new in the life of the Church that it had become a point of contact between religion and the thousands of people untouched by the Church, and this over and above its normal activities as the centre of the diocese. It was found that certain criticisms such for example as that the Cathedral stood for what was vague and indefinite arose from a mere lack of information and were unjustified and negligible, and hence it was agreed that the liturgical experiments now being made were such as the situation demanded and that these developments should continue, subject of course to the control of the Bishop as Visitor.

A separate and undated sheet reports on statements made at a meeting by five of the members:

Dr Masefield, Poet Laureate, in a speech on the importance of maintaining special services at Liverpool Cathedral said he felt that more than anything else, the artists of our day needed a place – a holy place – where they could take their work. Such a place to many of them is Liverpool Cathedral. Professor Myres said that to him the ever-enlarging and embracing attitude of Liverpool Cathedral was the most hopeful thing in the spiritual life of our day. He hoped there would be an altar for the Greek Church and a rostrum or reading desk for those whose worship is not best expressed at an altar. Mr Eeles, as a liturgical student, said he hoped the Dean and Chapter would continue to make use of old treasures. No other Cathedral had discovered their richness and adapted it so effectively. Lord Crawford pleaded that Liverpool Cathedral Chapter should not be self conscious in its work which made Lancashire men turn to Liverpool instead of (as they used to do) to Manchester. The Lord Bishop of Chichester pleaded that whatever else is done at Liverpool, the Chapter will continue their consecration of the imagination.

Only a short time before the College was established, General Smuts had played a significant part in an 8.30 service in the Cathedral to celebrate the Centenary of the British Association for the Advancement of Science, when he was the preacher. That statements such as that which follows were made in the Cathedral by members of the Counsel and then published indicates the ways in which Dwelly fearlessly set out to use eminent men with differing specialisms and to identify them strongly with Liverpool Cathedral.

Science, which it is my honour to represent in this Cathedral, has proved probably the most important factor in human destiny during the last two centuries. It has opened the new world order which it is your privilege in this Cathedral to dedicate to God.

In many ways science has prepared mankind for fuller revelations. Many people thought that when the Bible was closed the revelation of God came to an end. Nothing could be more erroneous. The revelation of truth is continuous, and I believe there has never been in all the pages of history a deeper revelation of the truth of God than in these last centuries in the great scientific movement. It has led to most amazing changes, not only in the power of material civilisation, but in our view points and in fundamental aspect of our civilisation.

Today we stand, perhaps, before one of the most momentous periods in the history of our civilisation. The old world seems to be sinking; the old authority is going; the old lights by which we steer our course seem to grow dim and faint and today perhaps more than for many thousands of years of our history, we are beginning to ask ourselves fundamental questions. Whither are we going? What are our objectives? It is partly the result of scientific change, partly the result of the inevitable growth of modern civilisation, and largely it is the result of that tragedy through which we have passed in a lifetime.

Today mankind is confronted with a serious crisis in his destiny. I do not believe there is any single agency that can see us through, but it may be that science, the truth based upon fact and not upon authority, that disinterested pursuit of truth for its own sake, may prove one of the most potent forces in helping us through the crisis.

For, thanks to science, we now look upon the universe as ordered – a reliable system in which we could have faith. Science finds no deceit, trickery, or wrangling in the universe; it is truth, sincerity, and perfect honesty from beginning to end. Science has also taught us the unity of all life. Further, science has taught us humility (such as this our Cathedral impels its worshippers to feel), it has taught man how to climb down from his high place among the angels, and to take a humble place with the rest of God's creatures. Such humility has done us no end of good.

The spirit of self-sacrifice is a much deeper motive in human society than the craving for comfort. Science will more and more take a form and have an effect on human society which will be of a spiritual more than a material character. The disinterested, fearless pursuit of truth is itself a spiritual pursuit and must have far reaching results. Science is going to be a great purifier, it will enlarge not only our knowledge but our imagination. It will reveal more and more the principles of harmony and beauty in the universe and bring us closer to the heart of life.

But science is only one of the great values. We want religion in order to realise our foremost human stature, as by this service religion affirms that it is one with science. In recent centuries these have been in a watertight compartment, the great change to which we can look forward in the not distant future is the drawing together of all great values. For failing such a unification, disruption is ahead of us.

As in this Cathedral praises have been offered for men of science and art; so it ought to be a common avowal that religion, art and science must join hands in a new world order, and new order of culture. For divorce between religion and

science has come up to an end. Some great synthesis, some great unification is now, as here, being effected. Already by faith we see the lineaments of this new order appearing. It will make one of the biggest changes, not only in our culture but in human destiny.

Let this cathedral never cease to rejoice in the evidence of this new order of life.

The Right Honourable Lord Dawson of Penn was installed to the College in February 1933 as an important member of the medical profession, being President of the Royal College of Physicians, as well as President of the British Medical Association. It is interesting to read the opening paragraph of his address in the light of the Unitarian controversies which flared in the same year:

The Order of Counsellors in this Cathedral – men gathered from diverse walks of knowledge and activity – bears witness to the comprehensives of the English Church. Happily you do not inquire whether those you receive into the privilege of your brotherhood subscribe to the Articles of your creed. Rather do you accept all disciples of truth as a way of fulfilling God's purpose.

Today you extend that fellowship to the profession of medicine; of this the Counsellor has the honour of being representative though the responsibility for these reflections is individual. Where viewed in its completeness, this profession has a wider range than perhaps any other calling. Its knowledge is based on natural history and in increasing measure of an exact science. The methods are observation and experiment. Its practice requires that knowledge, and further, the application of that knowledge to the individual man – his make-up and circumstance.

And in these days when we study not only disease, but health and its early lapses, we have to deal not only with those cloistered by sickness but with man in his daily life and vocations, and therefore have to so extend our outlook as to take stock of individual and social relationships. Further, we need ideals of service without which our practice would be as 'sounding brass or tinkling cymbal'; on the one hand, intuition and charity to perceive and understand, and on the other hand, strength to guide and sustain. It is here our work has contact with religion – not in its beliefs, but in its care for the individual soul and the way of the living.

The disciples of medicine are thus concerned with two parallel but different kinds of knowledge. Between these varieties there should be contact and tolerance, but not compromise, which though helpful in the world of action is out of place in the world of thought. To the profession of medicine belongs the narrow road of knowledge, wisdom, and understanding. The magical and miraculous are the broad road which leadeth to destruction.

Here let me find illustration and inspiration by thinking of a great citizen of Liverpool who was recently laid to rest in this Cathedral – Robert Jones. Scientific thinker, inventive craftsmen, teacher, leader of men, he gave himself and through his disciples great service to mankind. For him the thread of a life was 'strung with the beads of thought and love'.

It is a natural sequence to pass to the consideration of the relations between religion and science. Here I omit reference to those who accept belief from the authority of the Church (though their opinions call for respect and even reverence), and concern myself with the outlook of Protestantism. Religion and science represent two different aspects of experience. Religion belongs to an inner world. It rests upon – first, experience, and later, conviction; its concern is life in its fullness. Science belongs to the outer world of the senses and the intellect. It rests upon external observation, and later objective corroboration. But life has to be lived, not only thought about, and through life run these different but equally indispensable threads of reality – the experience of the outer world which makes life possible and the inward conviction which makes it strong.

What of the world in which these forces move and have their being? Look in what direction you will, there is the unrest belonging to rapid change. The growth of mechanical invention, and the changes in industry, concentrate attention on material civilisation. The advances of science are so extending that, though enlarging the ambit and worth of life, they disturb established habits of thought and bring perplexity to the mind of man.

Comprehensiveness which began as an intention in the early Prayer Book 'to keep the mean between the two extremes' of Catholicism and Protestantism is, in these days of a larger world, a soil favourable to progressive thought, and should prevent unconsidered rejection of new ideas and methods of living which need guidance rather than a rebuke.

The essence of life is movement, as the design of this great Cathedral, and the thought and the vision it comprehends, bear witness. It can truly be said that today, in the realm of thought, materialism does not hold sway. On the other hand, in the realm of dogmatic belief there are noteworthy changes, and also in those habits of observance and worship which in the minds of our forefathers were naturally, but not less arbitrarily, regarded as essential ingredients of the religious life.

For a large and increasing body of Protestant people dogma, today has less appeal. It fails to stir. Some, indeed, it even estranges. Religion for them is more rooted in experience and less in belief. Is there not, as the result of this develop-ment and change, such a disparity between the current forms of expression and actual conviction as to either jar or numb sensibility?

Belief which has been attenuated cannot activate a spiritual life. Yet it cannot be said that the people of today are not religious. Perhaps they need a firmer accept-ance of the fact that the way of life for all must be 'No cross, no crown'; but the manifold contacts I have had with the ranks of the people, in my hospital life and during the war, impel me to speak humble and admiring tribute to that faith which gives them trust, to that courage which gives them patience, and to that kindness that never lets the left hand know what the right hand doeth. Though scant of form and expression, surely here is Godliness! Judged by the Christian virtues, assessed by the Sermon on the Mount, those of today hold their own with preceding generations of stricter belief and narrower tolerance.

It is values which are altering. It may be they are feeling their way back to the Gospels with their universal appeal and small concern with set forms. They are leaning more to expression by drama and poetry, and perhaps that spirit of which is embodied not only in the lesson of today, but in that litany, of unsurpassed beauty, to which we have listened. Is it not a fact that this large body of a religious feeling exists, and is half-consciously searching for expression and shelter? Is it not in the power of the Church of England, with its tradition of comprehensiveness, to enfold it?

And does not this service at which we are now present supply the answer?

I make no apology for quoting in full a third installation statement from a member of the College because, for me, these public statements reveal so much of the spirit which energised the Cathedral under Dwelly's leadership in the early years and which remains significant today.

John Masefield, Counsellor in the Cathedral Church of Liverpool, to the Dean and Chapter, Greeting; and to all of the brothers of the Cathedral Fellowship of what-ever quality and degree, Greeting.

I have been asked to write down what a Cathedral is, and should be to one like myself.

To most of us a Cathedral is a big and beautiful building, made from four to seven centuries ago by men of extraordinary genius, as an offering to God, and as a place where large numbers of citizens might draw near to God, and as a house for the throne from which the Bishop might watch them draw near. Usually such a building is kept in good repair; it is often thronged by sightseers, who sometimes

The Dean frequently visited even the most inaccessible parts of the building site.

in the course of the year contribute large sums towards its upkeep. Sometimes the sightseer is slightly inconvenienced by the presence of a few very old infirm men and women, gathered in a corner to listen while a man in vestments gabbles something, but the inconvenience comes seldom and is always slight. The sightseer is usually more pestered by guides, who will tell him that such an arch is late thirteenth and the other window early fourteenth, and expect money payment for the information. Looking into his guidebook, he will read that Ruskin thought that such a tracery was the last quite pure tracery to be traced by an upright heart, and that somebody else thought that the profound knowledge evident in every line of the Bishop's throne marks the culminating point of the Cinquecento.

Coming away from such a place, the sightseer sometimes reflects that the place is dead and had better be buried.

As it happens, I have only once, and then for only two weeks, lived sufficiently near to any Cathedral to have felt its influence in my life. Cities today have become too big for the citizens to have a civic sense; a city dweller may well be five miles from his Cathedral: so it has happened to myself. Often a city dweller cannot see his Cathedral without making a special journey. This brings me to my first point of what a cathedral should be.

It should be, first of all, a place plainly to be seen by the citizens, and by those in the district. The Parthenon at Athens is the most perfectly placed of all great temples. The sites of many castles would be perfect for cathedrals. Amiens is well placed, so is Durham; so are York, Gloucester, Salisbury and St Paul's Cathedral. So is this great Cathedral of Liverpool. A Liverpool Cathedral should be readily seen from many parts of the city, and, above all, by the Life of the City, the river, with its ships and docks. All Cathedrals should be made specially conspicuous by tower or spire, and these again should be made more conspicuous by some great figure of white and gold, the guardian of the city; and some further glory of windvanes telling the windshifts, and great bells telling the hours and their quarters, and ringing for the city's joys; in this city for the ship launched or the ship come home. And in this city I would have the tower such that Mariners, who are the life of the city, could adjust their compasses by it, and see the storm signals and the time signals upon it, so that it should be their tower pre-eminently.

Then Cathedrals have been made great in the past because their citizens have believed in them, and had given greatly and of their best to make them glorious. In their great times they have provided for all great artists the opportunity to indulge the imagination to the full. They have used the best skill of their time. The skill in a nation does not vary very greatly from century to century, but in some centuries it is encouraged, and greatly used, in others it is neglected, in others it is depressed and abused. Cathedrals in the past have taken the very best skill of their time and encouraged it to the full. Their builders, sculptors and painters, their metal workers, paviors, glaziers and carpenters have been of their best. All the skilled ones of the time have had the joy of contributing; and the rich ones have had the joy of helping. Poets, perhaps, have been looked at somewhat askance by Cathedrals in the past (I do not blame the Cathedrals wholly), and the results of the coolness may be seen in hymnals. Still, some of the noblest Cathedral decorations known to me are illustrations of Dante; and there was a time when at York and at Coventry, if not elsewhere, poets gave of their best to link the life of the city with the city's holiest place.

Certainly a Cathedral, besides being visible at a distance, should be splendid within, with the best that all artists and citizens can offer. This splendour should touch and mark all her parts and precincts, and not only her building, but the many institutions attached to her, for teaching, healing and relieving. She should be the place to which all the generosities of her citizens as well as those of the artists of her time, should turn and flow.

Then since the main purpose of a Cathedral is worship, and the Dedication of a Cathedral is to some special attribute of what is ever to be worshipped, that Dedication should have its Feast of a solemnity great and touching, in some way that many might share and all feel. Here the arts are needed, for by the arts men are linked, as by the intellect men are set asunder.

How the touching of all souls may be wrought, is for inspiration to show, but no Cathedral can be serving Life that does not draw Life to it, all the Life of its community. Sports, contests, exhibitions, draw whole communities: they always did and always will; contests and spectacle cannot fail. Yet they have always yielded their place as chief attraction to the sincerity of men in earnest.

This Cathedral of Liverpool, the greatest of modern Cathedrals, is a Church of the Resurrection. It comes into the life of our time, in a decade when all the ways of life known to us from childhood have to be remade, when the nation has to be re-created, with what difficulty we do not yet know, but no doubt with much. This Cathedral therefore, should be the symbol of that Resurrection: and at the same time its standard. What has been muffled and in shrouds and buried down deep after being broken by the soldiers, should emerge here and be triumphant. Then indeed it would be a Cathedral that Is and Is as it should be.

Together with Raven's *Liverpool Cathedral*, public statements such as these gave voice to the sentiments which are at the heart of Dwelly's vision for the Cathedral. Previous chapters have tried to give insight into some of the organisational and political problems of the new Cathedral. The rich variety of the service papers in the archives give ample evidence as to how the Cathedral was used by its regular daily and weekly worshippers and also the vast numbers who annually attended the wide range of special services.

One special service held on 6 June 1937 was indicative of Dwelly's all-embracing vision for the Cathedral community. The success and significance of the service was recorded in the Minutes of the Principal Chapter, convened half an hour after the end of the service:

The Chapter records with great appreciation the Empire Broadcast Service of Affirmation held in this day in the Cathedral shared by Clergy and Ministers from all denominations in the City and Diocese, the first actual personal witness together by Christians to their common experience of God which has been held since the Reformation.

They extend to all of their brothers of the Clergy and Ministers their deep gratitude for the presence and friendship of this great act of worship. And a further record of their opinion that gatherings of this kind afford a most effective means toward the promoting of increasing unity between the Clergy and Ministers and the members of their various Churches and Congregations.

For evidence relating to the devising of this service, Liverpool Cathedral is indebted to the Reverend Alan Wilkinson for references to it and its Dean in *Dissent or Conform?* (1986), and to primary source material from the papers of his father. The Reverend J. T. Wilkinson was an eminent Free Church Minister who came to Liverpool in 1932 and, as President of the Free Church Council, he developed a strong working friendship with Dwelly. So strong was Dwelly's commitment to his Free Church colleague that he sought legal advice about ways of appointing Wilkinson to some office in the Cathedral. Dwelly's solicitors wrote to him on 15 September 1938:

> As you know I have been actively engaged for some months in considering proposals by the Cathedral Commissions for the revision of the Statutes of Liverpool Cathedral. In view of these proposals I deeply regret that it is not possible to carry into effect what was, I know, one of the many schemes in your mind for developing the joint worship of the Anglican and other religious bodies by the appointment of a nonconformist to some office within the Cathedral.

A copy of the solicitor's statement was sent immediately to Wilkinson, together with a handwritten, and difficult-to-read, letter from Dwelly. Some of the words are impossible to decipher but the strength of Dwelly's feelings of regret is clear: 'This post is the unhappiest I've had. All my hopes so carefully builded are dashed ... Not only is the blow to me the greatest I feel I have failed a friend for you so generously co-operated in my scheme. I am grieved and sorry and ashamed and unhappy for I so badly wanted you.'

For the writing of *Dissent or Conform?*, Alan Wilkinson had considered carefully the religious inclinations of his father and the Dean and found much in common. He described the Dean as being 'an innovative and a romantic genius who could be affectionate, seductive and pastoral, but also difficult and obtuse ... Dwelly's understanding of Christianity and the Church was liberal, platonic and mystical rather than credal, Catholic and sacramental, and this was exactly my father's a outlook. Dwelly was less interested in the Eucharist and the statutory services than in pioneering, devising and staging colourful dramatic pageants of worship, expressed with original ceremonial and accompanied by fine music.'

Ullet Road Unitarian Church, the church of Lawrence Redfern in Liverpool.

After the Unitarian Controversy and the Bishop's ruling, Dwelly no longer extended invitations to Nonconformists to play any part in the Cathedral services. After the Jubilee Service for King George V, one leading Free Church Minister, Nicol Grieve (not one of Dwelly's devotees), wrote to complain about the Dean's stance:

> In St Paul's Cathedral on Monday 6th a Free Church Minister took part in the conduct of the service, in the presence of King George V, and we may surely assume it was with his sanction at the very least. I understand that the Archbishop of Canterbury had urged that where possible the services throughout the land should partake in a like joint character. But despite the King's sanction, nothing of the kind happened in Liverpool Cathedral, not even at one of the many services held. For years many of us have been proud and grateful that among all other Cathedrals Liverpool seemed to be taking the lead, even on striking out new lines, to further the fact and witness of unity, but this honour is here no longer. She seems to be lagging behind others. Apparently Liverpool has faltered and turned back for some reason, the nature of which I can only guess ...

A group of Free Church Ministers met with the Dean in February 1937 to discuss with him their hurt at the obvious change of heart on the part of the Cathedral authorities. Handwritten notes were made by one anonymous minister after the meeting and preserved with Wilkinson's papers. The writer showed great respect and sympathy for Dwelly but was anxious that matters be taken forward:

Sir Frederick Radcliffe and Sir Giles Gilbert Scott, both close friends of Dwelly throughout his Liverpool years.

The Dean has been quite consistent all along, and I am convinced that he gives to these affirmations of unity that profound sincerity which he expects of all others who take part in them … So that I would plead earnestly and affectionately with Dr Dwelly not to be content with engaging the Holy War for the University of the Spirit on the one level only, though that may be a very high plane , as it always is, in his case, but to come down also to a more pragmatic level – the level of stimulating unity by such means as are still open to him, and us, working together.

Similar feelings were expressed by the Rev Dr John Pitts, of Myrtle Street Baptist Church: 'I was much impressed by Dean Dwelly's transparent honesty and obvious sincerity … From our point of view the situation is far from satisfactory. It seems as if the clock has been put back …'

At this distance of time, it is impossible to discern Dwelly's motives in taking such a hard line. He may have been protecting himself against legal charges; he may have been determined to keep faith with his Unitarian friends; he may have been determined to stand out for genuine ecumenical relations for all Free Churchmen within the Cathedral; or he may simply have been awkward. Whatever the truth of the situation, it was with Wilkinson's help that Dwelly devised a spectacular ecumenical event in the summer of 1937 for which the Cathedral was filled to capacity.

Dwelly had sent invitations to all the Free Church ministers and this was followed by a personally signed letter from Wilkinson on 16 April. 'Such an occasion of our

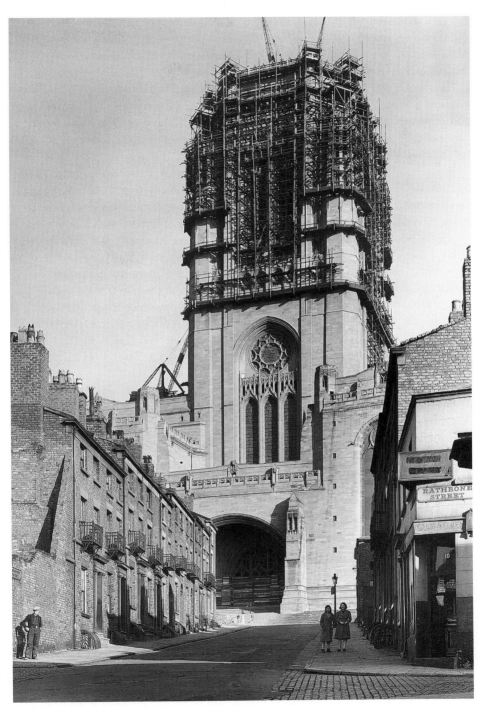

The unfinished tower covered in timber scaffolding.

united affirmations in worship, as that to which he invites us as Free Churchmen, should be regarded as a sincere and valuable opportunity. It forms a new kind of witness to the unity of our common faith. Further, as the service is to be broadcast throughout the Empire, it is unique. The listeners will number many millions.'

The service was held on 6 June 1937 at 4.15 p.m. and entitled 'Affirmations of those who call themselves Christians'. From Wilkinson's report it is known that 161 clergy and ministers attended and 1955 singers from churches and chapels throughout the Diocese took part. As many as 4,300 people wanting to attend the service could not be accommodated.

One person who had not expressed his intention of attending was the Bishop because he already had an engagement elsewhere. Dwelly with great political skill, or cunning, actually used Wilkinson to persuade the Bishop to be in attendance at the service. Dwelly went so far as to draft a letter, most of which was used in Wilkinson's letter to the Bishop. 'It is with real concern – indeed, even with a dismay – that I learn that you will not be present ... You may reckon my own sense of its importance when I say that I can think of no engagement so important that I, personally, would not myself rearrange in order to be present. You, my Lord Bishop, have a place in the Free Church thought in England, which is unequalled. There is no Bishop to whom Free-Churchmen look with greater hope and confidence in this matter of Christian unity, than to yourself.'

In a hand-written letter on 8 May, the Bishop assured Wilkinson of his presence at the United Service.

Looking back on the situation after fifty years, Alan Wilkinson was to write: 'How ironic it was, in view of the history of Anglican–Free-Church relationships over the centuries, that a Dean needed to use a Non-conformist go-between in order to communicate with his Bishop, in order that both might express publicly a degree of Christian brotherhood for the Free Churches which they found so very difficult to express in their personal relationships with one another.'

Sir John Reith himself, Director General of the BBC, took considerable interest in the service and met the Dean to discuss possible future arrangements. Wilkinson gathered hundreds of written responses to the event and he quoted one Methodist Minister who reported on 'a simple brotherliness and utter lack of any spirit of condescension, ... the real bond of unity. On my left was a little deformed Pastor, humble, unordained and almost poor; opposite me was a Salvation Army Officer; behind me was the Bishop. One felt that there had never been anything quite like it since Gentile and Jew first mingled in the early Church.'

A radio broadcast by Howard Marshall entitled 'The Church in Action' appeared in the Listener, 14 April 1937. The broadcast gave important insight into much that the Cathedral community was attempting to achieve and quoted Dwelly extensively:

On Easter Sunday I was in Liverpool Cathedral for the morning service. The cathedral was packed and two thousand people had to be turned away from its doors.

Actually I saw more than that Easter service in Liverpool Cathedral. I saw enough to convince me that there is work in progress at Liverpool which touches the hearts and minds of mankind. The Dean was good enough to take me over portions of the cathedral which are now being built by Sir Giles Scott and the laymen who support him. I don't usually care much about looking at churches; certainly I don't normally like climbing hundreds of stairs early in the morning. But this was very different. It was like stepping into a new Renaissance. Here once more were craftsmen and scientists and engineers and inventors working together. And the building was alive, growing like any other living thing, growing, as they would tell you there, to the glory of God.

This service was to me the least important of all the things I saw there at Liverpool, but it was a very beautiful service, unfolding itself like an exquisitely produced pageant of worship ...

I could see the purpose behind it. It was a flowering of worship, the arts combined, the grandeur of architecture, music, singing, design, the vision of the poet, the craftsman and the mystic – all combined as the response of the Christian to the redemptive fact of Christ.

Forgive me, then, if I return to the unimportant fact that I personally found it rather overwhelming. This does bring us to an important distinction; for the Dean said to me: 'It is perfectly clear that we have to provide for two quite distinct classes of people – those who are liturgically minded – those, that is to say, to whom this Easter morning service appeals greatly – and the other class who don't want liturgical services but instead something very simple and related to every day life.'

At Liverpool they do cater for both of these classes of people. You may have your liturgical service exquisitely done, your singing and your symbolism. But also every Sunday night at eight-thirty there is a People's Service, where they have no choir, and a hymn or two is sung and this service is built round some social or international problem of the day. And the congregation communicates its views to the Dean. It is interesting to know that for this People's Service the largest congregation assembles. And out of it have developed groups – for example, a group of unemployed men who meet regularly at the cathedral on Wednesday afternoons to talk over not only the economic aspects of unemployment but the personal side of it. And out of this has arisen an interesting development.

The cathedral is interested in a school for the unemployed about twenty miles from Liverpool, where unemployed men can take a course, studying anything from six weeks to six months, finding out how to make the best use of their enforced leisure. When a man has been through this course he often gathers a group round him at one of the unemployment centres and the work has spread so much that unemployed men from areas as far afield as East Lancashire and the Potteries are anxious to go to the school.

I mention this at some length because it seems to me an important phase of the Church in action. And it shows, too, the function which is being fulfilled by

Liverpool Cathedral. The cathedral, in fact, is working like the leaven in the lump – quietly, and unostentatiously, but always active, co-ordinating the lives of people in the district, drawing them together, seeking a common and communal purpose relating all to an eternal truth.

It is a little difficult to explain activities which in a sense are rather abstract and certainly undefined. But the cathedral itself is the symbol of the work that is being done. In the cathedral you see the communal effort of men of so many varying talents – the architects and engineers, the craftsmen and labourers, the artists and scientists.

And here, if I may quote the Dean again, is the purpose behind it all. For as he said: 'Many of the problems of the day would be solved if the outlook of artists and scientists could be fused into one creative vision. And as with the actual building of the cathedral so with the life of the diocese and the City in which it stands. Here again you have so many different forms of endeavour – different kinds of business being carried on – every sort of activity of man. And all the time at Liverpool Cathedral men are looking for the unities in these various manifestations of life.'

Perhaps this also may seem abstruse; and I admit it isn't easy to explain but it does seem to me to be religion in action.

I asked the Dean what he meant by unities and he quoted me this example. 'Well,' he said, 'we had an extremely difficult time when we were trying to deal with the problem of what our responsibilities were as a community to the man who was unemployed. We tried to find out what various sections of the community thought about it. And we found it was almost impossible to get them to meet on common ground. For example, it is only natural, I suppose, that Trades Union representatives and the employers of labour shouldn't see eye to eye. So one day we invited the Bishop to gather them all together. At first, of course, they were all tied rigidly to the outlook of the groups to which they belonged. One group would be opposed to public grants, another group would be suspicious of training the unemployed and so on. But gradually, out of our discussion, one vital truth emerged: it was that we all had responsibilities for the unemployed man's personal welfare. Here was a unity. Here was one human fact upon which we were all agreed. And this representative group felt that actually all the other issues didn't matter and that now they had found this common cause of agreement they could work together perfectly happily.'

Well, there are unities of that kind everywhere, if only we can discover them and act upon them. And that's what they're trying to do at Liverpool Cathedral. They'll tell you there that they can give you very few definite answers; but they can go out with you and seek the true principles by which your attitude to life should be determined. As the Dean said: 'One of the great difficulties is that so many people are seeking answers to their problems – definite answers – and they expect the clergy to give them a lead, so that parsons are frightened into producing solutions and taking up attitudes. Nobody can say that we ought to do this or that. What the Church should offer instead of answers is community seeking. The cathedral is for ever looking out and searching for signs of the coming of God in the mind and purposes of his creative creatures and as the cathedral is for ever searching it is for ever rejoicing – it seems as though joy cannot die. We are prepared to go out together to find the eternal truths.'

The Dean went on to explain other ways in which the cathedral was working out the application of religion by co-ordinating – by drawing together – various phases of life and giving people a sense of sharing in the activities of the cathedral as well as in the actual growth and development of the building itself. 'All through the summer,' he said, 'thousands of people go over the cathedral, and, of course, and we have our own voluntary helpers whose job it is to interpret the building to them. We try to make them feel that cathedral worship is not just a matter of what the parson is doing in taking the prayers or what the choir is doing. But here, in this worship, you have the whole of the arts and crafts represented – the glass workers, the sculptors, the engineers and inventors and so on. And we try to get them to feel that their own job is represented in this offering of worship which contains work from so many different sections of the people.' And then the Dean added something which seemed to me very important. 'There is no true act of worship,' he said, 'without an offering of mind or will or experience. Our work is to gather the affirmations of our time as they are to be found in every walk of life.'

And so we went on to discuss worship and the Dean said that this was the pivot of everything. 'We affirm,' he said, 'the thing that is worth while, and in affirming what is worth while we shall be able to get into touch with the spirit, the quality of life which makes the worth while thing; and so it will be easy for us to approach him who is the creator. I know of only two walks of life from which affirmations never come, and these are walks of life where money and position are given for themselves and not for what they can give the community.'

'And so,' the Dean went on, 'as our groups are seeking contact with people of all kinds, we discover the unities, the worthwhile things – the creative spirit, if you like – and we come into the cathedral to affirm these things. We will affirm in a special service, for example, what one branch of science has discovered for the good of humanity or the beauty that certain artists have brought into people's lives And in affirming these eternal principles, these creative activities, we believe we are helping to prepare for that new spirit which we are persuaded is coming into the world.'

Then the Dean showed me some of the forms of service used in the Cathedral. There was one with a special service written by John Masefield called Kinship with the Sea. Then the remembrance services held right through the week, in which there is a reading from the Bible and then a reading from a secular author. In one week I found quotations from such a variety of authors as Wordsworth, A. N. Whitehead, D. H. Lawrence, Edward Carpenter, and T. E. Brown. I found also mentioned in the services Isaac Newton, Florence Nightingale, Robert Burns, W. G. Grace and the Lancashire cricket crowd.

So you see in Liverpool Cathedral they range widely through life. And they have something to offer all conditions of men. Some of you may not agree with the way the cathedral authorities set about the job. But I can imagine that others will be saying: 'Well, why aren't there more cathedrals and more churches of this kind?' . . .

I asked whether something couldn't be done to break this organised machinery of the church. 'I'm afraid not,' said the Dean. 'The trouble is that the taskmaster is the victim of the machine that he himself has called into existence. Worse still, his machine must not fail. It cannot afford to fail. This is unlike the method of Christ, whereby an acceptance of failure is essential, as it is with the artist and the true scientist. Don't forget that John Bunyan said that the Valley of Humiliation is the most fruitful of valleys. Unfortunately centralised and organised religion doesn't agree with John Bunyan . . .'

Their outlook at Liverpool is very simple. As the Dean summed it up to me it is this: 'With all its faults the cathedral is the encourager of goodwill. It attempts to establish an actual communication of friendship with men who seem to be moving in bewildered ways and, as far as possible, to give them support, understanding, sympathy and encouragement.'

Owen Pittaway, Clerk of Works, Dean Dwelly and Sir Giles Gilbert Scott.

CHAPTER TWELVE

In time of war

W HEN THE CONGREGATION ARRIVED at the Cathedral for the morning
service on 3 September 1939, they read a sombre message printed at the head
of the service paper: 'Because of the evacuation of the children of the choir the daily
services in the Cathedral will be non-choral. The congregation is asked to sing with
full heart and voice all the music of the Sunday Services.' During the latter years of
the nineteen thirties excellent progress was being made on the building itself and
year by year the great central tower was rising and the central space started to give
evidence of the huge area soon to be added to the worshipping area of the Cathedral.
Meanwhile in Europe, German troops occupied the Rhineland in 1936; by the end of
1937 Hitler was re-arming Germany; and Austria was overrun in 1938. The nineteen
thirties were tempestuous days for the Dean too, as the Cathedral experienced brilliant experimental services which pushed forward the horizons of Anglican worship,
as well as episodes of bitter and destructive conflict.

Just as the morning service was commencing on that September day, Prime
Minister Neville Chamberlain broadcast the news to the nation that Britain was at
war with Germany. Dwelly and the Cathedral were preparing themselves for whatever might happen as they sat after the first hymn 'O God, our help in ages past, our
hope for years to come', and listened to the words of The Hallowing wherewith the
first Christians accepted the trial of their faith 'though it be tried by fire'; 'wherein
ye greatly rejoice though now for a season, if need be, ye are in heaviness.' In his
fifty-ninth year, Dwelly led his Cathedral company through six years of war, during
which the port of Liverpool withstood night after night of heavy bombing. Scars
remain even now, sixty years later.

At the 8.30 People's Service Dwelly himself was the preacher and by great good
fortune a typescript of that sermon still exists, one of only half a dozen sermon texts
to be preserved in the building. I do not think anyone would judge it to be a great
sermon, but it is a remarkable insight into the preaching style of the man and worthy
of being recorded here in its entirety.

Bishop Albert Augustus David and his family before his retirement.

DWELLY SERMON, 3 SEPTEMBER 1939

I would like us at this first service after the announcement of the great decision to begin, as I hope you and I will continue in these days, counting up the causes for which we have to rejoice and I would like the first word of the hymn we are going to sing to be the keynote which marks us all with a definite stamp of our belief in God and in the magnificence of Liberty. It is not of prayer that I would speak to you – your own hearts will dictate your prayers during these days. My duty is to remind you that the Church came into existence with a shout of joy, with a note of triumph, with a rejoicing in tribulation and so we will begin this our first service in the time of war.

'Rejoice, O Land, in God thy might.'

'Being justified by faith we have peace with God. Let us wait upon the peace of God. Let us joy in the peace of God, through Jesus Christ, in whom we have access by faith into this grace, our most sure ground, wherein we stand. Let us set our hope in God. Let us rejoice in the hope of God, triumphing even in our troubles, knowing how trouble produces patience; patience produces endeavour; endeavour produces character; character produces hope; hope putteth not to shame. And the peace of God shall keep our hearts and minds in Christ Jesus. Rejoicing in hope, being forward to honour one another, never letting zeal flag, maintaining the spiritual glow, steadfast in the hour of trouble, serving one another as though serving the Lord himself. Attending on prayer, that the thought of encouragement, promoting steadfastness and hope, may lead us to wait upon God who inspires steadfastness and encouragement. In him shall all peoples find hope. May the God of all hope fill us with all joy and peace in our faith that we may abound in hope in the power of the Holy Spirit. Blessed be the God who hath begotten us again unto a living hope.'

The reading which I have had printed for you this week is from the first century – probably about 50 to 80 A.D. Most of this you will recognise as coming in your own New Testament but the letters of St Paul and St John come down to us in many forms. They are what are known as manuscripts. It is as if you wrote to a friend on a very valuable piece of parchment and wrote, 'Our King on the first day of the war, said this,' and you write the words which you heard him say to his country and to the world, and each one of you wrote what you heard him say, and then these papers were discovered a hundred years later and each one would be a little different but together you would all be giving the main purpose, the main meaning, you would all give the same strength – giving thoughts though the phrases would be different. The one thing which the King said on the first day of the war was, 'The liberty of which God has given us is at stake for all civilization. It is for us to declare afresh our belief in it, so to rejoice in this most precious thing that in our very faithfulness we become calm and say, No, no. Do not destroy liberty.' These are not the actual words of the King, I will read them to you later, but the tenor of it would perhaps be something like that because that is

the tenor of the King's message. It is a sudden calling up of this sense of the great
value of a very precious jewel: it is a sudden calling up of the spirit of all Britons
saying, 'This treasure we will keep and we will not allow it to be destroyed.'

You will find here a word which for the early Christians meant everything. You
will find it is repeated again and again. They are very clear in their minds. Their
faith is based on past experience. So many people think that faith is something you
live and look forward to. For them – and their sufferings were worse than we have
ever known – for them, faith was based on their experience and so the hymn
singers and songwriters of their day would say how the Lord had blessed them.
How he led them out of the wilderness: how he fed them and cared for them, and
so they continued to give thanks, 'For his mercy endureth for ever.' Blessed be
God for his mercy. You see what I am trying to give you – I want you to catch
this thing for this is the basis of the early Christian faith, the habit of blessing.
Blessed be God who has given us eyes to see. Blessed be God who has given me
a country that can feel for other people who are suffering. Blessed be God who
has given it me to live in a day when the whole of humanity feels, and it is willing
to feel to the uttermost. Now this is a habit I want you to get please. Will you
agree? When you go to bed will you please think of the many blessings you have?
We may never meet again at eight-thirty but we will remember that at the eight-
thirty service we were never preached to – we just talked of our experiences and
so now you have to be calm. I cannot give you calm, but I can tell you the way
to be calm, and the way to be calm is to say Blessed be God who has given me
strength. Blessed be God who has given me peace. I will preserve it. I will keep it.
Blessed be God who has given me feeling for others. I will exercise it. I will not
bother about myself.

If your Cathedral is to do the work which she has hitherto done, I must be able,
as day by day I come here, I must be able to recall that the people of eight-thirty
are linked together by habits. Again and again I have said to you, I do not bother
about your prayers, your prayers will arise out of your own heart. You will pray
all right and you will pray as God would have you pray if your heart is calm your
purpose set. It is the habit of lessing that will put you right so that you cannot help
praying. Say tonight, Blessed be God for Old England. Blessed be God for my
country. Blessed be God for our Empire. Blessed be God for the human heart.
Blessed be God for the Germans who may not say it aloud or hear it said. Blessed
be God for the freedom that shall be his. Blessed be God for the overflowing heart
of the German that shall yet overflow again. Blessed be God that persecution shall
end. Blessed be God that the days of oppression are now measured and will pass.
Blessed be God for this great hope.

And now you can add to that, and this I want you to do. Put it on a piece of
paper, write to me what are the things we ought to bless God for next Sunday and
we shall bless God for them corporately, thus shall you build up strength that will
enable you to endure – calm endurance. That is how St Paul and St John built up

the Christian Church – they rejoiced in their tribulations. Now let us read these sheets I have had printed for you. Let us not bluff anything, let us not hide anything. If those bombs come tonight – don't let us become emotional – for these are facts you have got to face and so you need to be calm for the sake of those in your house and here lies calm for you, the peace of God. Blessed be God for the peace of God; for the peace of God shall keep your hearts and minds. 'Rejoicing in hope, being forward to honour another.' And when we say 'Blessed' we mean the German people too – we must not confuse the German people with the Nazis. There are two words which the King used and which we will remember, 'resolutely faithful'. He also summarised the 'ultimate issue' – the ultimate issue. That the peoples of the world shall not be kept in bondage of fear. And now as I think his boyish lovingness calls forth greater reverence than is demanded by the King, let us stand as I read his message to you ...

God save the King.

After you have gone home tonight, after the Cathedral is closed, we shall take all the treasures that are here and they will be hidden away – this is our duty for they are not ours, they have been given to the Cathedral that future generations might see and love them and find in them links with the past, that they may know the faith in which we have been venturing. There are many secret treasures here of which few of you know – some of them not because of their intrinsic value (they would fetch very little in a pawnshop) but valuable beyond all count because of their associations – the lovely things of Chavasse, the Bishop who boldly and bravely saw a great Cathedral in his heart and mind. I could go on enumerating them: tonight we shall gather all these treasures and secretly put them away in safety. We shall not forget them, we know them and so you, my good friends, must put away, hide as one of the greatest, if not the greatest treasure that is yours, the word peace, the secret of the Christian faith – the peace of God which is yours. Wrap it up, keep it calm. Let nothing disturb it. Blessed be God for the peace of God. There will be a day when we shall bring that word forth again and rejoice in it, for it is not only for the heart and mind, but for England and the whole world, the greatest and most precious jewel of the crown of life. We are not disturbed because one person dares to try to destroy it. Of that our most treasured possession we now constitute our selves the Guardians – the guardians of this peace. Pacifism is no word for us now. It is the great secret treasure toward which we of this Cathedral secretly, steadfastly, faithfully, calmly set our will.

You were so good that Sunday evening a while ago when we rallied together around the peace ballot. You and I rallied around it and the cry was heard by England, by the whole world, that cry of England's great vote for peace. Oh don't regret it men and women. I know what you are saying in your hearts and I say it myself. We helped to hinder armaments and that men took advantage of us. It failed but it is not the failure of struggles for the right that are any cause for shame. We shall often fail our great efforts for the right, but we shall not ultimately fail.

It is necessary that we try and try again, but there are times in between when the secret must be held, guarded, preserved, kept warm within the secret confines of your soul, waiting for the moment when it will burst forth with glory. And so as I superintend the putting way of the treasures of this place will you let me hold in my mind and heart that you are enthroning peace and pledging yourselves to be guardians of it. Guardians who are at once ready and indeed happy to do whatsoever the country bids us to do. We cannot, we ought not, we must not contract out of society but humbly, above our fears and hopes, accept the situation, and having accepted it, breathe deep the peace of God. This then I call you to do tonight, to accept the situation. This is not an intellectual proposition I am putting before you. The most practical way we may help each other is to accept the situation and be calm. You know when you have failed your friend, failed your home – you have not wanted to become fussy – it is because you have not accepted the situation but when the moment comes that you do accept the situation, then you begin to breathe deeper and stand again calm. My greatest gift to you tonight is this – I bid you accept the situation, accept the privilege, accept the honour and be the guardian of the peace of God in the human heart. Have I made it clear to you so that I know when you go home to night you are accepting the situation?

I am so anxious to give you this secret of calm. I know it is a gift you can give to Liverpool. I know you can take it here tonight from God. Let me be very homely for a second time. How often have you said, 'Oh well, I accept the situation.' That is only a free and a homely way of saying something which is very serious. And so tonight I want you to accept this great honour which God has given to England, the honour of doing that which he called one by the name of Moses to do. For forty years Moses had been feeding sheep in the wilderness. For forty years he had been making money. He had a lot of sheep and so he was a wealthy man and one day he saw a fire and he heard a voice, 'Whom shall I send?' and he said, 'What shall I say?' And the voice answered, 'Let my people go.' When you hear over the wireless that Hitler has commanded that no German people may listen to any foreign wireless message or they will perhaps be killed or certainly put into confinement – when you hear that command, you at once say, 'These people are oppressed' and God speaks to England as he spoke to Moses and he says, 'Come I will send thee. Let my people go.'

There is another story, the story of the birth of our religion. Do you remember how it speaks so simply of a little child, a little baby who is called the Prince of Peace? Do you remember how the angels called it the Prince of Peace, peace on earth? Still only a baby even in our day. Do you remember how the Hitler of that time commanded that they should be brought forth and slain? Do you remember the Hitler of that time speaking to the wise men, 'Come and tell me where he is so that I may go on and worship him.' Was there ever a closer parallel between the so-called statesmen trying to deceive, Herod trying to deceive, Hitler trying to deceive. When Chamberlain in his greatness went forth last year and risked his

The temporary wall as backdrop to a wartime service.

own reputation and dared then to make a great trial of the faith of this man Hitler: Dared to trust him, dared to take his word, dared to bring his words home written on a piece of paper and written by Hitler – dared to wave it in London and say, 'I have brought back peace for all time.' It was only a little baby. Chamberlain did so bravely and nobly but he was dealing with a statesman not unlike Herod. And when Hitler entered Czechoslovakia he slaughtered the innocent and the Bible tells us the story of how an angel appeared to these wise men in a dream and a voice said, 'Go back another way.' And so it seems to me that God speaks to the Church and to every peace organisation in the country, to us who have worked so hard for peace 'Go back another way.' Will you accept that? Today we go another way. Do you remember the last thing in that story how the mother then wrapped the little baby in swaddling clothes and hid her secret away and by night fled into Egypt? Hid away the treasure until that time when Herod was dead. Even so, like for the wise men of old we worship the Prince of Peace for we place before him our treasures this night, this our Cathedral, the spirit of this Fellowship, the heart that can feel and know what suffering is, the readiness for the myrrh if these bombs say so. Gold, frankincense and myrrh. So shall we prepare for that great day which yet shall be, the day when we shall shew forth the gospel of Christ, the day of which the angels sang and the world has sung again and again, the great day when we have all shared in the fellowship of his sufferings and shall see the reign of the Prince of Peace, but until that day we hear the voice, 'Follow me.'

One other story let me remind you of. A magnificent story that steels the heart and makes you ready to rejoice and bless God that the human heart is capable of such things, that you and I are so made that we can feel and see beyond the far horizon, beyond that which the natural eye can see – magnificent it is that you and I are so made that we can dare to the uttermost and be calm in the doing. Holding the Peace of God. The night when he accepted the situation his friend Peter came and said, 'Lord shall I smite?' And Jesus said, 'The cup which my Father hath given me to drink, shall I not drink it?' And he set his face steadfastly towards Jerusalem and his friend later wrote of him, 'Who for the joy that we set before him endured the cross.'

Fellow Christians – you and I have often sung of the cross, we have talked of the cross – it has become just a word with us and to some it has become something that is hung about them and looked at but we are about to experience it. Are you calm, can you accept it? Will you accept it? Will you rejoice in it for the joy that is set before you, the joy of giving freedom and peace to the world? Shall we accept it? 'For the joy that was set before him, he steadfastly set his face towards Jerusalem.' Will you? I will, cheerfully. And to that end, the habit of blessing God, the habit of rejoicing in blessings and everyone will find peace and calm. You won't fail – don't worry. For in that moment you will find the Peace of God has calmed your hearts. I am not pretending that in these moments you won't have any fear. Don't bother about it. It is the bondage of fear that matters. Fear is sensitiveness and that is worth everything to you. You don't want to be insensitive. It can make you sensitive to the Peace of God and to the Unknown and so shall we be able to rejoice in the peace of God. When Jesus calls us o'er the tumult he says, 'Follow me.' 'And he set his face steadfastly for the joy of giving peace to humanity.'

If I have not made it clear to you, please write to me. I am your servant. Bless you, you fine things.'

217. 'Jesus calls us o'er the tumult.'

There are four main types of Cathedral material which help to throw light on Dwelly during the war years: the service papers, a series of typed reports from someone

King George VI and Queen Elizabeth with the Dean during their wartime visit.

identified only as W.J.; the unwritten memories of a small group of members of the Cathedral company; and the letters, particularly a rich sequence of letters from Sir Giles Scott, his wife, and even his elderly mother.

As was the case in many other densely populated cities, children were evacuated to less potentially dangerous areas of the country. The Cathedral choristers attended Liverpool Institute High School for Boys and the whole school was evacuated to Bangor in North Wales. The evacuation was not to last long and the choir was back to something like normality by spring of 1940. This was before the serious bombing of Liverpool began, but once it did begin it was devastating and the Cathedral from the air was a prominent and significant target. The Chapter was informed by the Air Ministry that 'at certain times the roofs of the Cathedral looked, from the air, like a lake and might be a guide to hostile bombing planes at night.' Dwelly had himself been flown over the Cathedral by the Royal Air Force to see for himself the highly reflective pale green patina on the copper of the roof. As a result of this warning, 4,798 square feet of roof were painted battleship grey at a cost of £139.18.10.

Although there was little structural timber in the Cathedral, the roofs of vestries, Lady Chapel and Chapter House were of timber and the whole of the unfinished tower was encased in timber scaffolding and highly susceptible to attack from incendiary devices. Fire watching teams were established with the result that the unfinished Cathedral was never left, day or night, and the Dean himself began to spend more and more of his time in his Cathedral. He wrote a letter to his mother-in-law on 5 December 1940:

My dear Mrs Darwin,
    Thank you for understanding my anxiety to have somewhere prepared for Mary in case our home becomes impossible. As my night duties at the Cathedral increase I feel the anxiety more. Indeed, apart from what we feel, it is my duty to keep Mary fit, so that when the war is ended she may be alive and able to do the marvellous work she does, giving in her gracious pleasantness new hope and new life to women. There is no other woman in Liverpool city or diocese who does this as Mary does. It is a duty to the need of our country to keep her in safety that she may live to do it.
    I am also thankful that we agree that when Mary feels the moment has come – not until then – she can feel she has her own place ready for her to sleep in safety, and from which she can come and continue her work which makes you and me so proud of her. I am deeply grateful to you for understanding that Mary is the best and only judge as to when that time has arrived.
    Again thanking you for being ready thus to share your home.

We do not know the exact date when Dwelly took up permanent residence in the Cathedral but we do know that he made an inhospitable little room half way up a steep flight of stone spiral steps leading towards one of the east end turrets into his bedroom. The Cathedral's heating system does not extend even now to this room,

The Dean with Admiral Percy Noble.

which can be bitterly cold throughout the winter months and baking and airless in the summer. At the start of the war there was one tiny window with less than a square foot of glass and it could not be opened. By the summer of 1942, the lack of ventilation must have become a serious problem and he looked to the architect for some remedy. Scott was not able to hold out much hope of improvements and wrote on 12 June 1942: 'I have your letter of the 9th inst. Regarding the window in your room in the south-east turret. I am afraid this matter cannot be dealt with at such short notice, as the treatment must be carefully designed and it means a good deal of cutting away and working of a considerable amount of new stone, all of which takes time, apart from which, I am doubtful whether a license could be obtained for doing the work now at all! However, I will go into the question and have a drawing prepared showing what I think will be the best treatment. It may, too, be desirable to reproduce the same treatment in the corresponding position in the opposite turret.'

Today, anyone who stands in the courtyard at the east end of the Cathedral and looks up to one tiny window high up on the south side will wonder why it is out of style with the corresponding window to the north. The answer is that Dwelly got his own way and, every day throughout the summer, I used to open 'Dwelly's window' as soon as I climbed up the steps to what was formerly his bedroom, then Archive Room and latterly Education Officer's office.

To the amusement of the choir boys, a wardrobe and a bed appeared in the Song Room and Hugh Reid, a Rodney Street consultant and friend of the Dean, took up residence. Edgar Robinson, Choral Conductor, moved into a vestry, and Christine Wagstaffe took refuge in an airless and claustrophobic area at one end of the old sacristy safe. Owen Pittaway, Clerk of Works, and his wife and sons were also to be found camping out in another part of the crypt. In the autumn of 1940, on four successive nights high explosive bombs landed dangerously near to the building, doing some damage to stonework and totally destroying some of the windows on the south side. Although the new central space was not really ready, a number of services had to be held there until the smashed windows letting in wind and rain had been boarded up. Dwelly himself must have felt that it was important that the events of those historic days be recorded for posterity and the first of a series of detailed reports is preserved in the handwriting of Christine Wagstaffe.

On Sunday 8th September 1940 the great congregation could not assemble in worship within the Cathedral. The roads approaching the Cathedral were still closed by the military and civil authorities. The work went on of removing and sorting of the debris of the houses opposite, wrecked by the bombs from the enemy aircraft on the night of September 5th, particularly the house numbered 31 Washington Street, presented to the Cathedral by Mrs. Swift Neilson, under the total collapse of which the Cathedral electrician and engineer George Siddall and his wife Milly and child Christine had been buried and done to death. Nevertheless the high altar of the Cathedral was prepared as usual for that which in ancient times of trouble was called the most comfortable Sacrament of the Body and Blood of Christ. The Dean, attended by Canon T. A. E. Davey, Canon C. F. H. Soulby, Mr. E. C. Robinson, deputy organist, Mr. H. F. Goodlad, steward, and Mr. G. Blade, sometime chorister, proceeded by the south aisle, rain falling on them through the broken windows as they went, to the choir crossing, and there began the Office of Mattins.

As the Apostles' Creed was being said a heavy burst of gunfire was heard and the sirens in the city gave warning of an air raid. The Dean repeated the ancient salutation 'The Lord be with you' and thereupon directed those with him to repair to the deeper shelter arranged for them by the Building Committee in the part of the Cathedral not yet used for worship, while he fetched from the high altar the vessels and the Bread and Wine.

This they did, but without the music of Bach's Fugue in C minor which Mr. Robinson had planned to play during the procession up to the high altar. It thus came about that the faint sighing of the wind in the broken windows, the grim wail of the sirens, and the answering challenge of some bagpipes heard in the distance were the only musical accompaniments of the movements of taking the sacred vessels to the place of celebration.

Those who had proceeded to the underground shelter were there joined by Mr. A. H. Harrod, Dean's Verger, Mr. Normal Blundell, gentleman of the choir, Miss I. C. Wagstaffe, Dean's Private Secretary, and Mrs. Jones, acting head of the Cathedral cleaners. Mr. O. Pittaway, clerk of the works, after the Dean had greeted him, withdrew to supervise and control the duties on which he was then engaged in his responsibility in the new part of the building. Mr. T. Douglas and Mr. W. Sands, vergers, were also prevented from joining in the service, it being theirs to devote themselves to watching and salvaging.

Underground beneath the great space that proclaims the majesty of God a rough bench of unshaved wood such as the carpenter might find useful was adapted as an altar, and on it the vessels were set out as best could be.

Here the Dean finished reading Morning Prayer, and used the form of intercessions set forth by the Lord Archbishop for this day of National Prayer. Here special remembrance was made before God of all who had suffered in the war, and the Dean particularly named George, Milly, and Christine Siddall, as was the more appropriate and to the mind of the congregation seeing that all present had known and well liked them for a long time.

After the silence that could be felt the Dean proceeded to offer unto God the place wherein we were assembled and ourselves – 'The will of the Lord be done'. 'Blessed be God.' Then were remembered 'those to whom the place is most dear' and 'those who have given of themselves to the building of it, particularly Sir Frederick Radcliffe and Sir Giles Scott.'

The Dean then proceeded with the Holy Communion, and every person present received, as hitherto in the expression of their mind making no complaint to God over the damage to the Cathedral building nor prayer for deliverance from any further sacrifice to which the Cathedral company might be called, but making thankful remembrance of all who have given the vision of beauty in stone and wood and of all who in those days were suffering to preserve the love of beauty and truth; and once again was remembered the man, the woman, and the child who had contributed graces of the soul to the Cathedral life. So in this impressive manner we lifted our hearts, with angels and archangels praising the majesty of God, and rejoicing in the truth of Jesus.

Just before the Dean pronounced 'The peace of God which passeth all understanding keep your hearts and minds' the city sirens gave the signal of the passing of the raiders.

Shortly afterwards, while entertaining the congregation to tea in the old wooden refectory outside the east end of the Cathedral, to recover them from the chill wind which blew through the shelter during the service, being now joined by Mr. O. Pittaway, the Dean gave instructions that a full record of the service and the circumstances in which it was held should be set down by members of the Cathedral company who were present, while memory should still be fresh and accurate.

And seeing that this was the first celebration of the Holy Communion in the new part of the Cathedral under the Central Tower the Dean instructed Mr. A. H. Harrod to mark on the floor a Maltese Cross where the primitive and rough carpenter's altar had stood.

The pressures under which the Cathedral community was operating in 1941 must have been extreme, but the Scott correspondence with Dwelly indicated that Cathedral spirits were high as the Dean presided, twenty-four hours a day, in his dangerously vulnerable building. Scott himself clearly stayed overnight in the Cathedral many times and found the experience exhilarating.

28 February 1941

... and now I must thank you for ... That wonderful hospitality of yours on my last visit and the music, how I enjoyed it all. I bet Wren did not have such fun when he was building St Pauls. Any way I am quite sure he never wandered through his Cathedral in a dressing gown on the way to his bath!

27 March 1941

What fun we had, and how right royally you entertained me. I am very grateful to you and Chris for all the trouble you take. I certainly do enjoy every minute of my visits, and only wish Louise was able to experience one night in a Cathedral, as my descriptions arouse her enthusiasm, but the real thing has got to be experienced to be really appreciated. Living actually in a Cathedral is a wonderful experience for which I have to thank Hitler as well as yourself.

There are members of the present Cathedral company who, nearly sixty years later, have a strong appreciation of Scott's sentiments. The Cathedral experience early in the morning, or in the evening when the public have departed, is very powerful. Throughout history, few deans can have had the opportunities Dwelly had to wander freely through a half-built cathedral and dream of future plans. I have been told that at one time, if Dwelly was not formally part of a service, the choir boys played 'spot the Dean'. He was always there somewhere – often high up on a gallery, savouring a fresh vision of the building.

The close friendship between the architect, designer of the building, and the Dean, designer of the patterns of worship, was important to both men. They were close in age and, though Scott was a Roman Catholic, the liberal mystical Christianity of Dwelly suited Scott's temperament. In an undated letter, Louise Scott thanked Dwelly for everything he had been doing for her husband: 'Thank you for your letter and mostly for taking care of Giles. I felt if he were with you and in the Cathedral nothing could happen to him only pleasure – We are so lucky to have you – I feel I ought to add a lot more to that last sentence but you know what I mean and would like to say.'

Scott was working in London in an office surrounded by devastating bomb damage during the worst days of the Liverpool May Blitz, but he wrote to thank

Dwelly 'for your kind thought in keeping me informed of the terrible ordeal all of you and my great big child have been going through.' (17 May 1941)

The enigmatic WJ has left posterity a full report of what was the Cathedral's most miraculous escape of the war. The account is a succinct, factual report of the events of a dreadful night and the final paragraphs are a brilliant evocation of Dwelly's feelings.

Tuesday, May 6th. 1941

A determined attempt to destroy the Cathedral was made by German airmen in the hours of darkness this morning.

The great building had a providential escape from serious damage and came out of its ordeal by fire and high explosive with little more than scars to add to those caused in the air attack last Autumn.

A system of fire watching at nights has been in operation here for many months, regular patrols being maintained throughout to ensure that any fires due to incendiary bombs are tackled without delay. Imagine, then, the feelings of those inside the cathedral – including the Dean and Mr. Pittaway – when, on Sunday night and again last night and the early hours of today, hostile planes singled out the building for attack – circling high above in the moonlight as anti-aircraft guns fired away in an effort to drive them off. On Sunday night large numbers of incendiaries fell, ringing the Cathedral, happily without doing any harm.

Then came this morning's attack. Once more incendiaries were dropped near the east end. It is fortunate that the wooden refectory which did duty at this end for many months was no longer there. It had in fact been removed precisely on account of this new danger of fire from the air. Incendiaries were also dropped on the north side and here again the value of foresight and precaution in this matter was demonstrated. To guard against the possibility of an incendiary entering the great organ, a wire casement had been placed against the north aisle window at the back of the organ. A fire bomb did actually hit this casement last night but, being unable to penetrate, did no harm. The organ was saved.

An oil bomb capable of setting fire to the largest of buildings dropped at the west end of the Cathedral and a fire raged among the contractor's offices, the setting-out shed and the machinery for sawing up the massive pieces of sandstone which go into the fabric of the Cathedral. Much spare timber also went up in flames. The wind at this time was due east and carried the flames away from the cathedral; otherwise the temporary west wall would undoubtedly have suffered. Tongues of flame reached across St James's Road. High explosive bombs followed the incendiaries. One fell into a basement of a house opposite the contractor's yard. A delayed action bomb fell at the feet of the steps of the King's Porch and was removed today by a bomb disposal squad. Two small high explosives fell just outside the Lady Chapel and while not removing a single stone of the fabric, chipped the steps in numerous places and caused hundreds, even thousands, of incisions in the walls.

The remarkable escape, however, was from perhaps the largest bomb of all. This fell on to the roof of the south-east transept. It broke through the roof and entered the space between roof and ceiling of the transept. By a happy chance, the bomb struck the top of the inner brick wall supporting the central beam of the transept and, being deflected outwards, burst through the outer wall and exploded in the air high above street level. There the chief damage was to the tall windows of the transept. The havoc that would have been occasioned had the bomb been deflected inwards so that it penetrated the ceiling to explode inside the transept is best left to the imagination.

It may be placed on record that the Dean, subsequently continuing his tour of the Cathedral and finding that the tower had survived and was undamaged, tried to sing the 'Te Deum'. In his own words – 'It simply would not come.' Just then a blackbird somewhere in the trees outside burst into song. That was the 'Te Deum'.

The bird's liquid notes heralded the dawn. The raid having ended, the watchers at the cathedral were able to look over the city to watch the light rising in the east. The fires left by the raiders were still blazing against the duck-egg blue of the western sky.

Before the outbreak of war, there had been an expectation that, when the newly completed central space of the Cathedral was revealed after the taking down of the temporary wall, there would be a service to rival the Consecration in pageantry and splendour. This was not to be, and yet the services on and leading up to Sunday 27 July 1941 must have been even more powerful because of the wartime tapestry against which they were being played. Dwelly's choreography had received world-wide acclamation, even when he had only a third of the planned Cathedral in which to work – the vast new central space provided spectacular new possibilities.

The new area was formally received by the Principal Chapter, the Archdeacons and the General Chapter. The following day, Edgar Robinson, the Choral Conductor, and the choir boys climbed all the spiral steps to take up their positions on the Corona Gallery, high above the new space and only a short distance below the under-tower vaulting. On Sunday morning after Morning Prayer and Holy Communion, the Chairman of the Building Committee led the Chapter from the older part of the building into the new, 'passing over the place in the crypt where during an enemy air raid a celebration of Holy Communion was begun in the older part of the building and completed at a carpenter's bench in the new; consummating the consecration in the choir at the first Eucharist in the Nave.'

The words of the order of service revealed the rich significance of all that was happening, as well as Dwelly's mastery of dramatic words and actions:

The Dean shall say: And first let us rejoice in his assurance, knowing that his promise never fails. Wheresoever two or three are gathered together in his name, there he is in the midst.

A space of silence shall be kept. Then the Dean shall continue:

It is written, Then came Jesus and stood in the midst, and said, Peace be unto you, And they worshipped him.

A space of silence shall be kept.

Children shall enter into the procession. When the leading boy has crossed the threshold, the reading shall continue:

Jesus called unto him a little child, and set him in the midst and said, Verily, I say unto you, Except ye become as little children, ye shall in no wise enter into the kingdom of heaven.

WJ reported on the effectiveness of the simplicity of one of the most significant moments – the Bishop's lone walk through his Cathedral, reminiscent of his walk in 1924:

There was drama in the very simplicity of the ceremony that followed. It had been prepared for by a magnificent rendering of the 'Te Deum' by the choir. The Bishop, Dr. David, who was the bishop of the Consecration, alone and unattended was on that day in the presence of their Majesties, walked 'the whole length of the fold of the Temple of God', passing down through the sanctuary, the presbytery and the choir towards the Nave. A tall, ascetic-looking, silver haired man, Dr. David was a stately figure as he measured the distance carrying his pastoral staff. All eyes were upon him. As far as is known, no other bishop has participated in two dedications of this nature.

The weekend was marked by a typical handwritten Scott letter of thanks: 'Phew! What a wonderful weekend, but especially I wish to thank you for what you did for us, in the midst of all your arranging and organising you still gave the impression that we were the only people you were attending to! Well it was one of the milestones of my life, and a weekend that I shall always remember.'

Dwelly had this special ability to make people feel their particular personal importance. He could be devastating in his criticisms but, by and large, he affirmed people and the role they played within the Cathedral, and former choristers tell many stories of the way in which they felt the full focus of the Dean's personal attention.

A particularly good example of Dwelly's brilliance with an individual was recorded over a year later when Sir Giles Scott's eighty-eight-year-old mother made her first visit to her son's masterpiece. From her letter to Dwelly we can imagine how Dwelly helped make the visit so special for her. Here again is the Dwelly so devoted to his own mother, and the Dwelly who was a devoted friend and priest to so many people throughout his ministry.

I was so overpowered and dazed on Monday that I feel I must try to thank you for all your kindness and thought for my comfort. If I had been the Queen you could not have been more careful with me.

I shall never forget my visit, which I had been looking forward to for years, but of late I had given up hope as I was not feeling well enough to undertake it. I was not a bit over-tired it was marvellous. It was a feeling of pride and astonishment to me to think my own son could produce such a glorious building and I am a proud mother of him personally and of his work. (He is rather nice isn't he?)

Dwelly must have visited Mrs Scott in the Lake District in 1942 and the old lady reported to her son that, 'We both talked so fast we had to stop now and then to take breath!'

Dwelly was attentive to the care of one elderly lady but equally attentive to the nightly needs of dozens of the inhabitants of some of the little streets near the Cathedral who nightly took shelter in the crypt, having more confidence in the protection provided by the Cathedral than by the inadequate and uncomfortable street shelters. Dwelly had realised that a little stealth was necessary to persuade the City Council into action. As Scott wrote, 'Your suggestion of putting this letter before them and saying "How am I to answer this?" is grand.' The subsequent letter gave posterity a wider vision of the Cathedral community sheltering each night from the bombing.

I had occasion recently to visit the public Air Raid shelters under the Cathedral. I went on two consecutive evenings, during one of which an 'alert' was on. I must confess I was shocked to find the conditions under which these poor people spend the night. They were lying about, covered with old dirty bedding, on rough boards supported by a few bricks. Old men and women, children of all ages – a pathetic picture, that made me feel I wanted to cry. Surely something better than this can be done?

At no point were Dean and Chapter responsible for the building work until the completion of any new part of the building – everything before was the responsibility of the Building Committee. However, Scott's letter showed just how deeply Dwelly was concerned with all of Scott's plans. A letter on October 1941 contained Scott's early ideas for the rebuilding of the area on the river side of the cathedral and a beautiful sketch signed by Scott. There were conversations about the chancel steps, pulpit, catafalque, west end, congregational chairs. Scott's admiration for the ways in which Dwelly was using the new Cathedral was obvious in all his letters; he clearly welcomed Dwelly's comments and felt it important to keep him in touch with all developments. Few deans can ever have played so significant a role in the planning and building of their Cathedral and I cannot think that any architect had greater admiration for his dean than Scott for Dwelly.

It is important not to give the impression that Dwelly's war years were insular, with the Dean residing in his Cathedral and wholly preoccupied with its internal affairs. Several isolated fragments preserved in the archives point towards what appears to have been a significant element in Dwelly's priorities. A piece of prisoner of war mail, 'Examined by Censor', was posted from Canada on 6 December 1940. It was written to Christine Wagstaffe by Fritz Wolff at Internment Camp R, Ottawa, Canada and expressed his profound gratitude to two men who had been attempting to secure his release. 'Whether I get freed or not, I shall never be able to thank him [Professor Budden] fully for his deeds – (nor the Dean).' Wolff was released and enabled to carry on with his studies but he, and his wife Lotte, maintained contact with Dwelly for some time. Lotte wrote on November 1942: 'This is out first wedding anniversary, and I do so much want to write to you; but my heart is so full that I am searching in vain for words to express what I feel. Somehow you are the invisible third in our marriage. It was you who blessed us, joined us together, and this your blessing is always with us, in our hearts and minds and sanctifies our union.'

There was an internment camp for over two thousand German nationals in Huyton, near Liverpool. From there in August 1940 Dwelly received a letter from Walter Simon, a German Jew: 'I thank you most heartily for your kind suggestion to take steps for my release ... I thank you once more from the bottom of my heart.' Ronald Jasper in *George Bell – Bishop of Chichester* wrote of Dwelly's communications with Bell, an old friend, on the matter of the indiscriminate internment of aliens. Dwelly briefed the Bishop on the situations in Huyton and on the Isle of Man before Bell raised the matter in the House of Lords. Dwelly and Bell visited the Huyton Camp on 19 July 1940 and Dwelly followed this with a long letter to the Bishop's wife:

20 July 1940.
   Dear Mrs. Bell,
   I feel it is only fair to give you a picture of what your Bishop has been able to achieve. His first task was to win the confidence of those in authority. He is the only bishop who has gone into the camp and, when there, (been) welcomed. I had no fear once I could get him into the mess. Success is a poor word – triumph sounds gaudy and yet the New Testament speaks of it.
   After that came the feeding of the hungry souls. I would have given all my savings for this sterile, publicity – seeking Church to have seen the sight I saw. There they stood, with heads leaned forward, with brows of broken faith in England beginning to quiver again – the signs of paralysis yielding, as when the masseur looks up with delight at the recovery of the feeling of pain – ideas of mighty men of learning and service to the community began to open again.
   George didn't know – he couldn't see. He was seated, like Jesus, just hearing them and asking them questions – as humble as that. He, the boy of the hope of the future and they the old, old wise men – men of deep learning in every depart-ment of life, the great discoverer of the Zeiss works, the mightiest gynaecologist today – so I might continue. And until now the Church has talked outside and a written its letters to *The Times*.
   I felt it only due to you, who can show our gratitude and better than we, that you should know I have seen the biggest thing done by your Bishop in the toughest of circumstances.
   Yours ever, F. W. Dwelly

August 1940 brought a telegram:

The Dean of Liverpool Tell Leopold Lindemann am in touch with his wife will apply on ill health grounds and David Oliver that sickness application has been made Please assure Heinz Daniels everything being done Stop Accept my sincerest gratitude: Abramowitz ++

Though there is no further material preserved in the Cathedral archive, the character of the existing pieces suggests that they were not isolated cases.

Liverpool Cathedral has not been encrusted with memorials as have St Paul's, Westminster Abbey and many of the ancient cathedrals, but on the wall of the South East Transept there is an imposing memorial to Admiral Sir Max Horton, Commander-in-Chief of Western Approaches, 1942–1945. A smaller panel in the North Choir Aisle commemorates his predecessor, Admiral Sir Percy Noble. Both men, but Max Horton in particular, were to become close friends of Dwelly. The Horton Memorial includes the words, 'My Lords Commissioners of the Admiralty recall that you assumed command of the Western approaches at a time when the United Kingdom was subjected to the most grievous attacks in its history. On the successful issue of the Battle of the Atlantic depended the future of the Empire and

The Dean with Sir Alan Tod. Sir Max Horton and Sir Leonard Slatter follow down the steps.

The formal election of Clifford Martin as fourth Bishop of Liverpool in 1944.

indeed of the World.' In one sense, Liverpool Cathedral had become the parish church of Western Approaches, with Dwelly as parish priest. As Horton was later to say when made a Freeman of the City, 'And there are others I would mention who deal in a different plane and helped in a different way. I refer, in particular, to our Dean of Liverpool Cathedral. What mortal man or priest could do to aid and strengthen us, he did – and I wish publicly to acknowledge the debt I and Western Approaches owe to him.'

In his book *Max Horton and the Western Approaches*, Rear-Admiral W. S. Chalmers was to write,

His sincerity and genuine desire to support the church in every way brought him into touch with Dr. F. W. Dwelly, the Dean of Liverpool – 'I often take the pulpit; the Dean is so difficult to resist,' They became close friends, and would dine together frequently in Horton's flat on the top of Derby House. They would talk late into the night on subjects which the Dean prefers should remain confidential, but we can be sure that Max with his scientific mind was seeking the Truth not only for his own enlightenment but for that of his country. He encouraged the idea that the officers and men should look upon Liverpool Cathedral as the 'Parish Church of the Western Approaches'.

On 18 April 1945 the Dean wrote:

My Dear Admiral,
   ... And I want again to thank you for the way you read those passages in the

Cathedral – old Lord Derby writes to me: 'The reading moved me more than I can ever remember.'

It means more than you can imagine that you should take the leading parts on those occasions, for well we know that we owe our very life as an island to the unconquerable resolve that you, Sir, have inspired, impelled and compelled. Thank you for allowing your cathedral to symbolise this without expressing it.

Yours,

F.W.D.

As part of the service of thanksgiving and celebration for Western Approaches Command, Dwelly, with Sir Percy Noble and Sir Max Horton, climbed to a high gallery on the South West Transept to make commemorative marks on the stone which were later carved along with an inscription.

The service papers continued to be bound in annual volumes, although not every service was preserved – one can only assume due to paper shortages. There are few papers for what might be called the standard services but there are a very large number of 'specials' – services created specifically for a group of people within the city or the nation, or to commemorate particular events. It is interesting simply to examine the titles of some of the services during the summer and autumn of 1942:

14 June, The United Nations' Celebration;

5 July, Commemoration of the Establishment of the Air Training Corps;

12 July, The Girls' Training Corps;

19 July, Sailors' Day;

26 July Annual Thanksgiving for the Consecration of the Cathedral;

26 July, National Fire Service;

3 September, Day of Prayer In Time of War;

13 September, Civil Defence Wardens' Service;

20 September, The Royal Air Force Commemoration of the Battle of Britain;

October 1942, the Celebration of the Prayers and Praises of the Western Approaches;

11 October Service for Rangers and Guiders;

25 October The Assize Service;

1 November, In Thanksgiving and Prayer for the Czechoslovak People;

13 December, Day of Mourning and Prayer for the Victims of Mass Massacres of Jews in Nazi Lands (bound alongside this service is one in Hebrew and English issued by the Office of the Chief Rabbi and the Jewish date appears on the Cathedral service paper – 5th Tebeth, 5073).

There can be no doubt that Dwelly, in his great unfinished 'citadel', throughout the most desperately difficult war years, ensured that the new Cathedral Church of Christ in Liverpool served the people of the district whether they be the residents of the city or the thousands of servicemen who were to pass through the port. The Scott letters give evidence of an almost boyish energy and delight in life even during the darkest days of the blitz. Residential life in the Cathedral cannot have been easy; he was no longer a young man and had to climb thirty-four stone steps to his bedroom, which must have been a stifling oven on hot days, and there is no evidence that he had any form of heating in the depths of the winter. The strain must have been immense.

The choir in the stalls and Cross Guild in procession through the Cathedral.

CHAPTER THIRTEEN

Dwelly the liturgist

I N JUNE 1945, right at the end of the war, the Archbishop of York, Cyril Garbett, preached at the annual Cathedral Builders' Service. Some of the words of his sermon lead conveniently into the crucially important topic of Dwelly the liturgist:

> Our cathedrals cannot accept too high a standard for the art which should be used as a handmade to worship.
>
> And the same principle applies to corporate worship as well as to the actual building and its adornment. There was a time when there was fear of using music, colour and beauty in the worship of the Church. It was thought that they might distract the worshipper from the solemnity of the act in which he was engaged. The result was that art became increasingly secular when it found the doors of the Church closed to it. But we are learning again that all art should be consecrated to God, and that it should be used as an offering to Him. Here directed by the skill of your Dean, your public worship has been made beautiful with music and symbolism. In the richness of their colour and pageantry, as well as in variety and originality, your services hold a place of their own in the Anglican Communion. The prayers and praises used are both old and new; the worship of the historic liturgies is combined with prayers for modern needs in present day prose. And the appeal is made to the eye as well as to the ear, and to the imagination as well as to the intellect.
>
> Your services have become popular in the best sense of the word. By this I mean that they have significance not merely to a small group of faithful who have been brought up to appreciate the ordinary worship of the Church, but to the people of a great city. Men of different professions and interests find in the special services of the cathedral worship which is relevant to their daily work and problems. Our worship should not be separated by a gulf from the ordinary life of ordinary men and women. No cathedral should stand apart from the life of those who live around it. It is nothing less than a disaster when Christian worship is treated as remote and cut off from the concerns and needs of the average man. Through worship the secular should receive consecration. As our Lord took the ordinary

Dwelly the choreographer.

food and drink of his day, the bread and the wine, and used them for the highest spiritual purpose, so he will accept and consecrate through worship the time and labour of all who use rightly skill of brain and hand. This is the purpose of some of the great civic and special services held here, they are opportunities of dedicating all public and private work to him, and in return those who worship receive from him ideals and help which will raise their daily business to a higher level.

We must never forget that worship becomes selfish and self-centred if it begins and ends with the building in which it is held. If here on special occasions the offering of work is made to God, it is made so that day by day it may be done for his glory. Worship within the house of God should flow over into daily life. Your cathedral with all its majesty and beauty would stand as a rebuke unless its influence spread far and wide. Its splendour and dignity should stir the citizens to emulate it in their public architecture. The wide spaces within it for prayer and contemplation should make them eager to provide without, spaces of peace and quiet for tired men and women and for the play of little children. The colour and glory within it should encourage attempts to bring more colour, variety, and interest into the lives which are spent in drab and dreary streets. Its splendour as God's Temple should be an incentive to provide houses for those who are meant to be human temples of God, but who herded into slums rarely attain to the greatness of their calling.

Easter celebrations.

As year by year you proceed with the completion of your great task, see that the life of the city grows too in harmony with the Cathedral which will be its crowning glory; so that men may say of the city as well as of the Cathedral that those who are responsible for them are seeking to express in their architecture, their order, their life and their worship something of the loveliness, the fellowship and the joy which are found only in perfection in the invisible City of God.

The choir in the stalls with the probationers in cassocks standing in front of Ronald Woan.

Nearly twenty years after the Archbishop's sermon, Dwelly's successor as Dean of Liverpool, Frederick Dillistone, wrote an unpublished article to mark the centenary of Dwelly's birth. A section of that piece provides an admirable foundation upon which a consideration of Dwelly the liturgist can be written:

> ... it was Dwelly who saw the possibilities for dramatic movement provided by the aisles and open spaces and who gathered around him a team of young lay men prepared to be trained for distinctive roles in ceremonial processions.
>
> This he achieved by forming a Guild of ex-choir boys. His earlier active participation in the Boy Scout and Boys' Brigade organisations provided him with a pattern by which the attainment of adolescence did not automatically imply severance from the movement. So, in the Cathedral, choirboys, even after their voices broke, continued to serve as maces, collectors, cross-bearers and above all as participants in the ceremonial processions.
>
> The result has been that no feature of the worship of the cathedral has been more impressive than that of the colour and orderliness of these processions. What may at first sight seem an undue proportion of the total floor-space has been kept open for free movement: the absence of fixed pews has made it possible to relate movements to the particular character of whatever service is being solemnised.

Far too often in English Cathedrals and churches fixtures for seating purposes have made it impossible for there to be dignified movement; and, indeed, to cover the floor with ugly pews or undistinguished chairs merely detracts from any proper appreciation of the building's architectural beauties ...

I do not know whether in designing the building Scott realised that he would make dramatic patterns of movement possible. Nor do I know whether Dwelly consciously interpreted their function in the total act of worship. It is nevertheless the case that the neo-Gothic design made movements possible in a way they never could have been in a traditional Gothic interior. The absence of pillars and a screened division between the choir and the rest of the building helped: the siting of the Lady Chapel apart from the main axis of the Cathedral also helped: in particular the provision of substantial arches on either side of the High Altar made it possible for processions from the eastern retro-Choir to enter the cathedral through the Sanctuary in full view of an assembled congregation. Simultaneously other processions could advance down the aisles on the north and south of the choir while, after the opening of the great central space, a procession could come from the west along a central aisle which was always kept some eight feet wide.

Dwelly recognised the immense importance not only of movement but also of colour. Those taking part in the processions wore robes designed to harmonise with the distinctive shade of the red sandstone out of which the fabric of the cathedral was constructed. Dominant colours selected for choir and guild were russet, green and that belonging to ripening ears of corn, all suggestive of the life of nature in the countryside. Dwelly, it seems, was eager to bring symbols of the natural order into the worship of God as Creator and this he tried to achieve through design, through colour and through movement.

Some time ago a Sunday paper carried the account of an interview with Martha Graham, the noted dance-teacher. She was born in Pittsburgh, the child of Scottish Presbyterian immigrants who would have found little place for dance in the life of religion. Though she broke away from her early ties, she continued to regard herself as religious and often turned to the Psalms for inspiration. 'The heavens declare the glory of God ... there is neither speech nor language'. In the interview she said: 'I often hear that, when I'm on stage. To my mind there are three sorts of language. First of all there is the cosmic language, which is movement. Next there is the language of sound. And finally the language of particular words. As my father used to tell me: "Movement never lies".'

The idea of three kinds of language is intriguing. Dwelly enjoyed considerable success in devising verbal forms which he used in prayers and sermons. These brought the vocabulary and concerns of the period 1925–1945 into the special services which he arranged. But only rarely did these seem still to be relevant and appropriate from 1950 onwards. He recognised the great importance of music but was in the main content to leave the expression of its language to those possessing specialised knowledge and experience. It was, however, in the first realm, 'the

The Dean receives his honorary degree from Liverpool University.

cosmic language of movement', that he made his outstanding contribution to worship in the Church of England. To some degree processions had been intro-duced into Anglican liturgical worship as a consequence of the Oxford Movement but generally speaking those followed mediaeval patterns, with a focusing of atten-tion on that which was being carried or on the dignitary whom the procession was designed to honour. In Dwelly's vision, all the participants had a part to play in the dramatic framework which, like that of the great cosmic recurring cycle, encircled the words and actions of the service itself.

A panel of glass, not part of a window, made by Alfred Fisher, a member of the Cross Guild.

In 1954, the University of Liverpool conferred the honorary degree of Doctor of Laws on the Dean and the citation spoken at the ceremony formed an appropriate public acknowledgement of the importance of all of Dwelly's work:

Into the superb edifice of the Cathedral which makes infinity so imaginable for us, Dean Dwelly puts animation which is always equal to the dignity of its purpose and its environment. Here is the great master of liturgical English to give perfect expression to the bidding prayer. Here is the creative artist of colour and of symmetry to convey that majesty and wonder of creation and revelation which made the stars of the morning sing with joy. Providence was indeed kind to all worldly impresarios when it made Dr. Dwelly a dean and left secular pageantry to their inferior talents. He makes art the manifestation of religion and not religion the manifestation of art. He habitually confounds the vulgar heresy that sanctity is greater where elegance is less: but he equally defeats those who would reduce fine ritual to the level of the aesthetic mummery of pagans and atheists. Dwelly, the Cambridge Master of arts, is always in harmony with Dwelly, the Oxford Doctor of Divinity.

As has been noted before, the service papers from the Dwelly years have been bound in annual volumes and preserved in the archives. From 1926 to the outbreak of Second World War, the vast majority of the papers have been preserved; from 1939 to 1953, by and large, only the special services have been retained. There is material for the most detailed textual examination of most of Dwelly's finest work, and there are substantial numbers of black and white photographs which form an accurate visual record of moments from the services. More important still are the memories of some of the people who actually participated in the services themselves, with those of one man particular being of supreme value. Ronald Woan, a choir boy and eventually Master of the Choristers, was associated with the Cathedral for fifty two years, and without his vivid memories this chapter could not be written.

Central to the study of Dwelly the liturgist must be the service papers for which he was responsible, although the success of any service depends not only upon the words but upon the whole staging and choreography of the event. The theatrical imagery is not inappropriate and it does not suggest falseness and unreality. A great service can be an intellectual, emotional and physical experience within a carefully designed setting.

Even before an examination of the content of a big Dwelly service, attention has to be given to the service sheet itself. The Cathedral not infrequently receives little parcels of old service sheets after the death of a former member of the congregation and I remember keeping a couple of papers from the early fifties of services which I attended and wished to preserve. Starting with the Consecration Service in 1924,

Dean Dwelly after the Judges' service.

these publications reached very high standards and went far beyond simply printing the words. In almost every case, high-quality cream paper was used, matching the colour of the choir surplices; in the most important services red and black were used in the printing of the text; font and type-size were well-chosen and layout was spacious. In the design of many of the papers, Dwelly drew on the skills of Edward Carter Preston, who designed many of the front covers as well as providing a set of

Princess Elizabeth descends the steps of the Rankin Porch with Dean Dwelly.

superb woodcuts to adorn the publications. The best of the service papers are works of art in their own right and must have had a powerful influence on the worshippers in the same way as the windows, stone, woodwork, music, vestments and choreography. Particularly impressive service papers include Consecration, Foundation of the Dean and Chapter, Solemn Entrance in Time of War, Enthronement of the Third Bishop, Western Approaches, and RAF Coastal Command.

This book is intended to be the biography of Dwelly and Dwelly the Liturgist is but one chapter in the whole story. There is a danger of this chapter becoming overlong because there is so much material which might profitably be examined in detail. I am having, therefore, to be highly selective in my choice of services for close examination and I am adopting what is to me a helpful categorization of services in order to try to give a reasonably comprehensive examination of this vital aspect of his work. Services will be considered under the headings of regular Sunday services; major services essentially for the Cathedral community; special – often referred to as vocational – services for a wide range of secular organizations; services planned for other churches.

On a standard Sunday, one without a special service, a simple service sheet gave basic details of the four services of the day. Morning Prayer, a Choral Matins, was celebrated at 11 a.m. and followed by a said service of Holy Communion in the Lady Chapel at 12.15. Choral Evensong was at 3.00 and the Congregational Service at 8.30 was preceded by half an hour of organ music. There is no evidence to suggest that anything other than *The Book of Common Prayer* was used for any of the Communion services, none of which was choral. Morning Service certainly kept close to this book and each service opened with what was called The Preparation, in reality a sung Introit from the choir. A single Psalm was sung to Anglican Chant, 'Te Deum' to a setting, Benedictus to Anglican Chant. Evening Prayer followed the same principles but mostly without Psalm or Nunc Dimittis. Organ music for Evening Prayer and Congregational Service is listed, though there is no mention of the morning voluntaries. These services were such as might have been experienced in all the Cathedrals of England and in thousands of parish churches able to maintain a choral tradition. What made the Liverpool services different were the processions and the choreography; the sheer size of the worship space, and the splendour made possible in what was to become the largest Cathedral in Britain.

On the great festivals of the Christian Year, the Dwelly liturgical genius was given a wider canvass, with such success that the Easter Day service was broadcast by the BBC for many years. The Christmas Carol Services brought into play all the musical expertise of Harry Goss Custard, Organist, and Edgar Robinson, Choral Conductor; outstanding musicians who respected Dwelly's musical good sense, and appreciated the musical opportunities which Dwelly's leadership gave them.

The Easter Morning service papers are preserved without gaps from 1926 through to the end of Dwelly's ministry. The 1926 service is similar in its material to that found in any church using *The Book of Common Prayer*: three hymns, Easter anthem, three psalms, 'Te Deum' to a setting, Benedictus to Anglican Chant, prayers, an anthem by Bairstow and a sermon. By 1934, the service had become far more elaborate and the service paper carried a short explanatory preface:

> The Festival of Easter calls for an offering of worship so wide and manifold as to justify the provision of a form of service added this day to Holy Communion and Morning Prayer. It begins with a selection from various sources of suggestions on which we may prepare ourselves for that which is prepared for us. Then in a procession from East to West, moving to the Resurrection hymn, is brought an ancient threefold Easter Blessing answered by the Hallelujah Chorus. Then follow readings from the Epistle and Gospel, with the Easter Anthem between them, leading up to the 'Te Deum', the Creed, and Collects. After an Anthem, written for the Cathedral by John Masefield and Martin Shaw, come our now familiar Intercessions, set to the music of Palestrina; the Sermon, with Hymns before and after; a reminiscence of the Eucharistic Thanksgiving, and, when the final blessing has been given, a Hymn sung by the congregation only as the Dean's company leaves the Choir.

All the words of the Preparation, sung by Cantors and Choir as the congregation remained seated at the opening of the service, were undoubtedly of Dwelly's choosing:

This is the day which the Lord hath made, we will rejoice and be glad in it. All praise be to God. He hath redeemed us. He hath burst the bonds of death. He hath smitten asunder the tomb of sorrow. He hath flung wide the gates of Life. Christ the King of glory, the Alpha and Omega, hath overcome the sharpness of death and hath opened the kingdom of heaven to all believers.

In thy Resurrection, O Christ: let heaven and earth rejoice. Praise be to thee, O Christ.

O come let us worship. I seek him in whom my soul delights. In his presence is fulness of joy.

Let not him who seeks cease until he finds, finding he shall wonder, wondering he shall enter the kingdom, and having entered the kingdom, he shall rest.

I seek for Jesus in repose, when round my heart its chambers close.

Abroad and when I shut the door, I long for Jesus evermore,

With Mary in the morning gloom, I seek for Jesus in the tomb;

For him with love's most earnest cry, I seek with heart and not with eye.

It came to pass as the disciples bowed their heads, a young man said unto them,

I know whom ye seek, ye seek Jesus, he is not dead, he is risen.

The Lord is risen. The Lord is Risen, indeed. Alleluia!

Then were the disciples glad when they saw the Lord,

And all the sons of God shouted for joy.

The archive papers contain music for some of these words, printed from the manuscript for Easter 1931, and after the final 'And all the sons of God shouted for joy' there is an instruction to other musicians: 'Drums – long roll – low A – to be followed without delay, Organ, Bells, Trumpets, drums and choir all together "Jesus Christ is risen today".'

After the Bishop had delivered the Easter Blessing from the chancel steps, the congregation stood as the choir sang the Hallelujah Chorus from Handel's 'Messiah'. Easter Anthems, A Vaughan Williams 'Te Deum', Martin Shaw's 'They buried him, and then the soldiers slept', and The Intercessions sung to music by Palestrina, made up the rest of the choir's contributions to the service. Creed, Versicles, Collects, Sermon and two more hymns formed the rest of what must have been an unusual and exciting variation of Morning Prayer.

Having created what appears to be a most effective service for one year, Dwelly was not content simply to repeat the same words the following year, though he retained the same principle of producing an elaborate and extended Morning Prayer. The archive papers for Easter Day 1933 contain precise details for the ordering and movement of four processions. The 1934 paper has been heavily marked (with typical

Dwelly thick, blue pencil) for Ralph Dawson, the Bishop's Chaplain, giving him details of the Bishop's movements throughout the service.

The Central Service for the Foundation of the Dean and Chapter, while containing elements of a formal legal nature, also provided ample opportunity for Dwelly's inspirational and dramatic qualities. The Preparation, the true start of the main service, was held in the Chapter House where the Chapter Clerk read a greeting from the Archbishop of York, a greeting which made reference to the special qualities of worship associated with Liverpool Cathedral: 'Liverpool Cathedral has won a distinctive place in the life of our church, not only by its splendid beauty, but by the varied expression which it has already given to Christian aspiration and worship. I have no doubt that it will, under the new conditions, continue to lead the way in freshness of devotional expression and in helping the new world of our time and the times that are to come to offer its best in the service of Almighty God.'

Dwelly welded this short legal prelude effectively to the main service out in the Cathedral largely through his use of the choir and the processions. Having led the Bishop to the Chapter House the choir, while standing outside, sang two verses of the hymn, 'The Church of God a kingdom is'. After reference to Bishop Chavasse, the choir sang a single verse of 'Let saints on earth in concert sing'. This distant music would have been audible to the whole congregation, so making them feel a part of the Preparation, and the choir's procession from Chapter House to stalls was accompanied by their chanting of biblical verses, one of Dwelly's conflations. The words themselves were wholly appropriate and the chanting of the words as part of an entry procession would have created a strong atmosphere of expectation and devotion.

The choir singing of the hymn 'Come down O Love divine' to Vaughan Williams' tune 'Down Ampney' preceded the main procession of ecclesiastics. It is interesting to note that 'The Dean's Own Sea Scouts' were part of his entourage – young men from the First Windermere Troop which he had founded over twenty years previously. The main part of the service began with the choir singing the anthem 'They buried him, and then the soldiers slept', specially composed for the day by John Masefield and Martin Shaw. Quite typically, the music played a prominent part in the service but its appropriateness to the moment militated against any feeling that the service was a splendid concert. There were two further anthems to the music of J. S. Bach; the Supplication was to the music of Palestrina, versicle and response, with three versicles sung by a single treble voice. The service made effective reference back to the Dedication of the Lady Chapel and then to the Consecration itself by surprisingly but appropriately singing verses from 'O Come, all ye faithful' and 'Jesus Christ is risen today'. 'And did those feet in ancient times', 'All people that on earth do dwell' and 'O worship the King' gave ample opportunity for congregational participation, while back at the Chapter House the choir singing of 'O for a faith that will not shrink' must have been a most prayerful, quiet ending to the whole service and mirrored the choir's singing of 'The Church of God a kingdom is' at the Chapter House at the commencement of the service.

The whole event exemplified Dwelly's strong structural sense which enabled him to design an effective service. His skill with words enabled him to write a meaningful and memorable text. His choreographic sense handled the processions and general movement which the service demanded. His musical sensitivity greatly enhanced the whole and the worshippers at that famous service must have left the Cathedral with the sense that the Dean had once again revealed his imagination, his flare, his sense of drama, his unerring ability to conceive of a service which would relate powerfully to the worshippers.

There are so many brilliant Dwelly services that it is difficult to select a few for comment in this context, but a sequence in July 1941 are particularly significant in Dwelly's development as a creator of effective services: from that time, he had the use of the great new Central Space with all of its dramatic possibilities and he certainly made the most of the first formal entry into the new space.

> Then the Building Committee, by the action of their chairman, shall put the Dean and Chapter into possession of the new portion of the Cathedral, passing over that place in the Crypt where during an enemy air raid a celebration of Holy Communion was begun in the older part of the Building and completed at a carpenter's bench in the new; consummating the consecration in the Choir at the first Eucharist in the Nave. During the procession the choir shall sing the hymn:
>
>> Lord, thy glory fills the heaven;
>> Earth is with its fullness stored;
>> Unto thee be glory given,
>> Holy, Holy, Holy, Lord.

When the action of the chairman has been duly acknowledged and the formalities of entering into possession completed, the chairman shall take his place in the westernmost part of the Cathedral, near to where the Building Committee purpose the building of the great bridge of the Nave, and the Dean shall say:

And first let us rejoice in his assurance, knowing that his promise never fails, Wheresoever two or three are gathered together in his name, there he is in the midst.

A space of silence shall be kept.

Then the Dean shall continue:

It is written, then came Jesus and stood in the midst, and said, Peace be unto you. And they worshipped him.

A space of silence shall be kept.

Children shall then enter into the procession.

When the leading boy has crossed the threshold, the reading shall continue:

Jesus called unto him a little child, and set him in the midst, and said,

Verily I say unto you, Except ye become as little children, ye shall no wise enter into the kingdom of heaven.

In the middle of the pomp and formality of this great occasion, Dwelly's choice of words and movements were a memorable example of his liturgical genius.

Dwelly's work showed a strong sense of his awareness of the history of the Cathedral and this feature is prominent in another war time service, that for the Enthronement of Clifford Martin as fourth Bishop in September 1944. He was coming to a war-battered city and, even though it was an occasion for rejoicing, the service clearly acknowledged the devastation and loss of life through which the Cathedral community were emerging. 'At intervals in this Service silence shall be kept for a space with intention to seek the blessing of God on those bearing the burdens of the war, winning victories for the free spirit.' The service also made reference to previous significant occasions in the history of the Cathedral. The new Bishop's entry to his Cathedral was particularly poignant, a nice balance between the spiritual and the theatrical:

> At five-thirty in the afternoon the Bishop shall knock three times at the door which opens from the carpenter's workshop into the Cathedral church. He shall knock with the same ivory mallet that was used by the late King Edward VII when he laid the first foundation stone of the Cathedral. The Dean shall order the door to be thrown open.
>
> As the door is opened the Keeper of the Door shall say in a quiet voice the words:
>
> Do justly. Love mercy. Walk humbly with thy God.

These same words were used again most effectively at the actual moment in the service when he approached the Bishop's Throne.

> The Dean, delivering the Staff into the hands of the Bishop, shall say:
>
> With this Staff may the Lord give thee grace to do justly, to love mercy, to walk humbly with thy God.
>
> When the bishop is come to the throne he shall be asked:
>
> What doth the Lord require of thee?
>
> The Bishop:
>
> To do justly
>
> To love mercy
>
> To walk humbly with my God.

In the repetition of these simple yet profound statements we observe the artistry of the liturgist. The words and their use would have made an impact on the members of the congregation but they must have had a profound effect upon the Bishop throughout the service. The same would have been true as the Bishop made 'his solitary journey' from West to East in the Cathedral: it would have looked impressive, but the symbolic significance lifted the whole movement way above the simply theatrical.

At the Font, before he approaches the Nave of the Cathedral, the Bishop will call to mind the love of Jesus, how he took little children in his arms and blessed them, how of them he said – of such is the kingdom of heaven; and then he will call to mind the command of Jesus to the Apostles to go into all the world and make disciples, baptising them, a boy singing:

Alone, yet not alone, my God, I journey on my way; what need I fear when thou art near, O King of night and day.

The Bishop's lone walk was not accompanied by trumpets and loud music but by the simple anthem, 'God is spirit and they that worship him must worship him in spirit and in truth.' After his arrival in the Sanctuary, part of the service echoed parts of the service of Holy Communion with a prayer:

Almighty God, unto whom all hearts be open, all desires known, and from whom no secrets are hid; Cleans the thoughts of our hearts by the inspiration of thy Holy Spirit, that we may perfectly love thee, and worthily magnify thy holy Name; through Jesus Christ our Lord. Amen
Lord, have mercy;
Christ, have mercy;
Lord, have mercy.

One sequence of prayers was followed by very short Epistle and Gospel readings, the Epistle by the Bishop alone: 'I bow my knees unto the Father of our Lord Jesus Christ, of whom the whole family in heaven and earth is named, that you may be filled with all the fullness of God.' All the incumbents of the Diocese together read the Gospel: 'That same day at evening, Jesus came and stood in the midst and said: Peace be unto you. As my Father hath sent me, even so send I you: Lo, I am with you always.'

The Eucharistic focus was continued in a section of the service called The Ministry of the Word in which there were short readings from the Psalms, Prophets, Epistles, Gospels, and Catechism. Here was a service wholly suited to the occasion: dignified yet simple; using good music appropriately and sensitively within worship; a service created for a congregation all of whom were active within the Church in the Diocese; but most of all here was a service created for a new bishop at his enthrone-ment. There is no separate sheet giving details of processions and other ceremonial for this service, but there is for the consecration of C. R. Claxton to be Bishop of Warrington in 1946. At that service there were forty-one named members of the Cross Guild taking part and there is no reason to assume that the team in 1944 would have been fewer in number.

Towards the end of his life when Dean of St Paul's, Dean Inge, had expressed a lack of interest in liturgiology, likening it to stamp collecting, but there were voices firmly in support of liturgical developments in the mid-twentieth century. As Stanley Morison was to write in 1943,

The Anglican Dean's comparison of liturgiology with stamp-collecting implies scorn for the frivolity he thought recognisable in men who satisfied an appetite for ceremony-mongering and dressing-up while evading the real problems of Christian worship. It now looks as if the millinery and play-acting stage has been passed. Liturgiology can no longer be identified with a programme to restore public worship into conformity with such conventions as east-windows, oak screens, elongated chancels and four-poster altars. We are likely to find religious bodies looking forward, rather than backward; spending less time on the 'beauty' of liturgical worship and more on the task of rendering it congregationally efficacious ... Today there is a new realization by those who profess a religious affiliation that public worship needs to be made more vital for more people. Moreover, there is a new realization on the part of those who make no religious profession that the retention by the Christian religion of its present influence in this country requires the expression of its faith and worship in contemporary terms.

Stanley Morison's *English Prayer Books* was to have been the first of a series of books under the general title *Problems of Worship* to be edited by Matthews, Dean of St Paul's and Dwelly. For whatever reason the whole series of volumes, to cover the nature of Christian worship, the drafting of services, the provision of music, the building of the fabric and the furnishing of places of worship, was never completed, but one chapter in *English Prayer Books* was entitled Present Day Vocational Services and devoted to specific examples of Dwelly's work. Morison was typographical adviser to Cambridge University Press for over twenty years and Sandars Reader of Bibliography at the University.

The first Service for Seafarers must have been held in the Cathedral in 1924 and though the service paper no longer exists, those for services from 1925 to 1929 do. They are all very similar in character and might well have been termed 'mutilated Evensong'. Morison must have been reliant on Dwelly in his judgements on the services:

A fine congregation of officers and men of the Royal Navy paraded. The chaplains and choirs sang handsomely to the accompaniment of coughs from the officers and men. The select preacher faced a congregation whose attitude was respectful rather than attentive. The next year the same offering was made. The failure was equally plain. Somebody at the time disposed of the service by describing it as a function of which 'nothing real happened'.

Dwelly was entertained to lunch by some of the Naval officers after one such service and the conversations on that occasion led to a radical rethinking of the whole service using the experience and advice of naval personnel.

At a later meeting agreement was reached that there should be two prayers: the official one, read by Captains at sea, should first be read by a captain; and a second prayer, building up to the Lord's Prayer, should be said by all. Strings of collects were never favoured, but the thank offerings and petitions as drafted became a permanent part of the revised service.

In the course of years the Benedictions of the sea have increased in number, and in degree of correspondence with the vocations of the men. Thus the mainstay of the Service was what was said and sung by men with experience of ships and the sea. The choir was dispensed from the task of singing elaborate responses and the single anthem was relegated to a position in the preparation. The sermon gave place to a business-like gathering-together of reflections which culminated in the seamen's petition to God, for help in relating their whole life with beauty of the sea and all to His love and His providence.

Everything Dwelly had said was clearly to be seen and heard in the service but, for some reason, Morison's text of the service is not exactly the same as the text of the service for Navy Day 1943: there are slight differences of order. Comments made here apply to the actual service paper for the day and not Morison's book. By the

The Dean takes the choristers into the building site near the foundations for what was to become the Nave Bridge.

standards of today it would probably be thought rather long and full of words, but the relevance of all that was being said and sung remains clear and it carries the sure sign of Dwelly in its design and in its text. Music was well-used and was never decoration. The service opened with the whole congregation joining in the hymn which would have been part of the thoughts of every one present: 'Eternal, Father, strong to save'. From the beginning of the service everyone would have had a sense of personal involvement. Then the Thanksgiving, Dwelly's words spoken by the Chaplain of the Port, would have sounded wholly appropriate to all present.

Terrible and magnificent is the sea in its proof through the ages of man's courage and strength, his endurance, his stern self-reliance, his gradual mastery of sea craft, his widening skill in ship construction, his dawning knowledge of science, of astronomy, meteorology, and engineering; his inventions, recordings, questings; his gatherings of infinite sums of knowledge and resource, bringing into being the great fleet of ships that sail the oceans of the world today.

Magnificent the unswerving fortitude, the enduring loyalty, the selfless sacrifice, of the men of the Sea, who keep watch over the great sea lanes, Safeguard the true freedom of the seas, giving battle for the ultimate world brotherhood of mankind, with our sovereign Lord the King.

We of the British Empire and Commonwealth together with officers and men of the navies founded in sea tradition are gathered in our Cathedral church to give thanks to Almighty God for the Kinship of the Sea.

The hymn 'Praise, my soul, the King of Heaven' preceded the single reading from Scripture. The reading is typical of Dwelly and might have distressed the purists: he has joined together verses from different books of the Bible into one continuous reading, in some instances not even using complete verses. The original text appeared without explanation; the italics are mine:

The Spirit of God moved upon the face of the waters. *[Genesis 1.2]*

And God divided the waters which were under the firmament from the waters which were above the firmament. *[Genesis 1.7]*

And the gathering together of the waters called the seas. *[Genesis 1.10]*

The waves of the sea are mighty, and rage horribly: but yet the Lord, who dwelleth on high, is mightier. *[Psalm 95.4]*

He layeth the beams of his chambers in the waters.

He maketh the clouds his chariot, and walketh upon the wings of the wind. *[Psalm 104.3]*

His way also is in the sea, and his paths in the great waters; and his footsteps are not known. *[Psalm 77.19]*

They that go down to the sea in ships, and occupy their business in great waters; these men see the works of the Lord and his wonders in the deep: *[Psalm 107.23, 24]*

How he maketh the storm to cease so that the waves thereof are still: *[Psalm 107.29]* and so he bringeth them to the haven where they would be. *[Psalm 107.30]*

I was in the spirit on the Lord's day, and heard behind me a great voice. *[Revelation 1.10]*

And the voice was as the sound of many waters. *[Revelation 1.15]*

And I turned to see the voice that spoke with me. *[Revelation 1.12]*

And I heard a great voice out of heaven, saying: Behold the tabernacle of God is with men, and he will dwell with them. *[Revelation 21.3]*

And he showed me a pure river of water of life, clear as crystal, proceeding out of the throne of God. On either side of the river was there the tree of life, which bare twelve manner of fruits, and yielded her fruit every month; and the leaves of the tree were for the healing of the nations. *[Revelation 22.1, 2]*

Dwelly has succeeded in welding together a range of material from various Biblical sources, giving them a unity through imagery and cadence. He had made no attempt to use Psalm or readings set for the day in *The Book of Common Prayer*, which, though meaningful to regular attenders at Anglican services, might have made little impact on a high proportion of the congregation. There is usually a sureness in the Cathedral's choice of both hymns and choir music and 'The Anthem of the Sea' by Vaughan Williams to words by Walt Whitman is dramatic and exciting musically, as well as being relevant lyrically:

> For the sailors of all nations,
> Whom fate can never surprise nor death dismay.
> All brave captains
> And all intrepid sailors,
> And mates,
> And all that went down doing their duty.

The imagery around which the Benedictions were written was close to the lives and experiences of the sailor and able to focus the vocational minds of all present more effectively than most traditional prayers:

Blessed the unending beauty of the seas and oceans,
    The ineffable, wondrous colour of sky, cloud and sea;
    The birds, the fishes, the sounds.
    The view of distant coast and hinterland from a ship's deck,
    The breathless loveliness of a tropic dawn,
    The cold blue grandeur of the iceberg.

        Response: Blessed the Beauty of the Sea.

Blessed the calms of the ocean;
Blessed also the storms and tempests,
    Which throughout the ages have challenged man's strength,
    Cradled his skill,

Called forth his vigilance, endurance and courage,
His sacrifices of self for the common good.

> Response: Blessed every Sacrifice of Self for the Common Good.

Blessed the headland, the lighthouse,
The mountain, the Cathedral tower,
The point of departure on a long trans-ocean voyage.
Blessed the first sight of land,
The emerging of a mountain from the clouds,
The looming of the light of a city at night,
The flashing beam of a lighthouse,
The tree-tops rising over a clear horizon,
The land-fall at the voyage's end.

> Response: Blessed the Land-fall at the Voyage's End.'

The Lord's Prayer was followed by the whole congregation joining together in the prayer 'appointed to be used at sea', 'O Eternal Lord God, who alone spreadest out the heavens, and rulest the raging of the sea ...'

The hymn 'O Lord, be with the men who sail upon the lonely deep' preceded the sermon and then everyone joined in saying the prayer of Lord Nelson, containing sentiments wholly appropriate to such a great naval service:

> May the Great God whom I worship grant to my country, and for the benefit of Europe in general, a great and glorious victory; and may no misconduct in anyone tarnish it; and may humanity after victory be the predominant feature in the British Fleet. For myself, individually, I commit my life to Him that made me, and may his blessing alight on my endeavours for serving my country faithfully. To Him I resign myself and the just cause which is entrusted to me to defend. Amen. Amen. Amen.

The service ended with the singing of the hymn, 'Onward Christian Soldiers', and the Blessing.

This might be an appropriate moment to hark back to what an American newspaper had to say about Dwelly in 1925: 'FIGHTS UNREALITY IN RELIGION: When in College Opposed Artificiality in Chapel Services'. Twenty years later, Dwelly's special vocational services for the Cathedral are ornate and carefully crafted, grounded in Scripture, but made specific and relevant to a particular congregation at a particular moment in time. The bound volume of service papers for the year 1943 gives evidence of thirty-seven special services, mainly vocational, and not taking account of weddings and funerals.

A number of letters in the archives give evidence that a range of people in the Church took advice from Dwelly over the preparation of special services. Although it is almost certainly impossible to trace every service which he helped to create, some of the most significant services are recorded. I am indebted to a letter written to Dwelly by Stanley Morison during the war years for what it reveals of Dwelly's involvement in Derby in 1927: 'The Hallowing of the Name of God in the New Diocese and Cathedral of Derby.' Derby Cathedral was created from an existing church and so it was not a service of consecration, but the service bears all of the Dwelly hallmarks. In format, paper colour, print style and colour, the service paper itself, right down to the bands of decoration, is typical of Dwelly.

Aware of my interest in Dwelly, the Very Reverend Huw Thomas, Provost of Cairo, lent me a copy of The Form and Order of the Consecration of the Anglican Cathedral Church of All Saints in Cairo, 25 April 1938. Although printed by the Nile Mission Press, Cairo, there are striking similarities both in content and appearance with the Liverpool service of 1924: whole pieces of service are identical, including Concerning the Meaning of Certain Ceremonies Preparatory to the Consecration, and the quotation from St Bernard, First Sermon on the Consecration of a Church.

There are no available records to suggest how many churches made use of material from Acts of Devotion within their own liturgy but we do know from the time of Dwelly's lecture tour in America in the spring of 1925 that the publication was known there and there were thoughts about an American edition.

My attention has been drawn by Canon Noel Vincent, Canon Treasurer at Liverpool and formerly of BBC Religious Broadcasting, to a book called Services for Broadcasting published in London in 1931. The book does not carry Dwelly's name but it has the stamp of his style and one service of Hallowing had originally been broadcast from the Cathedral. The prayers for fifteen orders of service are printed in full and even their titles are typical of many of the Dwelly special services: The Kinship of Life, Home and Friendship, Education Art and Letters, Business and Industry. The final section is entitled Meditations for the Close of Sunday Programmes and they are strongly reminiscent of the Liverpool 8.30 services. The use of a wide range of poetry is also typical of Dwelly: Browning, Hebert, Francis Thompson, Wordsworth, Langland, Arnold, Shelley, Shakespeare, Kipling, Houseman, Yeats, Vaughan.

CHAPTER FOURTEEN

Personal perceptions

ANYONE WHO HAD EMBARKED on a Dwelly biography shortly after his death might have had access to the memories of many people who had known the Dean well. Now, over forty years later, most of those people are dead. Fortunately, a few people who were close to him in different ways have been able to contribute uniquely significant memories. The service papers, legal statements and newspaper articles provide a detailed and lively picture of the public figure but the private Fred Dwelly has remained somewhat of an enigma. In the correspondence between Dean Dillistone and Alan Wilkinson there is evidence to suggest that there might be aspects of Dwelly's life better left unresearched. 'I can remember asking you at Alsager whether anyone was likely to write a life of Dwelly and you then said that there were then some people alive whose relationship to Dwelly if chronicled would be hurt.' (Wilkinson to Dillistone, 1 December 1986). 'There were personal developments in Dwelly's career which, I think, are better left unrecorded.' (Dillistone in a letter to Wilkinson, 5 December 1986).

Many former members of the choir retain vivid fragments of personal memory which help fill-out the picture of the life of the Cathedral for over thirty years, but few of these people knew him really well or over a long period. Fortunately there are a handful of people who knew him well enough to contribute fact and opinion of considerable importance in the search for the real Dean Dwelly.

Everyone from the Cathedral company with memories of Dwelly couples his name with that of Christine Wagstaffe, whose ashes are in the floor of the south choir aisle just below the Dwelly Memorial. We know that she had moved from Cambridge Road to the house in Grove Park when the Dwellys moved to Liverpool in 1925. She was to become his private secretary. Mrs Diana Luck, daughter of Bishop Albert Augustus David, remembered her from early days in the Cathedral: 'He had a very devoted secretary called Chris Wagstaffe, we always thought maybe she was a girl-friend, they certainly held hands, but he also was devoted to his wife – called Molly – who was never well so we did not see much of her. He loved grapefruit juice. I have such clear memories of going to see them both in the Dean's room after

Two choristers with Ronald Woan in the Song Room.

The Dean and Field Marshal Montgomery with choir and Cross Guild.

Sunday church (lovely pale wood everywhere) and seeing Chris squeezing grape-fruit juice.'

There are few recorded comments on Mrs Dwelly. Miss Mary Raven wrote of her, 'His wife I believe was a considerable recluse', and it certainly is difficult to paint a clear picture of her. Mrs Patricia Mollison, her niece, has pleasant memories of 'Auntie Molly' in the late twenties and early thirties. Mrs Darwin, Molly's mother, was seen as a very difficult women – Mrs Mollison even used the words nasty and cruel and said in conversation, 'Grandmother and Fred were always at daggers drawn'. There was Darwin family money for which Molly received interest, though on Mrs Darwin's death she did not inherit. The estate of some £30,000 went to the three children of Mrs Darwin's son.

Chris Wagstaffe's energy, efficiency and above all her total dedication to Dwelly were beyond question, and the older he became the more indispensable were her services.

No one has been able to enlighten me about the latter part of the Dwelly marriage. With the outbreak of war and threat of bomb damage, Dwelly took up residence, as did Chris, in the Cathedral. Mrs Dwelly may well have spent some time with her mother in Southport, but her home remained in Grove Park. Chris knew the mind of the Dean better than anyone else, though she has left no trace of her thoughts and feelings.

As far as his work in Liverpool Cathedral is concerned, there remains no one who knew Dwelly more closely than Ronald Woan, former chorister, member of the Cross Guild and Master of the Choristers. Ron has given me hours of his time as he has talked through many of his Cathedral memories and has allowed me to record his words. The kindness and hospitality of Ron and his wife Doreen have been a great support to me in this project.

The musical leadership at Liverpool Cathedral has been in the hands of a very small number of men whose functions have passed from one to another in almost apostolic succession. The first organist was Frederick Burstall who was succeeded by Harry Goss Custard. Master of the Choristers was Edgar Robinson, known affection-ately as Robbie, and he was succeeded by Ronald Woan. For much of his time in office Noel Rawsthorne was the organist. After the retirements of Rawsthorne and Woan, Ian Tracey was appointed Organist and Master of the Choristers, and later Ian Wells, former chorister, became Assistant Organist. Ron's musical memories of the Cathedral remain clear and strong. He prefaced his spoken memories for me in a letter, the opening paragraph of which is a powerful statement about the significance for him of Liverpool's first Dean:

> ... I have thought back over seventy years and considered the first three Deans of Liverpool under whom I worked during that period, and the fourth, who arrived on the scene some months after I retired. Far be it from me to draw any compar-isons; Dilly was among my closest friends until his death, and Edward Patey still is. I came under the influence of the first Dean in 1930 at the age of ten and

remained in close contact with him until his death. He was a second father to me and fashioned my future life in almost every aspect. In no way would I wish to diminish the work of his successors, but why is it that when I see the words Dean of Liverpool I see, in my mind's eye, as do others of my generation, the first Dean? Why do I think of him, after so many years, as one of the greatest influences of my life? I think it was his total, total, dedication to his Cathedral, his dreams for that Cathedral and his care and consideration for those who shared those dreams.

Ron, always Ronald to the Dean, joined the choir in 1930, prior to the foundation of Dean and Chapter, and he was thrilled by the sense of awe, wonder and mystery which seemed to pervade the Cathedral and its services. In those days the Cathedral, because of the newly cut stone, had a particular smell, as did the newly limed oak of the cupboards in the Song Room. The original choir robes were black and white but Ron was not the only chorister who remembered being measured for the new and distinctive robes: rust-coloured cassocks, with warp and weft threads of slightly different shades, and cream surplices.

The sense that Liverpool Cathedral was new and different seemed to have been held strongly by the choristers, who had their own rigid and self-imposed discipline. The boys were never to be seen until, fully robed and in procession, they appeared in operatic splendour processing through the south choir aisle. The Evensong sung 'senza trousers' must have been remembered vividly by one group of choristers for seventy years. The choristers attended Liverpool Institute High School for Boys, on the other side of Duke Street at the west end of the Cathedral. One afternoon as they were walking over, they were caught in a violent deluge of rain but they had no thought of entering the Cathedral from the west or through the Lady Chapel: they battled through the rain to their traditional entrance in the eastern courtyard. They were so wet that they had to sing Evensong in cassocks and surplices but without trousers which were hanging up to dry in the undercroft!

The choristers' outdoor dress on Sundays and formal occasions was no less distinctive than their choir robes: black jacket, striped trousers and Eton collars. The choir boys were also unusual prior to the 1944 Education Act in that they were all educated at the Liverpool Institute, one of the city's foremost grammar schools.

The Dean was a memorable figure to the choristers, 'this strange gatered person smiling benignly'. He was at the very centre of their Cathedral world: 'he was constantly there ... he seemed to be part of the fabric.' It was sometimes slightly disconcerting to a choir boy slyly embarking on homework during lesson or sermon, anxious not to leave ink marks on his robes.

Dwelly was deeply revered by his choristers, though they had no feeling of fear or domination; his was a warmly benevolent dictatorship. He was warm and enthusiastic in his praise for their performances – sometimes, to the ears of Edgar Robinson, not sufficiently critical. At the end of the service after the procession back to the ambulatory, he would bow to Can and Dec and declare as only he could, 'MOGNU-FICENT'. This high praise so annoyed Robbie that a coded message was introduced

The Dean on holiday.

on those occasions when the Dean was to be permitted enthusiastic praise. The choir recessed west down the chancel steps, turning left at the ambo and past the foundation stone at the entrance to the south aisle where a verger stood. If the performance reached Robbie's exacting standards, he would bow to the verger, who would in turn bow to the Dean. No bow, no 'Mognuficent'.

The Dean and Chris Wagstaffe were a part of the social life of the boys and they would arrive to support choir cricket at Riversdale Road on a Saturday evening. There was a trip to Blackpool when Robbie bought them all fish and chips which they ate walking along the prom. Photographs and service papers give evidence as to the numbers of former choristers married by Dwelly and the subsequent sons and daughters whom he baptised. He also had named photographs of his large choir team and, some years later, when in France or North Africa, they treasured a card or present at Christmas.

I am indebted to the late Gordon Pemberton, retired head teacher and former chorister, for his account of his admittance to the choir. 'We [five boys] were taken to see Canon Dwelly, as he was then. We sat down in his office and he asked us, in turn, about ourselves, so that he got to know something about us and we got to know something about each other. He then sent for the two senior choristers and we all went into the Cathedral to kneel at the Altar rail while Canon Dwelly said some prayers appropriate to the occasion. Led by the senior choristers we then sang three verses of 'All things bright and beautiful', and then each of us made his dedication to the Cathedral, reading from a card. He then blessed us individually and gave us each a 'membership certificate' in a large envelope, which he enjoined us to take home with great care. He then shook hands with us and congratulated us on becoming members of the choir.'

Gordon Pemberton also recorded a memory of the more severe side of Dwelly, a side not often seen but when seen not forgotten. Pemberton remembered one Friday evening after choir practice when Goss asked him to page turn at the organ for one of his pupils, a young man of about twenty who was studying for higher musical qualifications.

When we went into the Cathedral the lights were on only in the ambulatory and the north aisle and I suppose Stephen assumed, as I did, that all people had gone home except the Verger on duty. He practised for the best part of an hour and I enjoyed the experience though I had to stretch my arm to turn the pages for him. At the end of his practice he produced from his satchel a page of music manuscript and said to me, 'I've arranged this for organ. Tell me what you think of it.' He then proceeded to play a jazz song that was popular at the time. He played three verses, each with a different set of stops and I thought his arrangement was excellent, though I had some doubt about it being played in a place of worship. Nevertheless I applauded and gave him my opinion. He then locked the organ and we came down the steps, through the Chapel of the Holy Spirit into the aisle, where we were startled to see a figure standing. It was the Dean.

He had a very angry expression on his face. However, he retained his dignity when he told Stephen to take the keys to the office and not to return ever for any more practice. He then turned to me and told me I was suspended from choir duty for a month.

Pemberton shrewdly summed up Dwelly's leadership style:

From the start it seemed obvious that Canon Dwelly was in charge, though he was not bossy. When necessary he 'invited' people to do things and they always acceded to his requests. He used such phrases as 'I wonder whether you would like to ...?' And, 'Might I suggest that ...?' I have often used such phrases in my own career as a head teacher. However, it was an understood thing by all the clerics that they carried out his suggestions without question.

From the reputations which they both established, Harry Goss Custard and Edgar Robinson were musicians of distinction and their work contributed to the success of worship in Liverpool Cathedral. Dwelly was not a trained musician, though Mrs

Dwelly was a pianist and organist. I wanted to know from Ron Woan the extent to which Dwelly was directly responsible for the choice of music. He took time to reply and his comments were revealing. Early in one of our conversations he had reported, speaking of Edgar Robinson, 'he put the Dwelly thoughts into operation' and both he and Goss had some influence on the final content and character of *Songs of Praise*. Without any hesitation he referred to Robinson's judgement: 'Canon Dwelly may not know much about music, but his choice was impeccable.'

The service papers give evidence of the appropriateness and imaginativeness of the use of a single verse of a well-known hymn sung as part of the prayers; of a short fragment of a longer piece being well-used, for example the effective short Alleluia section of Peter Philips's 'Ascendit Deus'. Dwelly's readiness to modify a piece of music became notorious, though his decisions were invariably right. Some old copies of Charles Wood's 'Expectans expectavi' have a line through the quiet, meditative final section. The piece rises to a musical and emotional climax at the words 'to thy great service dedicate'. 'The piece stops there!' said Dwelly, and it did. In a secular Purcell piece 'with drooping wings, ye cupids, come' became 'with drooping wings, ye angels, come' when sung on Remembrance Sunday. Sterndale Bennett's 'God is a Spirit' became 'God is Spirit'. Even the Litany had to be altered: 'Ronald, I may be a sinner, but I'm not a miserable sinner.' Cranmer had to be modified. An incident at a choir practice in the stalls was typical of his eccentric genius at work. The choir were singing the hymn 'Bright the vision that delighted' but were interrupted by Dwelly who called up to the organ loft, 'Goss, before the next verse I want you to take my soul from the depths of hell to the highest pinnacle of heaven'. With the Willis masterpiece to help him, Goss did just that before the simplicity of the final verse.

Dwelly might be remembered by the general public for his magnificent services attended by the good and the great but for Ron Woan it was the many little incidents and attitudes which were to him typical of the Dean. As a very young man just before the war, Ron played the organ at St Alban's, a church in a rough, deprived area off Scotland Road in Liverpool. He started a choir and, to give him encouragement, when they were performing a special piece of music at the church, Goss played the organ, choir gentlemen sang the solos, and Dwelly preached the sermon. When Ron's father died, Dwelly arranged for the funeral service to be held in the War Memorial Chapel of the Cathedral and took as much care over the service details as he did over a service for a great, national figure – even though he had never met Mr Woan senior.

With the impending retirement of Edgar Robinson in 1948, Dwelly invited Ron to take over the choir but, as a young teacher starting a new job, that was not Ron's wish. However, he agreed to take over as a temporary measure. He attended Robbie's last Evensong as a mark of respect for his mentor. When Dwelly went into the pulpit to preach, all Ron's plans were wrecked when the Dean preached on the subject of the mantle of Elijah falling upon Elisha and he knew that he was trapped.

He worked closely with Dwelly for the next seven years until the Dean was physically and mentally unable to carry out his duties. During those years, Ron worked in the closest cooperation with the Dean and was forced to witness the painful final degeneration of a great man.

At the beginning all went well and Ron had the opportunity to work alongside the man who had become the greatest influence in his life. Every time he went into the Cathedral, he went first to speak to the Dean. On school days, when he was collected by taxi, a bottle of milk and a straw awaited him in the outer office before he went to speak to the Dean. Ron retains no memories of sitting with the Dean over the planning of specific services but they had much informal contact and their discussions were ongoing. He does have memories of dinners in the French Restaurant at the Adelphi Hotel, often with the visiting preacher, and that day's service paper being commented on as notes were made for the future.

More and more the 'clothing' of the ceremonial, the actual assemblage of the cross guild processions, was in the hands of Chris Wagstaffe, who, having worked alongside Dwelly for so long, instinctively knew what he wanted and she supported and protected him to the end. Both Ron Woan and Geoffrey Rimmer have remarked on her ability to use Dwelly's signature. There is not the slightest evidence that she sought power for herself but she did become more and more protective of the Dean.

Ron and Geoffrey were close enough to Dwelly towards the end of his time at the Cathedral to be painfully aware of his mental degeneration. Ron believes that Chris Wagstaffe found it hard to accept and acknowledge what was happening and she urged him to continue taking a public role. Ron dreaded the words from Chris before a service, 'Ronald, the Dean will sing the Litany; you walk behind him'. Geoffrey was often given the task of sitting with the Dean in his stall at services in an attempt to prompt his memory and to prevent unfortunate interruptions. There were times when Dwelly stood up and announced, 'God, save the Queen!', and the choir had to sing the National Anthem. Bride and groom at two wedding ceremonies were mildly concerned about the legality of their marriages, Dwelly having omitted parts of the service. Mrs Dwelly had died in 1950 and Chris Wagstaffe's health declined. She underwent surgery for cancer but despite her own weakening health she was immensely supportive of the Dean and in his latter days she it was who was responsible for much of the final drawing up of services. She knew his mind so well that the Cathedral managed to run smoothly despite the fading of the Dean.

In the archive papers from the Dean's final months in office is an intriguing letter from Mr and Mrs Vernon Dwelly in Los Angeles. One of the obituary notices made mention of an adopted son, as did a little handwritten note amongst the papers deposited by Granny Cotton, but no one to whom I spoke could give me any information on this matter. Then, in the summer of 1999, I spoke to a visitor in the Cathedral who introduced himself as Vernon Dwelly. We were able to spend only a short time together but later, thanks to e-mail and fax, another gap in the Dwelly story could be filled.

The man now known as Vernon Dwelly was born in 1921 of German parentage. His uncle had known the Dean and Chris Wagstaffe, who helped make it possible for the young man to be educated at Buxton College from 1934. The threat of European war and financial problems made it impossible to continue his formal education at the end of his school career, despite academic and sporting prowess, so through the Dean's close friendship with the Holt family, the young man was accepted as a management trainee with the Blue Funnel Line. Many years later he was to write:

> I loved the man from our first encounter and not just for the kindness to me. My home in Liverpool was with Miss Mabel Kelsall, Mossley Hill, an old and trusted friend of the Dean and Chris. They would come out to 'Helston', Miss Kelsall's home … She was about the kindest woman I have ever met – patient, tolerant, intent on helping others and dedicated to the best human sides of life … As a friend, that suited the Dean. He used to come for high teas on Sunday – sometimes, even Saturdays or during the week for that or a light dinner. Chris was always with him. She was his clock, organiser, reminder book – with a very good, dry sense of humour. The Dean was the creator, dreamer in some ways, but still also a no-nonsense, down-to-earth thinker. She was the pragmatist to get things done. These hours at Helston were quiet, relaxing, re-energizing – with both trivial and deeper conversations.
>
> You could recognize him from a distance: that soft, black, wide-brimmed hat pulled into his face, the lengthy dark coat, compatible with Liverpool weather, shoes with rubber over-boots which Chris helped him remove. Chris 'babied' him in some ways, as I now seem to recall. It's so long ago, I was young, much has happened since – so that some of my comments are images … There he stood in the big window to Helston garden – quiet, thinking, often with his hands folded behind his back, soft spoken, smiling, deliberate. Rodin's Thinker but standing … The Dean and Chris had strong wills and, at times, seemed to be ahead of the world around them. Some of these aspects of his life emerged over high teas at Helston.
>
> He was a total believer in God, the Holy Trinity, and shared his beliefs. There was no routine, monotony about his sharing. He felt that prayers and sermons alone might not fulfill and introduced musical events, plays, and other events within the great Cathedral walls. He must have been one of the earliest clergy to do this.
>
> He was a man of great contrasts. Extreme simplicity for himself in style, manner, clothing, food and the material demands on life – but unlimited colour and pomp for the ceremonial – processions would be spectacles of splendour and beauty, both sound and vision. His sermons consistently brought 'full house' from all directions and one never seemed to leave his service without a deep message. A man of soul, part of his life was dedicated to the poor, the underdog. He visited the under privileged and forgotten and did much to help. A man of amazing toler-

ance and open-mindedness ... I do not remember the context, but he told me one day that 'it is always so important to tell the truth, but not necessarily the whole truth'. I have often remembered that as good advice. His life, from what I know, was not the easiest but there was almost always a sparkle in his eyes and a sense of optimism in his words. Part of his life was very personal, almost secretive, enig-matic, made one wonder. He valued privacy and space and gave the same to others ... A man of kindness – compassionate, appreciative, controversial in his views on society and even within the church, determined, dedicated, able to deal with his labourers at the Cathedral, or the poor in the Port of Liverpool or the factory workers, or hospitals – as well as devising services for and entertaining the visits of the King and other Royalty, Air Chief Marshals, Field Marshals, Admirals, Government Leaders.

At the outbreak of the war, he was still a German national and as such interned as a potential enemy alien and shipped off to an internment camp in South Australia. His correspondence with Chris and the Dean was maintained throughout this difficult period, and he subsequently volunteered for service in the British forces, became a Captain and served under Mountbatten.

At about the age of twenty, he cannot remember for certain, he was adopted by the Dean and took the name Dwelly. Despite having moved about the world he has continued to treasure a collection of the most affectionate letters in Dwelly's own dreadful handwriting. The letters express his concern for the young man, the delight in his progress, and the depth of his affections.

My Dear Vernon,

A great pleasure to have your letter and even greater pleasure to sense your understanding of our gratitude for the way you sense our pride in you and delight in our family life together – Mabel and Chris, you and I: nothing like it. Then our talks – and your achievements – our mutual search for what we shall not reject – its all fine and thank you for making it so.

Love,

Yours, FWD

Thank you for giving me the chance to put my admiration in writing – I adore it – please telegraph me your new title when you have it for I am so like an excited mother and though so restrained in expression I am deeply proud of you. Bless you.

CHAPTER FIFTEEN

Dwelly and Raven again

WHEN THE WAR ENDED in 1945, Dwelly was sixty four years old and despite the rigours of twenty-four hour residence in the Cathedral and some of the immense pressures upon him, the Dean was still at the height of his powers and anxious for building to progress to add to the already vast worship laboratory. Four important letters exist in the archive handwritten by Dwelly to Charles Raven. Two of those letters are typically undated but the contents indicate their being written between 1945 and 1947. The earliest one must have been written fairly soon after the death of Raven's first wife in 1944. The letter offers important insight into Dwelly's mind at that time.

> Charles my dear,
> How wonderful of you to write to me when you are yourself so bowled up. Wonderful you – what I would have given to have been serving you and I did serve you – those years I loved it trying to keep up to your speed and to the rigorous way your mind adventured in the spirit – wonderful until Albert came under the dictation of Twitchett.
> You must be very very lonely now, you always needed what Bee gave you and with such understanding. But your great work with its mighty influence must in itself support you whilst it makes big demands on you.
> So you have Mary with you – lovely Mary – That also opens a door of delight in my memory – yes lovely Mary.
> As for us – I do not know – I cannot say. I only know I am a battered man; they who talk about suffering and keeping silent as I can only say the last few years have been heart breaking – to see saint after saint broken at the wheel of mechanis-ation as ruthless as A.L. did it and not know he was doing it. Ah! But how terrible to be able to do it and not know you are doing it.
> How often I have refreshed my soul by memory of you. Dear you.
> Yours gratefully,
> FWD

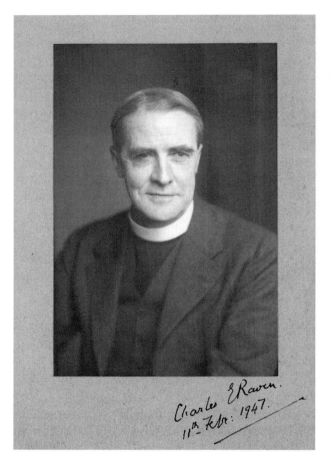

A studio portrait of Charles Raven, Dwelly's closest friend throughout their acquaintance. It was Raven who preached at the service in 1960 to mark the unveiling of the Dwelly memorial in the south choir aisle.

Raven tended to date his letters with day and month but not year but one sequence of letters refers to a series of lectures which Dwelly delivered in Cambridge.

Christ's College,
  Cambridge.
  17 February [1939?]
  Fred, my dear,
  I am writing as Chairman of the Divinity Board to say that you were unanimously appointed Lecturer in Pastoral Theology for the year 1940, your subject to be The principles and practice of public worship, six lectures to be delivered at dates to be fixed later, and the stipend to be £50 ...

There are no archive letters to indicate why the lectures were not delivered in 1940 but the war and all the concerns for fire-watching and the safety of the Cathedral must have played a part in postponing them until Liverpool and Cambridge were back to normal. A letter from Raven to Dwelly on 4 September [probably 1946] stated: 'Your proposals for the lectures are most intriguing; and I am delighted with the suggestion that the 17th century has help for us – in this as in so much else. Don't be too historical. It is the principles of worship that you know so well and that most of us totally ignore. Tell us not only how to collect material but how to arrange and employ it.' Another letter suggests that the lectures would finally be delivered in 1947.

A completely undated letter remains from Dwelly to Raven which must have been written immediately after the delivery of the pastoral theology lectures. It is so important that it has to be reproduced in full.

Charles my dear,
   And still I am in a dream of delight and gratitude to you.
   The magnanimity of your receiving me, then of your presenting me to the undergraduates, then of your sustaining me at what must have been a great strain in your staggeringly busy full time office – and marvel of marvels so doing it that composure was inevitable and freedom to let out things sacred to my inner life – nearly fifty years of accumulation of experiments in the experiences of worthship with wholeness.
   You have since 1916 meant more to my faith than any other man – and from such a confession you will imagine what a deep content came to me with your word of 'well done'. And that you should see fit to say this concerning the job you had given me to do in Cambridge.
   In Cambridge where alone without any help from tutors – but introduced by Goodchild and by Loewe – I discovered the ways of Eastern worship – swotted and concentrated only on 'oblations' 'dedications' and 'consecrations' in the five greatest uses of Christendom and with their many variants – very many – The which caused me the disgrace of the ordinary degree – I was badly directed, but with what a rich result – you recommended David to give me the consecration of the cathedral to compile – (still I observe it stands as the one pattern) and so I might continue through the achievements you have evoked.
   How I prayed that I might not let you down in the Divinity Pastoral Lectures – Thank you very much indeed for this letter from you which assures me I did not let you down.
   Thank you again.
   Yours,
   FWD

An earlier letter from Raven (29 August) mentions a Chinese bishop anxious for Dwelly's liturgical advice. 'I have just had a visit from Bishop Shen of China, now in England, who has been charged by his colleagues with the task of preparing a new prayer-book for the church in China. He has seen the Dean of York and been commended to the liturgical experts: but he is live and liberal, and not content with

Western traditions. He has begged me to give him an introduction to you ... I believe you can shape the whole public worship of China by seeing him.' Dwelly met Shen in Liverpool early in October.

A letter from Raven to Dwelly on 27 July [1944] raised an intriguing subject: the next Bishop of Liverpool. Albert Augustus was preparing to retire and Dwelly obviously had strong views about a successor.

Ralph [Dawson] came and told me the position. It is wonderful to know that some of you would like to have me; and I believe, in all humility, that much could be done. But I know Lang refused to consider me for a diocese three years ago when pretty strong appeals were (I believe) sent to him. Nor am I sure that my health would stand a big change at the moment ... You see my position, Fred. I can't say that I will leave: I can't in any case lift a finger to get myself invited to leave: I think it vastly unlikely that I shall be even considered for the work. But – And there I must leave it.

I think Raven knew he would never be Bishop of Liverpool; that he was better employed as Vice-chancellor of Cambridge University. But his Liverpool years, and particularly his deep co-operation with Dwelly, were immensely important to him: 'I don't know when I have been so deeply moved as I have been by this vision of you and the Cathedral. I always knew that Liverpool had left a great mark on me; and that it was our partnership there which mattered. But to come back and find that in spite of all these devastating years you and it are still growing – and still gracious and lovely to me, that is very wonderful.' The same letter refers to the Cathedral as 'a place of vital religion'.

The lectures in Pastoral Theology at Cambridge are not recorded in any way in the Cathedral archives but Dwelly's words on a second important Cambridge occasion have, in the text of the annual Hulsean Sermon, 'Before the University of Cambridge on Sunday, Thirtieth November Nineteen Hundred and Forty-Seven by The Dean of Liverpool The Very Reverend F. W. Dwelly, M.A., D.D. Queens' College.' As this is the final Dwelly sermon within the archives and delivered in such a significant context, I quote extensively from it. The text was Ephesians 1:19: 'The exceeding greatness of His power toward us who believe.'

By the spaciousness of the great rock salt mine of England, Hulse had an experience which might be described as 'Apprehending that for which he was apprehended by Christ.'

Stimulated by the questions of visitors about the geology of 'Wich' and by literature in his grandfather's library at Elworth, John Hulse came under the influence of Robert Boyle, and was fascinated by his faith and by his experiments. I need not remind you that making experiments and risking some failures was the essence of the life of Robert Boyle.

Robert Boyle was prepared to be tough and to have a lot of difficult and unsolved problems on board and yet be a worshipping mind. He wrote 'Beasts inhabit and enjoy the world: man, if he will the more, must study and spiritualise it.'

If we are to spiritualise it we must believe in it, enjoy the unveiling of new possibilities through it, and wonder at the things that are before us in the many vocations of our day. (As many as three hundred in a great City.)

If organised religion is to spiritualise the world, it must stop running after itself. Instead it must take on an ever new and refreshing outlook for the uncounted, great, good that has not yet been welcomed in the name of God. Some of the time spent in mourning evils must rather be spent in counting blessings, appreciating them and publicly acknowledging these gifts of the Creator. Then all the Angels of God will shout for joy.

Varying ways of acclaiming the good in several vocations should be the chief concern of organised religion today, if the world is to be spiritualised. Take a lesson from the I.C.I. Newspaper advertisements which are veritably works of art, and every time constructive healthy, purifying in their appeal.

The Lord Christ introduced his teaching with a series of blessings; He had been taught so as a child. Let us teach our children so to do and they will know how to enjoy the world by acclaiming the good.

The early Christians would turn to the parables of our Lord for the right mood: 'Without a parable spake He not unto them.' Often His parables grew out of the vocations of His disciples or their homes. Again and again He identified His spirit with their vocations. Sometimes the very words they used, He used. Always He spake within the understanding of their vocations.

To the fishermen: 'I will make you fishers of men.'

To the harvesters: 'Gather the good into My barn.'

To the servants on watch to welcome home the wanderer: 'Bring forth the best.'

To all the disciples who had cultivated a preference for joy over murmuring: 'Enter thou into the joy of thy Lord.'

Through the parables of their working life or home life, disciples who had educated their powers of appreciation and who now had eyes to see and ears to hear entered into His joy. 'Joy which no man can take from you.'

'You never enjoy the world aright till you see how even a sand exhibiteth the power and wisdom of God.'

'Yet further, you never enjoy the world aright till you so love the beauty of enjoying it, that you are earnest to persuade others to enjoy it.'

'Till your spirit filleth the whole world, and the stars are your jewels; till you are familiar with the ways of God in nature.'

'You never enjoy the world aright till the sea itself flows in your veins, till you are clothed with the heavens and crowned with the stars.'

'As it becometh you to retain a glorious sense of the world, so are you to remember always the unsearchable extent and unlimited greatness of your own soul, and length and breadth, and depth and height of your own understanding.'

The parable way of leading into the kingdom of worth-ship is very, very old. It is sufficiently elastic to serve all vocations. It demands that we educate our emotions and our powers of appreciation with constructive criticism.

The parable way is also good in accumulating material, identifying and sorting those experiences that attend upon every man, even to his first sight of death. 'At the first sight of death, cling to God; God who never faileth them that put their trust in Him; all whom we love are in God.'

'I have put on incorruption through His name, and have put off corruption by His Grace.'

'There hath gone up deathless life in the Lord's land, and it hath been made known to His faithful ones.'

'As the sun is the joy to them that seek for its day-break, so is my joy in the Lord.'

'Life and joy and light without stint to all those that trust Him.'

'As the hand moves over the harp, and the strings speak so speaks in my members the Spirit of the Lord.'

'My joy is the Lord and my impulse toward Him.'

Preparing the ways of the worshipping mind is hard work, but is there anything so satisfying? What joy indeed! 'All things are yours and ye are Christ's and Christ is God's.' 'I turned to see the voice ... and being turned I saw ...' 'If all be mine dear Lord, why then thy Grace is mine, thy Gifts are mine.' J. S. Bach wrote at the end of all his work 'A.M.D.G.' Ad majorem dei gloriam, to the greater glory of God. He was expressing the real spirit of worship.

Professor Myers and the scientists and artists who collaborated with him in shaping an act of worship for the centenary of the British Association on 20 September 1931, selected for the first oblation and acknowledgement of God, Praises for the glorious revelation that in Christ we are called to be fellow workers with God, and acknowledgement of the relationship of our vocations to His creative purpose.

In his address on that occasion Field Marshal Smuts said he believed 'the Spirit of God enables the true citizen to interpret the processes of nature, for the benefit of the life of man. In the common task of mutual enlightenment and public service, men's minds awakened to the revelation of that which works in all and through all, and their grasp strengthened on the principles and the meaning of life.'

The service was not an accumulation of blessings one after another, for that would have been making a catalogue instead of a form of worship; a colourless list of thoughts, not that glory of light and shade which you will find in all ancient beautiful forms of worship.

Glory to the Most High Trinity, God pure in essence, one Divinity; Equal Glory, Co-Eternal Majesty. Praise to the Father and to the Son and to the Holy Spirit Who subjects the Universe of the Spirit to His Laws.

May the Lord Jesus Christ fill you with spiritual joy.

May His Spirit make you strong and tranquil in the truth of his promises.

And may the blessing of the Father come upon you abundantly. Amen.
Let the Holy Spirit come upon us and bless us.
R. Come upon us and bless us.
May the Blessed Godhead of the Father, the son, and the Holy Spirit,
Who subjects the universe of the Spirit to His laws, grant us peace.

Experiments in worship are now recognised as essential for hallowing the ever
growing number of vocations in our age ... In a sermon on June 9th, 1945, the
Archbishop of York, Dr. Cyril Garbett, pressed the need for an accumulation of
experiences in corporate worship, additional to the Offices of the Church. He also
urged the duty of experimenting with the worshipping mind. 'Our worship should
not be separated by a gulf from the ordinary life of ordinary men and women. It
is nothing less than a disaster when Christian worship is treated as remote and cut
off from the concerns and needs of the average man.'

On February 19th, 1943, Dr. William Temple, then Archbishop of Canterbury,
writing of the worshipping mind welcomed experiments in vocational services ...
He said: 'The composition of these services in order that they may be effective and
worthy is by no means easy. Our traditional forms were brought into their present
shape through the use of many generations. If we are to supplement them by
another type of service bearing more directly upon the needs of life, we shall need
much experiment and many of the experiments will fail. But it would seem that
there are two conditions that ought generally to be fulfilled. The first is that the
service should be drawn up either by men and women actively engaged in the
occupation with which the Service specially deals or at least in close and intimate
consultation with them. The second is, that the actual shaping of the Service
should then be entrusted to someone who, by natural gifts and by the discipline
of serious training has acquired the art of giving to what is already guaranteed as
relevant, the dignity and note of reverence essential to any act of worship. As I
have already said, we shall reach our real goal only by making experiments and
risking some failures. But action along these lines seems to be called for.'

You may well ask: 'But who is sufficient for these things?' Traherne would make
reply: 'A magnanimous soul.'

'A Magnanimous Soul, if we respect its Capacity, is an immovable sphere of
Power and Knowledge, by its virtue and power passing through all things, and
God alone its sovereign Delight and supreme Complacency ...'

'Magnanimity includes all that belongs to a great Soul; a high and mighty
Courage, an invincible Patience, a divine, profound, uncontrollable sense of one's
own Capacity, a generous Confidence, and a great inclination to Heroical Deeds.'

'If you would have the character of a Magnanimous soul, he is the Son of Eternal
Power, and a Friend of infinite Goodness.'

Well, here is a reed of the worshipping mind. From natural good, reaching out
to receive supernatural good.

But some will say: 'Be more practical – How do we prepare for this duty of the worshipping mind?' By a calendar. A self imposed and then a unit agreed vocation calendar. Adding to the many and varied calendars, Mother Church set the example of registering appreciation, human and divine, in a Church Calendar. It is for us to add to it a vocation calendar. Add to it from among the devoted in art, in science, in any vocation which is known by experience to open 'the eyes to see or the ears to hear.' By the calendar we renew our thanks for the good received through benefactions. Instance Hort for his Hulsean on 'The Way, the Truth and the Life,' Creighton for his Hulsean on 'Tolerance.' Enlarge the calendar with names of those who have made possible that which seemed impossible, instance how one of our great Cathedrals would have utterly failed in its purpose had not two benefactors, Dr. Sir F. M. Radcliffe and Dr. Frank Neilson made possible that which seemed impossible.

In Victorian days every home had its calendar called a 'Birthday Book' or a 'Family Bible Record.' It is for us to renew the affections of heart and will continually by enlarging and using such calendars. Responsibility in one's job of work is made human by a calendar. Moreover by some such use of calendars comes release from individual pettiness in personal life and from centralised top-heaviness in our organised life, and we shall say 'Blessed be God who has placed our feet in a large room.'

Meanwhile, Gentlemen, those salt brine pans are still boiling in Cheshire as they were when the Romans over-ran the Midlands, and as they were when the boy John Hulse lived by them. Yes, and that vast, sublimely beautiful Rock Salt Mine is still there, with its crystal and bronze walls and roofs. I saw it myself only a few weeks ago, and then I understood what the boy Hulse apprehended. Only no longer is that dirty lane there, with its paid foster mother treating boys as of less value than a bucket of brine water. Grandfather picked the boy up on horseback and took him to his own home. At the age of sixteen Grandfather took him, on horseback all the way, to St John's College, Cambridge. Here the loveliness he had admired as a boy did what appreciation always does. Eighteen months of this felicity. Then news of his Grandfather's death brought an order that John must leave College and return to misery.

With this news our parable from life might have been cut off, but magnanimity stepped in. The Master and Fellows of St John's College saved John Hulse. The words were re-echoed 'Shall I yield to misery?' Magnanimity says 'No!'

Blessed be God for the 'spirit of magnanimity.'

Blessed be God for all 'natural good.'

Blessed be God 'the intercourse with Him.'

Blessed be God for 'the reaching in Him of the good supernatural.'

Blessed 'the environment.'

Blessed be God 'for the greatness of His power to usward who believe.'

CHAPTER SIXTEEN

'Gone from us ...'

T HE 8TH OF SEPTEMBER 1949 was probably a date with no special significance for Dwelly or the Cathedral but of considerable personal significance because that was the day I started as a pupil at the Liverpool Institute High School for Boys. The school lay in the shadow of the Cathedral and it was from that date that the Cathedral began to impinge upon my life. Unfortunately I have almost no personal memories of Dwelly: he remains a rather shadowy figure at the back of a procession and I have no memory of his voice.

As I have already commented, from the war years onwards only the service papers for special services were bound in the annual volumes, and at the end of 1953 even this ceased, though a few isolated sheets remain from Dwelly's final years in office. There is nothing in the service papers themselves to indicate any weakening in Dwelly's liturgical skills or powers of leadership. The service on 29 March 1949 was simply entitled Liverpool Cathedral and marked the occasion when Princess Elizabeth, accompanied by the Duke of Edinburgh, formally opened the Rankin Porch. The service had been prepared for two days before when the sermon was preached by Bishop Albert Augustus David who highlighted the significance of the Cathedral building enterprise in the rather desolate post-war years: 'No longer can it be said that the days of great architecture inspired by religious faith are all in the past. Modern art moved by modern faith and interpreted by modern craftsmanship has still something to offer not unworthy to be compared with the masterpieces of the Middle Age. This Cathedral is standing proof that we of this generation do not lack the power to achieve greatness. Within these walls we may take fresh courage as we face colossal tasks of other kinds crowding on us now – tasks of re-building the national life of our country and the broken life of the world.'

The Archbishop of York's sermon reprinted in the 1949 commemorative service paper is in a similar vein: 'The common purpose which has united all who have given and worked for this Cathedral has been the worship and glory of God. Their purpose has not been to erect an architectural monument, nor a super concert hall, nor a luxury auditorium for ecclesiastical and ethical lectures. Their purpose has been to raise a house in which the worship of God may be conducted with devotion, reverence and dignity. When a visitor enters the Cathedral for the first time, he is at once impressed by a sense of vastness and spaciousness; the grandeur and majesty of the building fill him with awe, and impel him to adore in worship. But he also is soon impressed by the care taken over every detail. He sees nothing which is cheap and shoddy, but everything of the best, for all within this building is an offering to God, and is intended to help in His worship ... Our Cathedrals cannot set too high a standard for the art which should be used as a handmaid to worship.'

Early in the morning of 7 March 1950 'all that could die of Mary Bradshaw Dwelly shall be borne into the Cathedral'. At the fully choral funeral service at noon, different parts were led by the Rev. Ralph Dawson, Canon Soulby, Bishop Gresford Jones, Canon Bezzant, and Bishop Clifford Martin. It will probably never be known what went wrong with their marriage. They did not live together for the last ten years of her life, though Dwelly went to visit her regularly and sometimes she called at the Cathedral.

A little handwritten note dated 20 May 1951 from Vere Cotton is the earliest indication in the archives of another personal worry. 'I was coming along to see you after afternoon service today when Bezzant told me of your great anxiety and I thought you would probably prefer to be alone ... This requires no answer, it is simply a note of sympathy from us both and to say you are much in our thoughts. I hope each day brings better news of Chris.' Her cancer had necessitated several operations and after later surgery she refused to remain in hospital over-night because she would not leave the Dean by himself.

October 1952 marked his twenty-first anniversary as Dean and, as a surprise for him, the Cross Guild commissioned a new piece of music and presented it to him in a handsomely illuminated leather binding with the inscription:

Master Dean

We the Members of the Choristers Guild, who serve with you to the honour of this Cathedral greet you with affection on this Twenty-First Anniversary of your becoming First Dean of Liverpool.

During these Twenty-One Years you have achieved the great work of shaping a lovely and generous tradition to the praise of God, which will live and grow throughout the centuries to come.

We know, amongst many other things, of the order which you have brought into the services in the Cathedral, of your endeavour to raise the standard of music and the status of the choir.

We thank you for the inspiration, encouragement and ready help which you have given to us in our work, especially in our further education and for your unfailing kindness to us in times of trouble.

As a way of marking the occasion in the spirit of this tradition, we commissioned Christopher le Fleming, Composer of Tonbridge, Kent to write a Magnificat and Nunc Dimittis. He undertook his commission with much delight, and visited the

One of a series of four studio portraits, each one revealing different facets of the Dean's personality.

Cathedral when you were on holiday to hear the choir sing and to learn of the acoustics of the building.

Here is the manuscript of his music, the Magnificat and Nunc Dimittis in D, contained in this folder which Kenneth Wood has designed. We ask you to accept it as a mark of the love which all members of the Choristers Guild, old and young, near and far bear towards you on this happy day.

In 1952 Bezzant resigned his chancellorship to take up an appointment as Dean of St John's College Cambridge. There are twelve Bezzant letters in the archives, written between October 1952 and July 1954. The first is addressed to 'My dear F.W. and Chris' and the rest to Chris, though they are not private letters to her but rather letters intended for the Dean of Liverpool. The most significant topic recurring in all of the early letters concerns the appointment of a new Canon to Liverpool Cathedral and it is quite clear that Dwelly wanted the Bishop to appoint Ralph Dawson, Vicar of St Edward's in Cambridge. Ralph and his wife, Freda, are several times described by Bezzant as 'dithering' but Bezzant was trying to help Dwelly in his plan: 'I want to help you in getting the one person you want.' There seems little doubt that as he moved towards the final years of his time in office, Dwelly, and a number of people around him, was keen to protect the traditions and standards which the Dwelly regime had established and fostered. There is one very barbed comment about the man who was eventually to be appointed Chancellor: 'I hear reports of Dillie's goodness but insufferable dullness.'

Thoughts about an eventual successor to Dwelly were raised in a letter from Colin Dunlop in December 1952. The letter is a reminder that he had first been a guest of the Dean twenty-one years before, at Easter 1931. The letter is full of gratitude and admiration from a fellow Dean and Bishop:

> ... I feel I owe to you and Chris a very great debt for your abiding friendship and affection and I have no idea how to repay it. God bless you. I do hope the B[ishop] will appoint someone whom you will really like and trust. It ought to be someone who could learn and then succeed you – a Coadjutor Dean. I hope he won't send some noisy gas-bag who thinks he's 'evangelising' whenever the urge to 'shoot off his mouth' gets too much for him. You do deserve a good sensible disciple who could perpetuate and develop your work in days to come. There is so much a man could learn from you over a course of years and then turn to good account later on.

A letter from Bishop Clifford Martin on 26 February 1953 gives news of the new Chancellor: 'I think that it is right now to offer the Canonry previously held by J.S.B. To Canon Dillistone. From what you said about him I imagine that you will approve this suggestion.' Until his death, Dillistone remained one of the Cathedral's most significant contacts with the first Dean. In a letter to Alan Wilkinson in September 1983, Dillistone wrote, 'When I first met him in 1952 he was already a shadow of his former self: Parkinson's Disease robbed him of his powers and he was shielded from the outside world by Miss Wagstaffe.' In another letter to Wilkinson in December 1986 he wrote that 'after the war there began that decline in his powers which was sad to watch'.

Dwelly had always maintained excellent relations with the Holt family of the Alfred Holt Blue Funnel Line. There is an unusual short personal note from Lawrence Holt on 14 May 1953:

> My dear and honoured Dean Dwelly,
>
> When I saw you come out from our friend, Chiropodist Coates, it flashed though my mind that you might like a voyage next winter to Australia and back, with your trusted lady companion. We should all rejoice to take you both as our welcome guests.

There was no restful trip to Australia and in a letter to Chris on 26 September 1954, Francis Neilson expresses his concern over the health of both Chris and the Dean.

> I am very sorry to hear of your physical condition, and I do hope that Hugh Reid will be able to give you relief. It is too bad that you cannot take a long rest and

really recover. Surely, the heavy work at the Cathedral is over for a time. What a year it has been for you! ...

Now about the Dean. I presume that you are saving him from exertion in every way and that you think it better for him to carry on as long as possible because you fear his successor may not be in sympathy with the tradition you have established. Well, you know I rely on your judgement, and I feel sure that you will decide for the best.

The decline of the Dean's mental faculties is part of the Cathedral's folk memory about which no one is happy to speak and when someone does is it with great sadness. As Ronald Woan has reported, Chris Wagstaffe's behaviour seemed almost not to register the signs of his degeneration but strange behaviour in a Dean in his Cathedral cannot be covered for long. He would act strangely in services, failing to respond within the liturgy and interrupting services by his suddenly crying 'God save the King'. On occasions, Ronald Woan would be conducting the choir when he became aware of the Dean at his side and heard the words 'Everything all right, Ronald?' A member of the Cross Guild, the Dean's Remembrancer, used to sit alongside him in his stall and try to prevent anything from going wrong. That the real seriousness of the Dean's condition was kept secret for so long is testament to Chris Wagstaffe's ability to keep everything going. She had known him so well and for so long that she knew what he would have said or done had all been well. As Colin Dunlop was to write to her on 26 June 1955, 'You have been so much bound up in the work at Liverpool that to the outsider it is not easy to know where you begin and the Dean ends or vice versa.' Spare copies of all the old service papers were kept and from what existed new services were compiled.

Whenever I have worked on private papers in an archive collection, I have had an uncomfortable feeling that I was prying into someone's life. To read the final letters in the Dwelly archive has been a powerful and distressing experience. I have no way of knowing what proportion of the letters sent to the Dean and Christine at that time are preserved in the collection but they are from a wide range of people whose warmth of feeling is palpable.

The opening letter of the whole sequence is a signed copy of his letter of resignation.

The Right Hon. Sir Anthony Eden,
Prime Minister.
9 June 1955
Dear Sir,
With a really heavy heart I feel I must ask you to acquaint our Sovereign Lady that I would like to retire from being Dean of Liverpool at the end of September. I have not been too well for some time and I feel this is best.
It is a long time since I have had the pleasure of welcoming you in the Cathedral. With kind regards,

Yours sincerely,
F. W. Dwelly

P.S. I have not yet informed my bishop or chapter of my decision. I would be
grateful to know how soon it would be in order for me to do so.

The copy of the original letter is signed but not with Dwelly's own fine pen but with
Chris's broader nib: from the start I had the suspicion that he had not signed it himself
and I held this suspicion long before I was told that Chris could sign his signature and
people could not tell the difference. Such a letter as this from one who had been a
master of the grand style is painful to read. With 'I have not been too well for some
time and I feel this is best' there is a sense of 'how are the mighty fallen', but in 'It is
a long time since I have had the pleasure of welcoming you in the Cathedral', with
its tone of mild rebuke, there is still the faintest flicker of the great man.

The final letter written by Dwelly in the archives is dated 18 June 1955. It is a
duplicated letter, signed, and addressed to the senior members of the Cross Guild:

With a very heavy heart I want you to know before it is made public that I think
the time has come for me to retire – without your help I would have done so over
a year ago. I have asked the Prime Minister to acquaint the Queen that I have
decided to retire at the end of this September. I am not worried about the future
of what I have tried to do here for the last thirty years – it will be safe in your
hands.

I think we'd rather not mention this – I want to carry on well and to talk about
it is too upsetting.

I don't know what our plans are but I will remain in Liverpool because without
you to come and see us whenever possible we would be too terribly lonely.

Please don't think of presents, it sounds funny to mention this, but I know you.
Presents would give me a feeling of actually parting – your present can be that we
aren't and that you carry on my work and to teach others to do so.

Yours affectionately,
F. W. Dwelly

There must have been a great many letters to Dwelly as soon as the announcement of his retirement appeared in the press, but what is even more remarkable is
the number sent personally to Chris Wagstaffe – clear acknowledgement of her
significance in the Dwelly story, especially in the final years. One of the first letters
she must have received was handwritten on 18 June by Clifford Martin:

My dear Chris,

Thank you very much for writing a personal note with the other letters. I feel
very sad for the Dean and know how deeply he must feel his impending retirement. He has indeed been a wonderful leader in the magnificent work that has
been done at the Cathedral.

I feel equally heavy at heart for somebody else but I mustn't say more because she wouldn't like it. Let me just say this. Thank you and bless you for a wonderful job done with courage and devotion. Few people may know what we all owe to you but one who knows something of it is

Yours affectionately
Clifford Liverpool.

An equally important letter arrived the following day from Bezzant in which it is clear that he believed the retirement decision was actually made by Chris:

My dear Chris,

What a decision to have to take! But I can, I think, fully understand what it means, and I am sure it would not have been made unless you were convinced that it is right. But after 30 years! It's like the end of life, isn't it? Anyhow, that is how I feel about it. I can only say this on the other side. What has worried me has been what we have so often said about a different matter, i.e., families looking after sick relatives. Time wearies most of them. And though you would have a much larger team of loyal supporters, if F.W. did not get better but became worse, in time many would forget all the great achievements and he achieved them he did so. And it has seemed to me that that would be a terrible end to such endless good and hard work in his (and your) literally living for the place. Better to go while all is well and the memory of great things is still green. But I am sad – for him and you – and apprehensive about the future. If Cliffie has a deciding influence in the future appointment, it will be someone of whom he is sure that he can 'boss' and who will never seriously oppose him – and it may well also be someone who will undo the great tradition.

Albert Augustus David had left Liverpool to live in Cornwall after his retirement and he died in 1950. After the acrimony which seemed so destructive of the relationship between Bishop and Dean it may seem surprising that the Bishop's widow, Eda, should write with such warmth and feeling to Chris:

Dearest Chris,

I was not surprised at the announcement in the papers when I saw the Dean last week, I knew it must come soon. Please God, when he has complete rest, he may get back some of his strength and vigour – I can imagine what leaving that lovely place will mean to you both and I don't like to think about it. But the past few months must have been an awful strain for you and it must have been an agonising decision to make. I am so grateful that I saw those two lovely services and Canon Dwelly in his place in the Cathedral. It will be the last of many lovely memories. Will you write now and then to tell me how Canon Dwelly is. I feel very anxious about him. Much love, my dear -

Bless you.
Yrs affectly
Eda M. David

Vere Cotton had been deeply involved with the Cathedral community since 1924 and he wrote separately to the Dean and Chris by the same post, saying: 'To those who know this Cathedral best can but appreciate what you have done for it and the strain under which you have had to carry on these last months. To say thank you seems a very inadequate expression of gratitude and admiration but perhaps this is an occasion when few and simple words are the most fitting.' The following day Elfreda Cotton wrote to Chris in sympathy with the great changes which were to happen: 'Such changes in anticipation seem cataclysmic, but when the time comes, the reward of a right decision comes too, and one is surprised to find great happiness and contentment. May these be yours, you have so very many friends, young and old, and all Cottons in these categories know how much they owe to you.'

Lionel Jacob, a Liverpool vicar, knew Dwelly and Chris well and wrote directly to her: 'But any appreciation of the Dean must also include another appreciation and that is of you, yourself. No one will ever be able to evaluate what you have meant to him and his work. And my little note is just to say a very deep appreciation of all you have been and have done for him.

I know you will say that this has all been LIFE to you, and that you would never have offered any less help than you have done. But that does not alter the fact that the LIFE of the Cathedral owes you a debt of gratitude again quite beyond repayment. The way you have devoted yourself to this task calls out the admiration of all who possess some knowledge of the inner life of the Cathedral.'

Dwelly himself was to receive letters from the widest range of people: from the Cathedral cleaners to the Prime Minister and the Archbishop of York; from friends way back in Chard to current young members of the choir; and, of course, from the many clergy who had known his work over many years. There was a warmly appreciative letter from Frederick Dillistone, the man eventually to succeed him:

My dear F.W.D. Sr,

Thank you for your letter received this morning. I am very grateful to you for your consideration in letting me know personally about the very big decision which you have now made.

It is almost exactly three years ago that we first met. Since that time I have had the privilege of entering more and more into the splendour of the tradition which you have done so much to create. There have been unforgettable services for great occasions – none I think finer than the three which came so recently over the week-end of June 12th. There have also been the quieter, more intimate week-day evensongs which we have shared together. And through all there has been the sense of the affection and loyalty which all within the Cathedral company feel towards yourself.

To me personally you have been most gracious. You have spoken many words of encouragement about my work: you have made possible for me a large measure of freedom to read and write. I am most grateful for all that this has meant to me.

We have all been sensible of the increased difficulty you were finding in working as in former days but you have, I know, carried on just as long as you felt it to be possible. I can well understand that it must be with a heavy heart that you have now made the decision to retire but what you have established in the Cathedral will not cease when you finally lay down your own responsibility. Meanwhile I need hardly assure you that I shall be ready to do every thing that I can to help both during your own last months and during the time which must elapse until your successor arrives.

   With affectionate regards and every good wish for the days that lie ahead.
   Yours as ever
   F.W.D. Jr.

Colin Dunlop, a Bishop and the Dean of Lincoln, had been visiting the Cathedral since 1931 and was an enthusiastic yet discerning admirer of Dwelly and his work. His letter is no formal courtesy letter to a dignitary at the time of his retirement.

My very dear F.W.D.
   I have heard from Chris that you are retiring in September. Archbishop Davidson said that his decision to retire was the hardest and most painful of his whole life. I hope it has not been so with you, though it could not have been easy.
   But what a lot you have to look back on with thankfulness and pride. Few Deans can have ever had so much as you and it has been hard slogging work all the way I imagine. Yet you have always kept yourself fresh and vital and ready for any challenge that came along. Yes, even if you do not look back with pride, your friends do. It has been a wonderful regime. I just cannot imagine the Cathedral without you. I shall, dutifully, come in October, but I shall not know where I am.
   God bless you my dear man and may you be rewarded for all your kindness and goodness, as well as forgiven for all the other things, and may your time now be full of peace and quiet growth of the things of the spirit.
   Yours ever
   Colin

From the Deanery of St Paul's came a letter from his old friend and associate W. R. Matthews:

My dear Friend,
   How can I tell you what I feel about your resignation? It is a sad and heavy piece of news to me and the cause is sadder still. I don't know how you are and I don't want to add to your burden but I must say that my thoughts and prayers are with you. I hope that you can reflect on the wonderful work you have done for your great Cathedral and be glad and I hope you will reflect upon the number of people who are your grateful friends; among them I count myself. Your friendship has been something of great value to me and I am happy that I had some very small part in your work in Liverpool. May God bless and keep you, my dear friend.

Always affectionately yours
W. R. Matthews

By 1955, Christopher Chavasse, son of Francis James, was Bishop of Rochester.

My dear Dean,
    I don't wonder that you are most sorrowfully afflicted with feelings of real bereavement, as you contemplate laying down your work as Dean of Liverpool Cathedral this coming September. The Cathedral has been at once your life and your child. You have been wedded to it as any bishop to his diocese, and you have created its worship and made it the wonderful thing that it is. Don't mind going too much. This must come to us all sooner or later, and you can thank God that he has allowed you to carry on so long. The great matter is that you have achieved 'immortality', and now will live in the worship of the Cathedral, which will always be associated with your name. A hundred years from now, and more, people will still be talking of 'Dean Dwelly of Liverpool'.
    May God give you 'light at eventide'.
    Ever yours affectionately
    Christopher Roffen

One letter from the Bishop would not satisfy his wife Itza, who wrote by the same post:

... Christopher has just whispered to me the sad contents of your letter. One feels like going into mourning – except that you would dislike that more than anything in the world. I think it is impossible to me, at the moment to think of the Cathedral and yourself apart. Every time I have been there I have marvelled afresh at the glorious thing you have created – surely the most elusive – a tradition of worshipful worship – and glory and dignity – ... Thank you for all the happiness that Liverpool Cathedral has always given me.

A letter came from the Palace at Chichester from his old friend, George Bell.

My dear Dean,
    It is with great sadness that I read of your retirement from the Deanery of Liverpool. But I cannot resist this slight expression of admiration and gratitude for your splendid and creative work in that wonderful Cathedral during all these years. The Church owe you a deep debt for the pioneer work you have done in worship, in drawing industry, art, learning, education, commerce to find in that great Temple their benediction and inspiration from Almighty God. I am sure that your work will live – and prove an illumination and a beacon to Christians – and to those who are on the frontiers also – showing how great an appeal God's House can make, what reverence and imagination unite as they had so nobly united in you. I shall never fail to value our friendship – expressed in such a notable way in Archbishop Lang's enthronement, but not only there. I hope you are able to find

a home for retirement, and refreshment acceptable to you. But your heart will always be in Liverpool and its Cathedral. And your love for the stones on the building and the artists and craftsmen cannot fail – Oh builder and Dean combined!

May God bless and keep you, my friend.

George Cicestr

Bishop Gresford Jones, himself an old man, had served with Dwelly on the chapter since 1935 and recognised the real agony surrounding his friend's decision: 'I hasten to assure you how closely I am with you in what must have been a decision of real agony. For it is your own genius, your own sympathy, your own inter-relation to so many diocesan minds of what our Anglican worship may be ... made Liverpool Cathedral what it is, and the aching pain of laying all this down must be unbearable.'

It is difficult trying to prevent his chapter becoming inordinately long; there is such a range of letters, many of them with a unique tiny insight into some aspect of the man. The way in which people from his distant past kept contact with him has been noted in previous chapters and at the end of his ministry there were letters, too numerous to quote, from people who knew him at every stage of his ministry.

In today's 'Chard and Ilminster' paper, I read of your retirement, and felt I must write and wish you well. Your name always brings back such happy childhood memories of Cheltenham. How adept you were at writing your name in treacle on bread and butter! I still have my school-girl autograph book, in which you wrote a quotation from Robert Browning. The date February 1916.

It seems an age since the Harvest Festival services in St Mary's Windermere.

I remember your dear Mother and Father well, and still remember how pleased as a child I was when Mother took me to visit 'Grandma Dwelly', one particular visit stands out from my childhood memory of about fifty years ago, Dora Dwelly was staying there, and played the piano and sang the song 'Daddy' to us, I thought it was so sad I burst into tears, you were there too, and you sat me on your knee and comforted me, and since then how many sad souls you must have comforted.

... take the opportunity of thanking you for preparing me for confirmation at Emmanuel very many years ago. I expect you have forgotten now what a lot of trouble you went to, urging our parents to let us be confirmed in the year the service was held in our own church, and preparing us in your own home during our school holidays.

Needless to say, there were many powerful letters from his own musicians and Cross Guild members:

I too have a heavy heart. twenty-four years of my life is a big span, and during that time we have shared so much.

I can only hope that you feel as great a measure of satisfaction when you consider your creative life of such magnitude and success, as I feel pride in the knowledge that I have grown up in the centre of that life and watched its expression grow to a full climax of glory. That its light will shine long and glorious to guide those younger friends I am certain.

One doesn't boast of one's affinity with the great, but in my heart I have known the joy of our deep understanding of each other: our common faith and love, and our 'oneness' in those things inexpressible in words.

It has been all so inestimably worth while, that whilst I share your heavy heart – and mine is so heavy, I try to rejoice for you with the intimacy and understanding of part of that which you have created.

Yours very sincerely,

Ronald [Woan]

I have had the happiest days of my life singing in your Choir and I am sure I should never have been appointed had it not been for you. Tom Coulthwaite.

I welcome this opportunity of saying how much I valued the kindness and friendliness which you always showed to the gentlemen of the choir. A. C. Bartlett

Dear Master Dean,

And friend of 32 years!

It will be terrible without you but your decision is typically courageous.

I guess we'll all have to try our best to help your successor to keep growing the tradition which you have so marvellously planted. This won't be an easy job, but then you've trained us for it ...

I owe a tremendous amount to you and Miss Wagstaffe more than I can ever set down but I'll just recall two things – my long apprenticeship to words at Cambridge leading up to the wonderful opportunity to read music that you created for me. Thank you for your inspiration at all times and for your encouragement in periods of difficulty. Thank you for your friendship over all the years and may we always keep it bright.

With love to you both,

Lawrence [Lawrence H. Davies]

We are very sorry to hear you are retiring shortly. We shall all miss you in the Cathedral each week. Michael Norris [chorister]

I regret to learn of your impending resignation and I hope that this will not mean that we are to lose you completely. Reg Evans [chorister]

My dear Master Dean,

It is impossible for me to express my thoughts on reading your letter, I cannot yet realise that our beloved Cathedral is to lose its first Dean and Father, for the very fabric is engraved for all history to see the name Dwelly, all that is done within its walls are the inspiration of the man called to be the first Master of its household.

I have had the deep and lasting honour, sir, of serving you for the past twenty-six years, I so well remember, as a choir boy, your installation as Dean, opening up a chapter of very proud and happy memories.

But now, sir, your time has come to lay aside your duties and to take your very well-earned retirement, but not in loneliness, you have a large family in the Cross Guild alone, sir, to whom over these many years you have been a Father and whose deep and sincere love for you will continue throughout the whole of your retirement.

I am certain that there will be no Goodbyes, sir, for there will always be some well-known face knocking at your door to enquire of your health and happiness, and, if I may have that privilege, I include myself. We shall also, surely see you at the Cathedral from time to time and we shall look towards your stall to see that all is well with you.

You need have no fear that the great tradition which you have set will not be carried on, for every member of the Cross Guild will, I know, dedicate himself and teach those who follow to carry out the traditions set for them in the past by a master of art, culture and tradition, and I can well imagine all things being carried out according to the Dwelly plan.

I am proud, sir, to have shared your friendship which I value above all others, and I sincerely hope that this may continue for many years to come.

May God bless you with a happy and comfortable retirement surrounded by friends, old and new and may your life be long so that it may continue to be an inspiration to all who know and love you.

Yours very sincerely,
Kenneth Wood

People wished him a long and happy retirement but the discerning must have faced the reality, and no one more feelingly than Eda David whose words formed the title of this chapter.

It is lovely to read all the appreciations of Canon Dwelly and I do hope he enjoys them. He must know what people feel about his work – but it is good to have it put into words. Do write and give me news of him. It must be a terribly hard time for you both, inspite of all the love and good will that is being poured out. I felt when I saw Canon Dwelly in June, that he had already gone from us into a world of his own – I hope there he will find peace and rest when all the turmoil of leave-taking is over.

CHAPTER SEVENTEEN

Dean Emeritus

T HE DEATH CERTIFICATE recorded, 'On 9 May 1957, Frederick William
Dwelly, Male, 76 years, Dean Emeritus Church of England (retired) died at 6
Grove Park'. Cause of death was stated to be (a) Hypostatic congestion of lungs
(b) Cerebral Arteriosclerosis. On a high catafalque in the Presbytery his body lay in
an oak coffin, draped with the Cathedral pall, with four tall candles on oak stands at
the four corners. As the congregation arrived and read their service papers, the
opening poem must have seemed so apt.

> Strange is the vigour of a brave man's soul.
> The strength of his spirit and his irresistible power,
> The greatness of his heart and the height of his condition,
> His mighty confidence and contempt of dangers,
> His true security and repose in himself,
> His liberty to dare and to do what he pleaseth,
> His alacrity in the midst of fears, his invincible temper, are
> advantages which make him master of fortune.
> His courage fits him for all attempts,
> Makes him serviceable to God and man.
> And makes him the bulwark and defence of his being
> And his country.

There was a mood of solemn triumph at the service: the choir sang Psalm 121 and
Bach's setting of the words *God liveth still*, and choir and congregation sang the hymns
Who would true valour see and *The strife is o'er the battle done*. There was no sermon but
Hugh Reid, Rev. Ralph Dawson, Canon J. S. Bezzant and Dean F. W. Dillistone led
parts of the service. An anonymous newspaper reporter described the final part of the
service – a service which might almost have been written by Dwelly himself:

> The full Cathedral Choir led a procession of clergy and Cathedral and Diocesan
> officials into the chancel. The great procession, moving slowly in a measured
> majesty created by Dean Dwelly himself, took five minutes to pass.

The funeral of Dean Dwelly. Bishop Martin can be seen on the Bishop's Throne on the right.

After the last hymn there was a moment of silence. Then, as all the congregation stood, the organ led the choir into Le Fleming's *Nunc Dimittis*, a work commissioned in 1952 as a mark of affection for Dr Dwelly by the Cathedral Chorister's Guild. Two choristers removed the red and gold Cathedral pall from the coffin. As the coffin bearers took it off the catafalque, a chorister snuffed the four candles standing at the corners. A path was cleared through the wreaths massed round the Presbytery. The *Nunc Dimittis* faded to a silence as the coffin passed between the choir stalls. Then, as the procession reformed and the coffin was borne slowly down the Nave, the Cathedral organ burst into Chopin's *Funeral March*.

Out through the main entrance and down the steps, with the great Bell of the Vestey Tower tolling over it, the body of Dean Dwelly went from the Cathedral for the last time.

It is difficult to know how much notice a biographer should take of obituary notices and memorial sermons. In Dwelly's case, I have found it an interesting read in that, although they are the words of people who knew Dwelly in different ways, there is a large measure of agreement and the evidence for their judgements is clearly to be seen in his life and work.

The monthly *Liverpool Diocesan Leaflet* for July 1957 carried a piece from the Very Rev. V. Spencer Ellis, Dean of St Asaph instead of the monthly message from the Bishop.

It is difficult to think objectively of a friend – possibly that is the reason that all the appreciations of F.W. that I have read seem so very unsatisfactory – and why this will appear quite inadequate to any who may read it.

My first meeting with him was on the departure platform at Euston at midnight. Bishop David had entrusted to him the task of making all the arrangements for the consecration of the Cathedral and on the journey to Liverpool, Dwelly sketched the work involved as he already saw it. He had pierced to the heart of the matter – The Act of Consecration culminated in the Bishop's Eucharist on the Sunday morning. All the ceremonies which preceded that were but the preparation – all that would follow throughout the years would be the fulfilment of that act whereby all men, all activities, all hopes and chances should be caught up and offered to God for his glory and so be transformed with the pattern of Christ's glorious Resurrection. The Rite must express this: the ceremonies must clearly interpret the manner and spiritual meaning of the Rite. The building itself was already testifying in stone to the all compelling Majesty of God – and all that should be done within the Cathedral must teach the same lesson, whether in word or sound or movement.

Here was the tremendous task that was committed to him – and, I believe, every action of his life finds its explanation when it is seen as a way by which he sought to fulfil the task the Bishop had entrusted to him.

None can question the rightness of the choice for Dwelly had, by nature, and by grace, those gifts which the occasion needed. His infectious enthusiasm gathered round him men who shared his vision, and who were prepared to work wholeheartedly for its realisation. In result, the first stage of the Cathedral's life reached a magnificent climax on the day of its Consecration.

Let it be remembered that at that time Dwelly was not even a member of the Chapter – his office was that of Ceremoniarius – a title which aptly described his chiefest contribution to the life and work of the Cathedral, and through it to the diocese and the Church at large. Provincial recognition was given to this aspect of his work when the Archbishop of York at the Southport Congress claimed that Dwelly was an asset to the whole church.

From the day of Consecration onwards Dwelly used every opportunity that could be found, to integrate the life of the diocese and city into the worship and witness of the Cathedral. Thus, he welcomed people and organisations of every sort and bade them feel at home in their Cathedral – where every art that appeals to eye, ear and mind was used to convey the message of the new life in Christ, and the unity which is theirs who love the Lord Jesus in sincerity and truth.

Perhaps less understood was his zeal to compel those afar off from 'organised religion' to come in. But it was all a part of that sense of mission of the Shepherd whose scattered flock must be brought within the fold. No man had a larger heart than he – no man was less of a Controversialist – 'First give thyself wholly to God! Then to the task which he has given thee.' These words may well have been the motto of his life – and few men have ever so completely embodied the ideal for which he strove.

'Remember unto me, O my God, for good, all that I have done for this people'.

The *Emmanuel Messenger*, the magazine for the Southport parish, carried two pieces about him in the June 1957 edition. The first was described as 'The substance of the sermon preached by Canon W. E. Harston Morris in Emmanual Church on Sunday, May 19th, at 10.45 a.m.'

'What went ye out for to see.' St Matthew xi, 8.

I have chosen this text and the thoughts that flow from it because I think they are tremendously applicable to him whom we bear in mind this morning, Frederick William Dwelly.

He was – if anyone ever was – a leader, a worker and a teacher, no 'reed shaken by the wind', but a strong man, of strong views, and strong to put them into action – no 'man clothed in soft raiment' but 'a man of the people,' who understood the people and became one with them. A prophet? Yes, one who saw the present and lived beyond the present.

I dare say there were those who disapproved of his changes and innovations, but he knew that 'the old order changeth, giving place to the new,' and that new thoughts must be met by new methods. To this end he brought his studied and expert knowledge of beauty in all its forms – architecture, music, colour, ceremonial, liturgy – and in the application of these things to the worship of Liverpool Cathedral, he set a standard which will be permanent in that Cathedral and which has influenced the Church throughout our country.

If I were asked to pick out one characteristic of his personality, I would instance his wonderful power of attractiveness. He drew people more than any person I have ever known. For five years Curate of Cheltenham Parish church, for nine years Vicar of this church of Emmanuel, Southport, for thirty years Canon and Dean of Liverpool Cathedral – in each of these spheres, he drew the people to the worship and service of God.

I have known him for nearly forty years, and have been the more closely associated with him for nearly twenty years in my membership of the Cathedral Chapter. I have never failed to be impressed by the affection which was felt for him by every member of the Cathedral staff – clergy, choir, vergers, cleaners. He was so full of thought for them. Only time prevents me from speaking about his wonderful work, during the war, with the Navy personnel of the Western Approaches.

And now he has finished his course here to serve God in some higher sphere. But the work of the first Dean of Liverpool will live and never be remembered without thanksgiving.

Do you remember those noble words of Tennyson in his 'Ode on the Death of the Duke of Wellington'?

> Speak no more of his renown
> Lay your earthly fancies down
> And in the vast Cathedral leave him.
> God accept him, Christ receive him.

The same magazine also carried an appreciation by Ralph Dawson:

It is difficult and probably impossible to give a truly objective picture of another human personality. All that we can do is to attempt to express how that personality appeared to us and this in these few words I must try to do. I think that one of the characteristics of Dr. Dwelly was his deep interest in and affection for people. Whenever people talk over their memories of him, whether those memories be years ago as Vicar of Emmanuel or after that as Canon Dwelly, or when he became Dean, it is always the same – for they speak of remarkable acts of kindness and of exceptional thoughtfulness and generosity. It was people he cared for more than causes, and nothing gave him greater or more sincere pleasure than to be able to be of service to a friend. For many years he went up to the Sea Scouts' Camp in Windermere every summer with unfailing regularity, not because he enjoyed camping, but because his friendships there dated from the years when he was a curate at St Mary's, Windermere, and his loyalty and affection would not allow him to do anything but go. This was entirely typical of him.

Another characteristic was his gift of encouraging. I remember that, when I was a curate at Emmanuel and was stuck for a subject for a sermon, he told me to preach on Barnabas because Barnabas was always ready to believe the best in people and to encourage the best. That he himself was always ready and eager to do. Time and again he would keep his own name in the background so that a friend should receive the praise which he felt should be his due.

One of his own great gifts was that of imagination, the imagination of the poet and the artist. One of his friends, the Liverpool sculptor, Mr. Carter Preston, said to me last week, 'He had a gift of true imagination which is very rare, very rare indeed. If you struck the match, for him the flame of it soared to the sky.' I remember also how another friend, the late Mr. Edgar Robinson, choral conductor of the Cathedral choir, said the same kind of thing in other words: 'It is a constant source of wonder to me that I, who am a trained musician (whose life's work is music) yet cannot see the possibilities of interpretation of a piece of music half as clearly as does the Dean.' Sir Giles Scott would say the same of the cathedral itself, for it is no secret that the furnishing and enriching of the Cathedral has been a partnership between the Architect and the Dean, in which the Dean gave that deep inspiration which enables a man to give of his very best.

I have no space left to write of other aspects of his personality, such as the creation of those acts of worship for which the cathedral was well known literally throughout the world. It must suffice to say that, when I came to Cambridge, my organist told me that he never realised what an Easter service could be until he heard a broadcast from Liverpool Cathedral.

Part of Bishop Clifford Martin's words in the *Liverpool Daily Post* under the head-line 'Dr Dwelly – maker of magnificence' are worthy of use here because they contain some material which is personal to him:

> Before my Enthronement the Dean asked me to go to the Cathedral not once but several times 'to walk over the ground' as he called it. In this way he helped me to become used to my part in that great ceremony and on the day to do it without flurry or anxiety.
>
> Dr Dwelly had a stern side. To many people he seemed austere and unap-proachable; others found him difficult and uncooperative. In actual fact he had a most loving nature. He would spare himself no effort or inconvenience to minister to a friend; and all the Cathedral company were his very dear friends. The welfare of his boys was his great concern. Their school, their career, their families, all these were near to the heart of the man who for so many years was the centre of our Cathedral company.
>
> One of Dr Dwelly's deepest loves was his love for children. He was marvellous with them and they loved him in return. A few weeks before my Enthronement the Dean arrived at our home bringing with him a cathedral hymn book. This he handed to our three young daughters with the instruction: 'Go into your father's study and choose the hymn you would like to have sung in the Cathedral when he is enthroned.' So he drew them into the Cathedral company, as he did our son, then a lad of seventeen. John was given the task of accompanying his father at every stage in the Enthronement ceremony. All this was Dr Dwelly's idea. It was part of his genius. Worship, according to his idea, was not something imposed upon the people but drawn out of them, so that they learned to offer their best to God.
>
> For all he has meant to Liverpool and its Cathedral we remember, with thanksgiving, Frederick William Dwelly.

A few sentences from the same Bishop in the *Liverpool Diocesan Gazette* have been much quoted by people writing about services in the Cathedral:

> You have to go to Liverpool Cathedral if you want to see how to walk to the glory of God. Every procession is an act of worship. Every boy in the choir, even the smallest of them, is helped to think of himself as an important factor in a common act of praise and prayer.

It was not until December 1960 that a fitting memorial to the first Dean was unveiled in the Cathedral – a life-size figure with chorister and cross guild members carved by his long-standing friend, Edward Carter Preston, using the death mask which he had taken three years previously. One of the sermons that day was preached by Gerald Ellison, the Bishop of Chester, who had known him for twenty years.

Can it be doubted but that the mainspring of his life was the intensity of his vision of the glory of God? I fancy that in his personal religion he was aware of God first as transcendent. He was acutely conscious of the greatness of God, his majesty and power and beauty. So, in his liturgical compositions and in the services he designed, there is the constant note of praise, the outpouring of thanksgiving and devotion to the Almighty God who has given so liberally and to whom man must respond by the uplifting of his heart and mind and soul.

It was because Dean Dwelly felt so intensely the awfulness of God that he could never be satisfied with anything less than the best in the offering of worship which man brought him. Shape, colour, sound, movement, all are integral parts of man's offering to God; and as such, all must strive for perfection. Himself a person deeply sensitive to beautiful things, he called upon craftsmen of all kinds to offer their skill for the worship of God, and he taught and trained others to bring what they possessed into the treasury of the divine offering.

So it was that he made Liverpool Cathedral renowned throughout the world for the splendour and beauty of its worship. It was indeed providential that as this great building arose, so Dr Dwelly was there to breathe life and spirit into its walls. In a memorable sermon preached here, Dr Garbett, then Archbishop of York, pointed out how fortunate it was that the opportunity presented by the new Cathedral was matched by the liturgical genius of its first Dean, so that within the new setting it was possible for sound liturgical experiment to take place. The experiment was original, but loyal to the ethos of the Anglican tradition. It was an enrichment of the whole Church.

Liverpool Cathedral came to be a by-word for perfection in worship. No detail was too unimportant to merit the most careful scrutiny and preparation. In a building which called for splendid ceremonial, Dwelly designed and put into effect the act of worship worthy of Him to whom it was offered. The music must be of the finest, the language fitting for the occasion. The colours of robes and furnishings must harmonise. The movement of officiants must be dignified. So, with infinite preparation and patience, the tradition was built up, one generation taught another, the great Cathedral became a great house of worship and prayer.

Of course Dean Dwelly had his critics and his detractors. There were those who regarded him as an eccentric, or dismissed him as merely a great stage manager. In lesser hands these criticisms might have had some justification. But in fact Dr. Dwelly was not an amateurish experimenter. He was a learned liturgical scholar, he had a considerable knowledge of the works of the mystics, he was deeply versed in literature and poetry, and he was an artist to his finger-tips. So, in the planning of a service, the designing of some new furnishing for the Cathedral, he knew instinctively what was wanted, how far to go, what was right. What in less skilful hands or with a less discerning mind might have become vulgar and offensive, was, under the Dean, uplifting and deeply satisfying ...

The Cathedral and all that it stands for is the wider, the more public expression

of Dr Dwelly's genius, and through it millions of people have been brought by him
to God. A smaller number, though doubtless large enough, were privileged to be
his personal friends, to enjoy his boundless kindness and to profit from his
generosity. His affection was without limit, and those of us who were his friends
know the lengths to which he would go to bring comfort and happiness to those
who needed him. His was a love which overflowed, a love which knew no
measure, a love which exceeded the bounds by which common-sense or prudence
might have limited his self-giving. We shall never know the number of people who
had reason to be grateful for his kindness and understanding; those in need who
were helped; those who were sad and who were made stable; the young men
guided as they planned their careers. All that can be assessed is that we, the indi-
viduals who knew him and were inspired by him, can never be sufficiently
thankful for what he taught us and what he gave us ...

The most important assessment of Dwelly's character and achievements by one
who knew him well for over thirty years is to be found in Charles Raven's sermon
on the Sunday morning the memorial was dedicated. It must be quoted in full.

In the 10th chapter of the Gospel according to St John and the 10th verse are the
familiar words 'I am come that you might have life and have it more abundantly.'
So Jesus describes the purpose of his mission as Life Giver, and on this Third
Sunday in Advent, when we commemorate the Ministers and Stewards of God's
mysteries and thank God for their work and example, it is peculiarly appropriate
that we in this great city and in this great Cathedral church should commemorate
Frederick William Dwelly, our first Dean, who was more than any other responsible for the implanting of the characteristic of life of this Cathedral and for its care
and development during the formative years in which he presided over our
chapter.

He was a man uniquely fitted to his time; a man dedicated to God in Christ and
to his own ministry in the Church of England; a man exquisitely sensitive to all
the appeals of art, music, poetry, literature, drama, liturgy; exquisitely aware of
the intuitive capacities which he possessed and singularly gifted in his approach to
people of all sorts, able to get along side of them and interpret almost without
spoken word their needs and express his readiness to help. But in addition, he had
singular gifts of administration, gifts of ingenuity in devising means for recording
and storing and making available all the experience he had gathered, whether from
his reading or his conversation, from his scholarship or from his contacts with men
and things. But above all, he possessed a genius for friendship, the capacity really
to care and passionately to help the folk who came to him and with whom he was
brought into contact. He was for us a steward of the good gifts of God in this place
and we owe him the building up of the community of this Cathedral which has
stood the test of economic depression, of world war and of radical changes in its
personnel and resources.

Of his life I need say very little. He was born and brought up in the West, in Somerset, without any special advantages of birth or prestige or privilege. Schooled for business, given a sudden conversion which transformed his whole way of living, going to Cambridge, to Queens' College – taking a degree without any special academic distinction – being ordained for a Curacy in Windermere, then going on for a short time to Cheltenham and finally coming after the First World War as Vicar of Emmanuel Church in Southport, where many of you surely will remember his very remarkable ministry. He and his wife made themselves known and beloved by a wide circle of parishioners. With all kinds he was constantly trying not only new experiments in methods of church service, but new adventures in the bringing of Christian help to the neighbourhood as a whole. They loved him as he loved them. I shall never forget how one of them, a man of high standing in Southport, spoke to me of him, 'We loved him. We knew that he cared for us. We knew that he would stand beside us whatever happened. We knew that if he was at the ends of the earth, he would come to our help if any disaster occurred.

This was the tribute to his many-sided service to his folk. And when he came to us at the consecration of this great Cathedral Church in 1924, when he came, bringing with him the trust of the Bishop, to order the great consecration service, we discovered not only the manifold range of his activities and knowledge, but his astonishing capacity to adapt himself to changing conditions, to improvise, to direct, and without the slightest self-aggrandisement, quietly, competently, devotedly to steer us all into the fulfilment of a design of which he was the master-planner. That great service gave to the Church of England something new, an artistry in worship which should I think have been used by the Church as a whole far more widely than it was, but which for us here and for the world-wide population that has passed through this Cathedral and city and taken part in these great services, an inspiration, an opening of the eyes, a quickening of the soul, a strengthening of the mind and an inspiration towards the common purpose and the common service.

He had the most extraordinary artistic gift of sensitiveness and intuition. You can see it in his discovery and encouragement of musicians like Goss Custard, or if I dare say so Benjamin Britten: of artists like the sculptor of this Cathedral, Mr. Carter Preston who is responsible for the memorial that we are soon to dedicate: of poets – he brought John Masefield here: – of statesmen – some of you will remember Field Marshal Smuts speaking from this pulpit: of doctors and scientists and thinkers, and men of letters: of industrialists and politicians: of soldiers, sailor, and airmen – the great Admiral of the Battle of the Western Approaches Max Horton not least – indeed of all sorts and conditions of men, craftsmen, and singers, visitors, tourists, all and sundry. To all of them he had an instinctive approach and I think that all of them, all of us, knew that we were joyful in his presence and that we went away from it better men and better women. He gave life and life abundant. And if he had singular difficulty in explaining the reasons for his intuitive judgements, he was always conscious of the need to consult others and by the end of his life when he gave his pastoral theology lectures in Cambridge, he startled me by the brilliance with which he handled an academic audience and academic subjects.

He was a man who grew continually in the range and extent of his resources. Yes, but of course, those resources were held together by a unity of purpose which gave them at once a sense of solidarity. People could perceive beyond the immediate interest which brought them into his company. This was his consuming passion to make of this Cathedral a house of God, a member of the Body of Christ, an instrument for the operation of the Spirit of God. And so he welded together into a living community all these diversities of people. He was capable of producing community, because his own many-sided interests and experience were held together by a single sublimating and integrating motive.

'En Christo – In Christ.' That was the motto of the great 8.30 services of which I had the privilege of being his colleague. Fullness of life, the first thing that Jesus came to give, must be held together by unity of purpose but unless it is combined with a measure of practical and administrative ability, the dreams will not of necessity come true. They need to be translated and I suppose the not least remarkable feature of Fred Dwelly's equipment was his mastery of means, the ingenuity with which he adjusted the available machinery to the purpose that he had in hand, the way in which he drew in human beings and found means of using their peculiar gifts, however small, however queer, in the common service, the ability to work and plan and adjust and organise until the dream came true. I suppose that the greatest quality in the life of the Apostle St Paul is that he was pre-eminently the dreamer whose dreams came true. I suppose it is significant of our faith in the incarnation that the eternal purpose of God can be transmitted and transmuted into the stuff of our daily lives. Thus, as the great prophet of this last year or two (Teilhard de Chardin) is telling us in his latest book, we can divinise, make divine both our activities and our passivities; and so in action and in the intimacies of our lives we can fulfil the will of God and share in some measure, dare we say it, the very nature of God.

A word or two about the cost involved and the sum of his achievement before we dedicate ourselves and his memorial. The cost of such self-giving, joyous as it was in the paying, freed from any sort of self-pity or I think of thought of self-aggrandisement, nevertheless was inescapable. Every prophet, every minister of the Gospel must be both a challenge and an inspiration; and in his case the challenge was manifest. He met with a certain amount of real malice, a good deal of misunderstanding and, of course, the immense difficulties which this city and our country had to confront at the time of the slump, just before I left Liverpool during the 'thirties', when the threat of war grew near and supremely during those years of blitz and terror, when its first Dean lived night and day in this Cathedral and when it narrowly escaped almost total destruction.

Those years, though at the end of them, when he visited us in Cambridge, he seemed to have lost nothing of his vitality and his friendliness and his charm, nevertheless, those years had brought their inevitable collapse. Fulness of life leads to a Cross. That is the price which we have to pay if the fulness of our life here is to become life eternal. And of the Cross which he suffered in his last years, this is neither the time nor perhaps the place to speak. Some of us watched the paying of it and will not easily forget the pain that it involved. Yes, but let us think rather of the splendid loyalty of the band which he had gathered together of workers in this great Cathedral, of the staff, the Cross Guild, the choir, the Sidesmen, the Vergers, and indeed of all those linked up with the direct service of this sanctuary, of Chris Wagstaffe and his own close friends among clergy and laity, of the splendid service which they rendered in maintaining the quality of life which he had seen and encouraged and indeed inspired, maintaining the quality of God manifest among us, taking new forms and gaining new resources, and employing new and splendid means. The cost was worth the pain.

Chris Wagstaffe.

And the purpose of it? There is one supreme need in the world at this moment, one manifest need. It is of course the need for community. In our over-individualist western world, as in the fear-dominated regions of communism, community is far to seek. Yet life is community; the fellowship of the holy spirit is the end product of the creative process itself as it was the immediate end-product of the ministry, the teaching, the passion, the death and resurrection of Jesus. And community is what this Cathedral church has always stood for and enabled. One world or none. That is the choice before us. We have the tremendous encourage-ment of a new partnership between science and religion, between the ancient traditions and the modern outlook, the partnership which is near ready for its sealing. We have an increasing partnership between the churches dedicated to the name of Christ and I think a new understanding of religion in all its phases. We could achieve a world-wide community for the first time in history.

We have already, and shall have within another generation at most, unlimited resources. If we can free the use of nuclear energy from its prostitution, its purpose of destruction, if we can see in proportion the rather childish business of inter-stellar exploration, if we can realise that we could quadruple the resources of the earth, overcome all drudgery, eliminate most disease, produce a condition in which the threat of increasing population was no longer overshadowing us, we might have, as Rutherford foresaw, a century in which mankind could sit down together to discover how this earth can become a home for the sons and daugh-ters of men. We could see the dream which Paul, the Apostle, dreamt that mankind might 'come home to the oneness of the faith, that is to the sensitive awareness of the Son of God, to a mature manhood, to the measure of the stature of the fulness of the Christ.' In his name we are dedicated. To that dedication our friend the first Dean gave himself. In that name we would dedicate ourselves. So in this great day of the Lord we may fulfil our high calling in God and his Christ, in memory of our past and in aspiration for our future: and to God be all glory.

CHAPTER EIGHTEEN

The Dwelly legacy

G ILES GILBERT SCOTT died in 1960 but the Cathedral he designed and built will surely last for a thousand years, so taking its place among the great cathedrals and churches of the United Kingdom. Frederick Dwelly, the man who more than any other created the Cathedral company and patterns of worship, died in 1957, and in 2004, the year being celebrated by the Cathedral as its centenary, the task of attempting to define and assess the Dwelly legacy is not easy. For the majority of people visiting or worshipping in the Cathedral today, Dwelly is a life-size stone figure on a wall in the south choir aisle. Only a handful of the Cathedral company have any personal memories of him, but for those who do, those memories are very strong.

All cathedrals, not just Liverpool, have changed markedly from the time of Dwelly's regime and it is hard to imagine Dwelly's autocratic ways operating in a world of administrators, bursars, catering supervisors, visitor and concert managers, personnel officers, heritage tourism, quantity surveyors, management theory, chapter politics and endless committees. I cannot see Dwelly functioning in a bureaucratic world. He would have been infuriated by the restrictions cathedral administration put upon him. At the same time, Dwelly's example shows just what can be done by a church leader with powerful convictions and the determination to put ideas into practice: an Edward Patey in the sixties and seventies and a Derrick Walters in the eighties and nineties.

I attended my first service in Liverpool Cathedral when I was in my early teens, worshipped there daily for nearly twenty years, and spent the last fifteen years of my professional life working in the Cathedral every day as its Education Officer. Having sifted through every last piece of the Dwelly archive over the last six years in preparation for this biography, I feel certain that the Dwelly legacy still exerts a strong influence – at the very least on the services – but not as a dead, restrictive hand from the past. Dwelly was never constrained by what he did last year as he constantly refined his ideas and experimented, polished and perfected into the future. Liturgy was not of antiquarian interest: it had to be right for the moment. The

American newspaper reporter back in 1925 had headlined Dwelly as one who 'fights unreality in religion'. This he did throughout his ministry and that is one of the great challenges which are a central part of the Dwelly legacy, the challenge to make the worship in the Cathedral fresh, relevant and memorable.

I hope that many parts of this biography have highlighted the characteristics and qualities of an archetypal Dwelly Liverpool service, 'its ceremonial, its music, its services', which 'enable folk to experience worship'. F.W.D. undoubtedly placed Liverpool Cathedral in the vanguard of Cathedral worship across the country in the twenties, thirties and forties. In the words of the second Dean 'Dwelly was a genius', but there was the obvious danger that Dwelly had imprinted himself and his services so strongly on the community that any changes after his tenure of office would be roundly resisted by any members of the community who might have been more caught up on the surface details of the 'signs and symbols' than on the truths they were trying to convey.

Frederick Dillistone had worked alongside Dwelly during his failing years, had recognised the quality of his achievement and quite rightly stayed very close to the patterns and styles which had been established for so long. The Chapter was not at full strength and there were some Sundays when the Dean was the only priest present at the services. Dillistone's quiet wisdom was just what the Cathedral needed after nearly thirty years of Dwelly's unique leadership. When Dillistone became Dean, the Chancellor's post went to Basil Naylor, a distinguished liturgist who was to serve the Cathedral for many years and whose choreography is still in evidence today. He was an admirer of Dwelly's work, the foundations of which were to remain, but he was a man who looked to the present and to the future as well as to the past. He was later to be made responsible for planning and writing the great service in 1978 to commemorate the completion of the Cathedral building in the presence of Her Majesty the Queen.

Basil Naylor was not appointed to Liverpool until after Dwelly's retirement but he immediately felt the continuing presence of the first Dean. 'Although he was no longer here when I arrived, I could sense his presence. Everyone from the Cross Guild to the cleaners were still hung around Dwelly. They had the tradition almost built into them.' Naylor recognised the virtues in Dillistone which enabled him to take the Cathedral into a new era: 'It needed a man of great humility to work with people who were themselves so attached to the Dwelly days. You don't want a man who was going to make noisy pronouncements or antagonize. Dillistone was unobtrusive but firm and he made the Cathedral a diocesan home again.'

It was under Dillystone's leadership that the Cathedral began to move towards replacing choral Mattins with Choral Eucharist as the main Sunday morning service. The choreography for that service was in the hands of Basil Naylor and remains basically unchanged today. Dwelly's ability to use space and movement symbolically was certainly inherited by Liverpool's new Chancellor. Naylor's admiration for Dwelly's work was clear but he was conscious of unfortunate division: 'I think the Cathedral company tended to think of themselves as a separate section and away from the diocese. There was a tendency to become rather like a Vatican chapel rather than the mother church of the area.' Such a tendency would have been anathema to the next Dean.

In 1964 the third Dean, Edward Patey, arrived from the recently completed Coventry Cathedral. He has readily acknowledged the Dwelly genius but was aware of the dangers:

We already had a great tradition of dignified worship and courageous experiment stemming from the first Dean, F. W. Dwelly, who was far ahead of his time in his imaginative use of a great building. But although we were a new Cathedral, I sensed that we were already in danger of developing a tradition which preferred to look back rather than forward. For some of the Cathedral company, 'what we did in the time of Dean Dwelly' was the yardstick by which everything was to be measured. Without jettisoning what good things had been inherited from the earlier days of the Cathedral's life in Liverpool, and from the much longer noble traditions of English Cathedral worship, we had to ask new questions and find fresh answers to the problem of relating the real needs of a rapidly changing secular society to the eternal truths of Christian worship and mission.

Some of Patey's friends, aware of the fresh experimental work at Coventry, feared that he might be taking a backward step by going to a 'huge unfinished sandstone edifice ... in danger of becoming a dinosaur surviving from another age, an Edwardian *folie de grandeur* out of tune with the mood of the second half of the twentieth century'. At Coventry he had experienced a freedom which left the company 'not tied to the past or paralysed by tradition'. A contributor to the *New Statesman* lamented of Liverpool Cathedral that 'the building is living many hundreds of years out of its time'. Local and national media comment on a Cathedral seen by its critics as a great anachronism demanded public response from the new Dean:

A young member of the Cross Guild wearing one of the green robes unique to Liverpool Cathedral, almost certainly the result of cooperation between Percy Dearmer and Edward Carter Preston. It is known that Mrs Carter Preston made some early robes.

The truth is that Liverpool Cathedral is probably used and appreciated by as wide a section of the community as any Cathedral in the country today ... The great space of the Cathedral provides us with a unique opportunity for liturgical and dramatic experiment. There is, I believe, no Cathedral in the country which so adequately provides the flexibility and adaptability which is an essential prerequisite of modern community worship.

Though Patey was apprehensive at the time of his move to Liverpool, he later admitted to me that Dwelly had been doing in the 'thirties and 'forties what Coventry had been doing in the sixties. 'I found in the light of my experience what a forward-looking person Dean Dwelly had been, twenty years or more before Coventry Cathedral was opened. Many of the experiments regarding community and worship and liturgy, which we were operating at Coventry, he had also pioneered.' As Raven had declared in the thirties and Ken Riley in the twenty-first century, the great services were designed to relate strongly to the people of their own day. Dwelly and Raven had been creating an atmosphere of 'discovery and inspiration' but they were not setting services in stone; we have noted the way Dwelly made minor adjustments to what had been successful services from year to year, though of course the famous festival services attracting vast congregations continued. To some people it may seem a strange notion but I believe it is true to say that experiment, evolution and change are significant elements within the Dwelly legacy. Bishop Gordon Bates, Precentor at Liverpool during the Patey years, wrote recently, '... because Dwelly had always wanted to be 'creative' it gave those who followed him the chance to be creative and innovative as well'.

Patey cycled to the Cathedral everyday, passing through areas of real poverty and unrest, and was moved to wonder was Cathedral worship 'a monstrous piece of escapism in the face of all the surrounding problems'? Was there justification behind the charge that 'the institutional worship of the church makes less and less impact on the community it is supposed to serve'? Dwelly had been acutely conscious of the thinking behind this charge and we have examined already the ways in which Dwelly laboured to solve some of the problems as he designed his 'special' services. Years later Naylor recognized the importance of what had been done: 'More and more groups are seeking to express themselves in a larger area than the normal city and urban life. A Cathedral is mother, servant, and teacher, and our services reflect community interests. It was here that Dwelly achieved so much by breaking away from simply using the old prayer-book formulae. When services are suggested, we ask the people concerned what they want to say, and tailor the proceedings accordingly'. Exactly what Dwelly had done with his services for the Royal Navy.

The Patey years are remembered for the number and the variety of the special events in the Cathedral, from Yehudi Menuhin to Tangerine Dream – events which attracted a wide cross-section of the community. The artist was welcomed into the Cathedral: 'We can say to them 'if you are trying to be genuinely creative, come and share your work and experience with us. For we honour God as the source of all true creativity'.' I retain vivid memories of students from the I. M. Marsh College of Physical Education as they celebrated Incarnation and Christmas in the Cathedral through dance. The superbly executed music and choreography of the Holly Bough Service on the Sunday before Christmas was continued and still today can produce a standing-room-only congregation, but Patey introduced a Christmas Service for young people built around folk and pop music. One year, a radically different service was produced for television and broadcast at prime viewing time on Christmas Eve; some viewers were scandalised while others were grateful for the powerful message of a radical experiment. Liverpool's great Deans and liturgists have been risk-takers and none more so than Dwelly. While Dwelly was referred to as the C. B. Cochrane of the Church of England, operating in 'God's Dwelly house', Patey was accused by one of his critics of being 'a beat age impressario'.

When Joe Riley published *Today's Cathedral – The Cathedral Church of Christ in Liverpool* in 1978, he produced an admirable summing up of the health of the Cathedral at that time and what he described was very much part of the Dwelly tradition: 'Liverpool Cathedral can probably claim to be the most exciting religious laboratory in the world ... One can only echo Dean Dwelly's famous exhortation, when he would encourage children to lie on the floor or on chairs, 'Look up! Look up!' This Cathedral is a sanctuary, a workshop, and a theatre of faith. We are fortunate to have had a succession of Deans who are fully aware of each aspect.'

Bishop Gordon Bates, who had been Precentor from 1973 to 1983, preached at the Cathedral during its centenary year and I asked him to comment on what he saw to be the Dwelly legacy. He had not known Dwelly but he admitted that his 'influence and style' coloured much of the worship in the Cathedral in the 1960s and 1970s:

It has always seemed to me that Dwelly was a great inventor and entrepreneur; wanting to create a liturgy and style which was peculiar to Liverpool and which in no way aped any other style (Roman or Lutheran). Some people described him as a 'decorated protestant', but that seems to me to be wide of the mark. He wanted and he created a Liverpool Cathedral liturgical style that allowed God to be worshipped in other ways than just words and music. It was Bishop Clifford Martin, I believe, who said that if you wanted to see how to walk to the glory of God go and observe the processions at Liverpool Cathedral. Now that seems in many ways to sum up one of Dwelly's great gifts to the Cathedral. The 'worship' started not with an opening prayer or hymn, but with the processions of choristers and clergy. That set the pattern for all that followed. Even now there is something left of the 'Dwelly style' in the processions from both ends of the Cathedral; though I must admit that some of the 'style' seems to have been curtailed somewhat, which seems a pity.

Then, of course, there were the 'traditions of Liverpool' that Dwelly created using as many young people (especially junior choristers) as possible. The very colour of the surplices and cassocks had to match with the colour of the stone; nothing was to 'jar' or seem out of place. That has been maintained and I hope

The youngest member of the
choir marks the consecration
cross.

always will. But what about the 'festival liturgies'of the Holly Bough and
Christmas Tree processions at Christmas, the daffodils at Easter, the red tulips at
Pentecost, the signing with water of the Consecration stone on the anniversary?
These were what gained Dwelly the title 'decorated protestant', I suppose; but that
is not enough. They were meant to be special signs and symbols of the passing of
the Christian year which were to become 'peculiar' to Liverpool Cathedral. They
were not copied from anywhere else and they were not for 'export' to other places.
They were (and, in a sense, still are) what singled Liverpool Cathedral out from
other churches and other Cathedrals. I suppose there was a period when these
traditions were followed slavishly; nothing could be altered and nothing missed
out from these processions and they did become a little 'twee': but the worshippers loved them and came from miles to witness them; so we kept them going,
and they should still be kept alive. But more than that we began to create new
'signs and symbols' and felt free and able to do this because it had always been
part of the traditions of Liverpool Cathedral. We could go on evolving the liturgies initiated by Dwelly and adding to them; and no one could protest because, of
course, they had been the style of Liverpool since the early Dwelly days. So whilst
some people saw the 'Dwellyisms' as limiting and time warped, I for one saw them
as useful examples and stepping stones to the introduction of new and amended

styles of marking the festivals and the special events in Cathedral life. Traditions need to be a stepping stone to further development and never a block to further progress and new vision.

I suppose that if I had felt I had to comply with everything Dwelly introduced and had been unable to make changes and to introduce new liturgical styles at all then 'Dwellyism' would have become a prison, a very limiting shackle around me. But because Dwelly had always wanted to be 'creative' it gave those who followed him the chance to be creative and innovative as well. So all in all I am very thankful for this strange character, who must have been very difficult to work with (especially in his later years), but who gave to Liverpool Cathedral not only an inheritance of style and panache, but also gave those who came after him the licence to be creative and innovative as well. Had it not been for the 'Dwelly legacy' then the liturgy and ethos of Liverpool Cathedral might just have been as uninspiring and pedestrian as many other Cathedrals in the country. Dwelly helped to create the uniqueness of Liverpool Cathedral and gave those who followed him the freedom to carry on and to develop this uniqueness. He saved us from 'conformity' and for that I remain very grateful.

In Dwelly's time there was no Canon Precentor; the Dean himself was solely responsible for the devising of services. But of 'those who followed him' I came to know three Precentors well and all have subsequently achieved higher preferment in the church: Nicholas Frayling as Dean of Chichester, Ken Riley as Dean of Manchester and Mark Boyling as Dean of Carlisle. I had a tinge of regret for each one of them, whose work I admired, in that each one moved on to work in physically rather small cathedrals. I am sure they must miss the vast 'Dwelly spaces' which Liverpool had provided.

The Very Rev. Ken Riley, Dean of Manchester, and a former Canon Precentor at Liverpool, reminded me of some of the ideas set down by Charles Raven in 1933 in his *Liverpool Cathedral – An Impression of its early years* in which he wrote of the 'creative adventure' of developing:

> . . . a life worthy of the community and of the age that had produced it. The eternal revelation in Christ must be presented in terms that can be understood by the people of today. Its theology must be a real interpretation of God to minds thinking along lines of modern knowledge: its ceremonial, its music, its services must enable modern folk to experience worship: its organisation must display the aspiration after fellowship and the ability of the Church to rise above legal and mechanical relationships.

It was Ken Riley who was invited to preach the sermon at the Cathedral Centenary Service on 19 July 2004 and much of what he said is relevant to any consideration of Dwelly legacy: he warned the congregation about 'the drag factor' on the church with the words 'Don't get stuck in the archives. Don't get locked in the past . . . Nostalgia has no place in religion, but history has.' He wanted to understand 'the spirit' of the earliest days in the Cathedral's history and returned to the words of a previous Chancellor:

> Writing of those days, Canon Charles Raven spoke of the creative adventure – 'At Liverpool the venture of faith which has enabled the building of a new Cathedral on so grand a scale aroused a keen sense of expectancy. Sir Giles Scott had given expression in architecture to the hope for a church which should stand for fresh and creative vision. To reproduce ancient formularies, to imitate earlier artistic modes, would be to betray the hopes of the community.' It is that freshness, that creative searching for the appropriate word, worship and service for each generation which has delivered Liverpool Cathedral from becoming a cocoon of nostalgia. And I dare to suggest that the creativity of which Raven wrote has now been taken up and is at the heart of English Cathedral life in general so that if things go wrong now, it is much more likely to be as a result of over-enthusiasm than of paralysing inertia. So we are not ashamed of what the Dean will refer to later in the service as the Liverpool Tradition, for that tradition has always been about proclaiming the gospel afresh, ever-new, ever-young in each generation.

The Dwelly legacy was not the province of clergy alone because from the day of the consecration onwards music was such an important feature in the Liverpool Cathedral world, and the Cathedral musicians form an unbroken line from the early days. Harry Goss Custard cooperated closely with the organ firm of Henry Willis and was the Cathedral Organist for over thirty years. He worked with Edgar Robinson as Master of the Choristers. On their retirements, their work was taken up by Noel Rawsthorne and Ronald Woan, who had both perfected their skills in the Cathedral since their days as choristers. Ian Tracey had been a pupil of Rawsthorne and Patey appointed him as Organist and Master of the Choristers and he was joined later by former chorister and organ scholar, Ian Wells, as Assistant Organist.

Big musical events in the Cathedral, prominent in Dwelly's day, became even more adventurous later. Ronald Woan had established the Cathedral Singers in 1958 and moved towards a tradition in which Bach's *St Matthew* and *St John Passions* were both performed in the Cathedral every year. Sir Charles Groves, the distinguished Conductor of the Royal Liverpool Philharmonic Orchestra, worshipped in the Cathedral and conducted major choral and orchestral works, sometimes combining Cathedral and Philharmonic resources. During Derrick Walters's era as Dean, a Liverpool Cathedral Festival was established to run for a fortnight every July and Verdi's *Requiem,* Walton's *Sea Symphony,* Mahler's *Symphony of a Thousand,* and Britten's *War Requiem* were just a few of the massive musical works performed within the Cathedral.

Because of building and refurbishment at the Philharmonic Hall, the Society needed to find a suitable venue for their 1994–95 season. Apart from the Cathedral, there was no other building in the city capable of accommodating the eighty musicians in the orchestra, a large choral society and a sufficiently large audience to make the season economically viable. That season the Cathedral played host to fifty eight concerts without the slightest interruption to any of the services. How Dwelly would have revelled in that extended musical feast! No other Cathedral in the country had ever attempted anything like it.

Liverpool's fourth Dean, Derrick Walters, was traditional in his tastes in music and liturgy; he enjoyed Haydn and Mozart masses, and Choral Evensong was a very important part of his everyday life. Cathedral music certainly flourished through the support which he gave to it and he was well served by his successive Precentors, Nicholas Frayling, Ken Riley and Mark Boyling. During Canon Frayling's time, the choir began to sing Evensong six days a week during term time. During a recent conversation, Nicholas Frayling told me of his strong memories of particular services for which he was responsible: the very quickly devised and memorable service to mark the football disaster at the Heysel stadium where thirty-nine Juventus supporters were killed; the liturgy for Holy Saturday and the Advent Procession; Darkness to Light, not a new service within the Christian church but a new service for Liverpool Cathedral and one of the most powerful and memorable of the whole calendar.

Many times I saw Canon Riley standing in the central space of the Cathedral, looking towards the chancel and trying to visualise aspects of the services he was devising. Some of his work showed an audacity similar in extent to Dwelly's: who but Ken Riley would have had cadets abseiling from the corona gallery down to the floor of the Cathedral because visually that expressed some of the Venture Adventure motto of the Air Training Corps? The Good Friday Service, The Way of the Cross, moves clergy, cross guild, choir and congregation all around the Cathedral in a manner not available to Dwelly in the unfinished Cathedral. At the very end, after the singing of the final chorale from the *St John Passion*, in a move of sheer liturgical genius, we travel beyond the tomb as the whole company walks in silence through the great west doors, beckoning us to life beyond, and reminding us that the gates of hell shall not prevail against us. This service is no copy of anything Dwelly devised yet it stands firmly at the heart of the Dwelly tradition. The Hillsborough Memorial Service to remember the lives of ninety five football supporters crushed to death in April 1995 was simply but brilliantly devised, very quickly, by Ken Riley and Ian Tracey. I do not think anyone present that day will ever forget the power of that service – the lighting of ninety five candles, the processing to the high altar of the Book of Remembrance, the solo treble voice rising from profound silence singing 'When you walk through the storm, Hold your head up high and don't be afraid of the dark'. Through the architecture of the building, and through the sensitivity and imagination of music and liturgy, personal grief was faced, shared, controlled. Only a handful of that vast congregation would even have heard the name Dwelly and yet for me that service carried the hallmark of the Dwelly legacy.

Twenty years after the Laying of the Foundation Stone in 1904, Frederick Dwelly devised his first services for the Cathedral. In 2004, to mark the centenary of the Cathedral's establishment, Mark Boyling produced his final services for Liverpool Cathedral before moving to the Deanery at Carlisle. One eminent member of the vast congregation at the service at 4 p.m. on Monday 19 July was heard to say, 'That service was eighty percent Dwelly!' That remark was no slur on Mark Boyling's creativity as a liturgist, but high praise that he had made his mark within the great tradition inaugurated by the first Dean.

Dwelly became famous for the high quality of the design and printing of the orders of service used in the Cathedral. The worshippers at the Centenary Eucharist and Festival Evensong were delighted by the style and quality of the orders of service. They were printed on high quality, cream-coloured paper and card; the text of the service was printed in black and the rubrics in red and the books were embellished with Carter Preston drawings from important services from the past. They were not ostentatious anachronisms but beautiful celebrations of the first hundred years of the Cathedral's life. That the Cathedral had commissioned a new mass setting by Sir John Tavener to celebrate the Centenary Eucharist was certainly within the Dwelly tradition. The richness and complexity of the music was nicely balanced by the simplicity of the Dwelly annual consecration ritual whereby the youngest chorister, this year Joel Dawkin, traced the Consecration Mark in the floor with water and the choir sang the anthem *Locus Iste* by Bruckner.

The Centenary Service itself was celebrated on Monday 19 July at 4.00 p.m. – the exact time of the Foundation Stone service one hundred years ago. The service was imaginative and dramatic with excellent use made of processions and human move-ment. The litany prayers had something of the character of material in *Acts of Devotion*. The service was no Dwelly pastiche but it certainly reflected the spirit of his ideas. In the section of the service headed 'For the future take us', the current Dean, the Rt Rev. Dr Rupert Hoare, linked the service to the work and example of the first Dean:

> Fifty years ago, Frederick Dwelly, the first Dean of Liverpool, chose and read the lesson at the service to mark the Golden Jubilee of the Laying of the Foundation Stone. He read from the Book of Revelation about John's vision of the worship of heaven. It was an appropriate choice for one whose liturgical genius had opened windows into heaven for those who worshipped in this great house of prayer.
>
> Dean Dwelly's liturgical achievement, which still shapes the tradition of this Cathedral, was to connect such a heavenly vision with the daily experience of the people of this City and Diocese in good times and in hard times ...

As Dwelly's first biographer writing almost fifty years after his death, the Cathedral Centenary's direct and indirect acknowledgement of the man's genius was heart-ening. Though the current Dean and Residentiary Canons had not known Dwelly in any way, Mark Boyling had devised celebratory services with something of the style and spirit of Dwelly, and Rupert Hoare acknowledged the liturgical genius of his great predecessor, with his ability to connect the 'heavenly vision with the daily experience'. He had established a great tradition but a great tradition rooted in the past, alive to the present and growing into the future.

I struggled to put three books in the public domain as my part of the centenary celebrations. Together with Colin Wilkinson and the photographic skills of Barry Hale, *The Cathedral Church of Christ in Liverpool*; the Centenary Edition of *The Building of Liverpool Cathedral*; and *Frederick William Dwelly: First Dean of Liverpool*. Words of Walt Whitman used as a favourite hymn of Dwelly might well be used as an appropriate epitaph.

ALL THE PAST WE LEAVE BEHIND
WE TAKE UP THE TASK ETERNAL
AND THE BURDEN
AND THE LESSON
CONQUERING HOLDING
DARING VENTURING
SO WE GO THE UNKNOWN WAYS
PIONEERS O PIONEERS

Ronald Woan and the choristers, a photograph paid for by the boys as a tribute to Dwelly at the time of his retirement.

Bibliography

N. J. Baron, 'The Record and Examination of the Life and Work of Frederick William Dwelly, First Dean of Liverpool', unpublished dissertation, Liverpool John Moores University (1998).

F. R. Barry, *Mervyn Haigh* (SPCK, 1964).

J. Blezzard, 'Holst and Vaughan Williams Manuscripts at Liverpool Cathedral', *Transactions of the Historic Society of Lancashire and Cheshire*, cxxxix (1990).

W. S. Chambers, *Max Horton and the Western Approaches* (Hodder & Stoughton, 1954).

V. E. Cotton, *The Book of Liverpool Cathedral* (Liverpool University Press, 1964).

A. A. David, *Who are Christians?* (Oxford University Press, 1934).

N. Dearmer, *The Life of Percy Dearmer* (Jonathan Cape, 1940).

F. W. Dillistone, *Charles Raven* (Hodder & Stoughton, 1975).

E. Dwelly, *Compendium of Notes on the Dwelly Family* (Private publication, 1912).

F. W. Dwelly (attrib)., *Services for Broadcasting* (BBC, 1931).

A. R. Ellis, *Lawrence Redfern* (Private publication, 1968).

A. Fox, *Dean Inge* (John Murray, 1960).

D. Gray, *Percy Dearmer: A Parson's Pilgrimage* (Canterbury Press, 2000).

A. Hastings, *A History of English Christianity, 1920–1990* (SCM, 1986).

W. R. Inge, *Christian Mysticism* (Methuen, 1899).

W. R. Inge, *Truth and Falsehood in Religion* (1906).

F. A. Iremonger, *William Temple* (Oxford University Press, 1948).

R. S. D. Jasper, *George Bell, Bishop of Chichester* (Oxford University Press, 1967).

P. A. Kennerley, *The Building of Liverpool Cathedral* (Carnegie, 1991).

J. A. Lee, *In Emmanuel's Land* (Private publication, 1998).

J. G. Lockhart, *Cosmo Gordon Lang* (Hodder & Stoughton, 1949).

W. R. Matthews, *Memories and Meanings* (Hodder & Stoughton, 1969).

J. McCulloch, *My Affair with the Church* (Hodder & Stoughton, 1976).

J. McCulloch, *Charming Manners* (J. M. Dent, 1932).

J. McCulloch, *Limping Sway* (Michael Joseph, 1936).

S. Morison, *English Prayer Books* (Cambridge University Press, 1945).

F. Neilson, *My Life in Two Worlds* (C.C. Nelson Publishing Company, 1953).

E. H. Patey, *My Liverpool Life* (Mowbray, 1983).

J. S. Peart-Binns, 'Albert Augustus David, "The Liberal Autocrat"', in M. Smout (ed.), *Four Bishops of Liverpool* (Liverpool Diocesan Centenary Committee, 1985).

C. Raven, *Liverpool Cathedral: An Impression of its Early Years* (Oxford University Press, 1933).

J. Riley, *Today's Cathedral* (SPCK, 1978).

E. Russell, *Not a Dead See* (Private publication, 1996).

C. Scott, *Dick Sheppard* (Hodder & Stoughton, 1977).

M. Shaw, *Up to Now* (1929).

M. Smout (ed.), *Four Bishops of Liverpool* (Liverpool Diocesan Centenary Committee, 1985).

A. Wilkinson, *Dissent or Conform* (SCM, 1986).

Newspapers, journals and letters in the Dwelly archive at Liverpool Cathedral and in archival material at Lambeth Palace Library.

Material from newspapers, journals and letters has been referenced within the text.

Index

Entries in *italic* type refer to illustrations or their accompanying captions.